An Overview Series Publication

Computer Networks

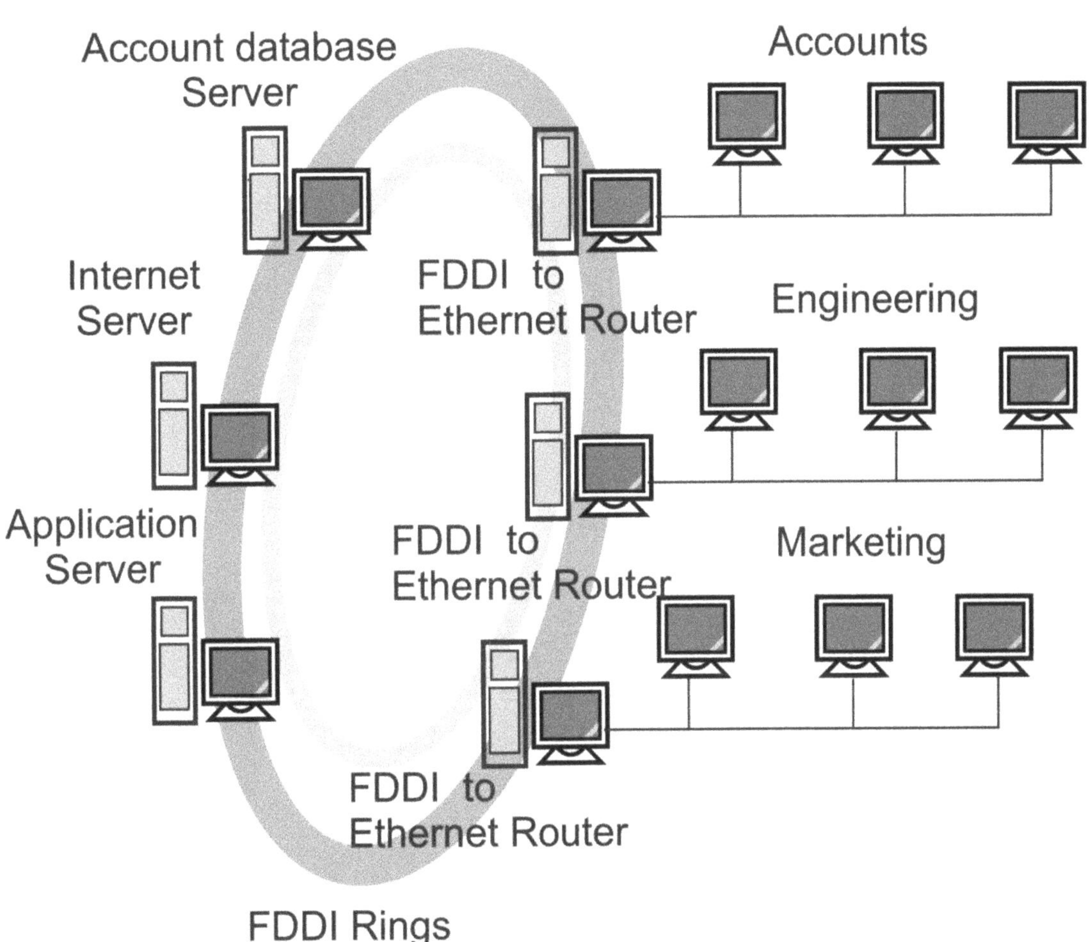

Dr. Goran I Bezanov PhD

This page is intentionally left blank

COMPUTER NETWORKS

AN OVERVIEW SERIES PUBLICATION

By Goran Bezanov PhD

Published by
MIG Consulting Ltd
31 Vicarage Road, London SW14 8RZ

British Library Cataloguing in Publication Data
A catalogue record for this book is available from the British Library

International Standard Book Number: 978-0-9558153-0-0

To my Sons

Ognen and Milos

This page is intentionally left blank

Preface

This text is a very brief overview of computer networks. My aim was to write a textbook that could be read and understood by readers who are not very familiar with modern computer networks. It was my intention that, from this text, they could gain sufficient understanding in order to know where to look for further direction. I cover briefly topics relating to general computer hardware architecture and the role of the operating system. Here I deal with areas such as process management and memory management in order to give the reader an idea of the type of workload a computer on a typical network may need to cope with.

General background to the technologies that are available for local and wide area networks are provided in order for the reader to be aware of these as options in network specification and design. I have also provide some guidelines to readers regarding the steps involved in the design of network infrastructure.

Network infrastructure solutions are the preserve of the large solution providers and very few individual consultants can claim to have taken on large projects to design and implement a corporate network infrastructure. This, in my view, is not because they could not do it rather it is because they could not do it in time. Corporate networks are designed and implemented to strict deadlines by efficient teams with the backing of solid technologies. Therefore it is difficult to provide a detailed account of all the steps that need to be taken in designing, implementing and maintaining a corporate network. Instead I have tried to give an overview and I hope the reader will find the material useful as a starting point towards designing corporate network infrastructure solutions.

This is my first draft and I shall revise and correct the errors in the next. Suggestions welcome to: mig@consultant.com.

Thank you

Goran Bezanov (December 2007, London)

This page is intentionally left blank

Contents

1 COMPUTER OPERATING SYSTEMS

1.1 Introduction

A computer operating system (O/S) is software that complements the hardware by providing a layer of services, which manage the resources of the hardware and permit the user to operate the system. Every general computer has at least one operating system. At present, for personal computers (PC), the most commonly used operating systems are Microsoft Windows, Linux (a variant of UNIX) and Macintosh OS X.

The operating system is primarily a provider and manager of machine resources such as the processor, main memory, input-output space and secondary data storage. Access to these resources is centralised and controlled by various software modules of the operating system. Figure 1.1 shows a generalised view of how the operating system interacts with the software programs and the computer hardware.

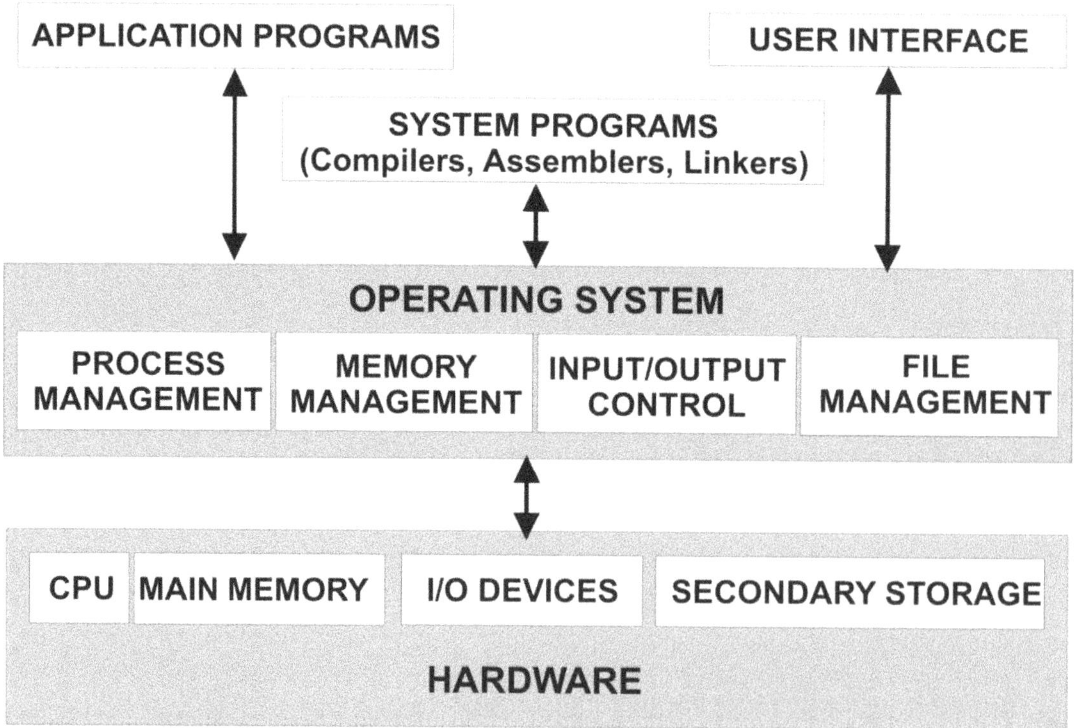

Figure 1.1. Operating system interacting with software and hardware

Operating systems perform several tasks, such as recognising keyboard input, displaying output to screen, keeping track of files and directories on the disk and controlling peripheral devices such as disk drives, printers, network interfaces, modems etc. It is also responsible for security, preventing unauthorised user access to the system. The block diagram of figure 1.2 illustrates some operations that an operating system is concerned with.

Most general purpose O/Ss support multi-tasking, which means that a number of different programs can run at the same time, i.e. concurrently. As seen in figure 1.2, one of the tasks of the O/S is process management. The operating system performs overall monitoring of tasks ensuring that different programs that are running concurrently do not interfere with each other. Since all tasks that are running have to be loaded into physical RAM, during process control the O/S also needs to consider the central processing unit (CPU) activity and also to look after memory management.

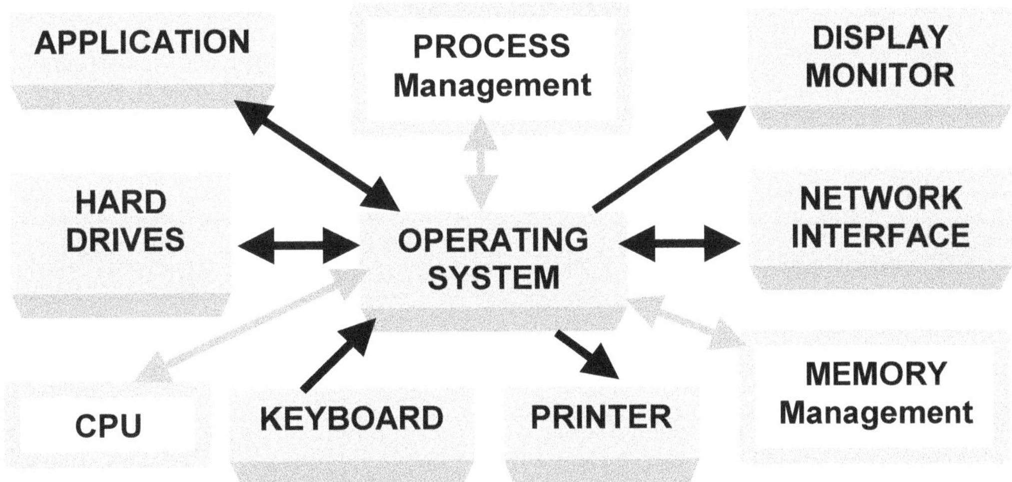

Figure 1.2. Operating system interfacing to programs and peripherals

Another function of the O/S is to provide a platform on top of which application programs can run. Typical examples of software applications are word processors, spreadsheets, media players etc. Management of peripheral devices such as the display, keyboard, printer etc. is another key role of the O/S.

Users normally interact with the operating system through a set of commands. For example, the DOS operating system contains commands such as COPY and RENAME for copying files and changing the names of files, respectively. These commands are accepted and executed by a part of the operating system called the command processor or command line interpreter. A menu-driven interface is one in which you select command choices from various menus displayed on the screen. Graphical user interfaces (GUI) enable the user to enter commands by pointing and clicking on objects that appear on the screen. The acronym WIMP (Windows Icons Mouse Pointer) indicates the principal elements of a Windows GUI. A simplified diagram of the software model for a user interface is shown in figure 1.3. Here different levels of interaction with the O/S are shown for different users. The GUI acts as the junction between a user and a computer program, and it allows the user to communicate with the program. This extends to programmers as well, who may also resort to command driven interaction for specific programming tasks. These include low level programming for system calls and also developing application programs through the API (Application Programming Interface).

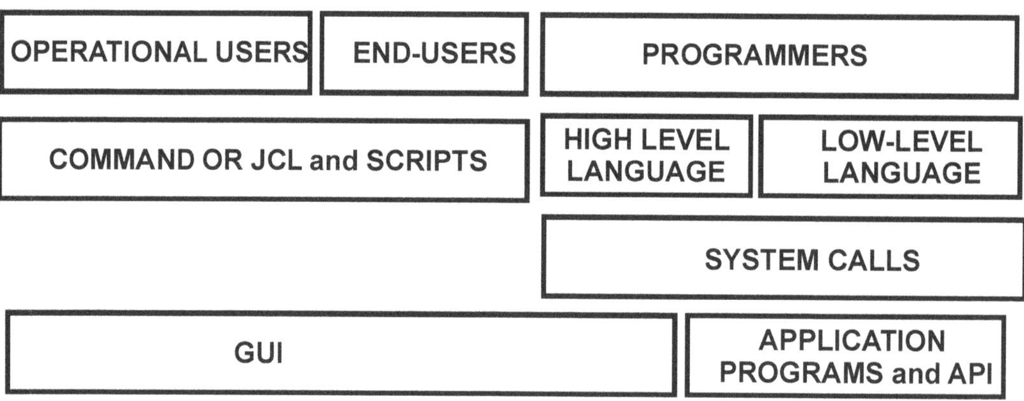

Figure 1.3. User interface software model

1.2 Types of operating systems

There are many types of operating systems, but the most common types can be classified into a number of categories. In a general sense computer operating systems can be classified as follows:

- **Multi-user:** Allows two or more users to run programs at the same time. Some operating systems permit hundreds or even thousands of concurrent users. (i.e. Linux, Windows, z/OS, Solaris).
- **Multi-processing:** Supports the running of programs on more than one CPU. (i.e. Linux, Windows).
- **Multi-tasking:** Allows more than one program to run concurrently (i.e. Linux, Windows).
- **Multi-threading:** Allows different parts (threads) of a single program to run concurrently. (i.e. Linux, Windows).
- **Real-time:** Responds to input within a specific time determined by the so-called real-time constraints (i.e. iRMX, INtime).
- **Network:** A network operating system performs the functions of multi-user, multi-processing and multi-tasking operating systems and additionally, implements protocol stacks as well as device drivers for networking hardware.

Network operating systems

A network operating system performs pretty much the same function as a desktop O/S, but does this across a network; therefore it provides an additional layer of services that use network protocols. Typical network operating systems are Unix, Linux, Windows 2003 Server, Novel Netware, IBM z/OS, Solaris etc. A brief description of some of the most popular network operating systems is given next.

Linux: Open-source Linux operating system provides Web serving, firewall security, Samba, and other features including wireless LAN support. [1]

Macintosh: Apple Macintosh computers support standard networking technology allowing them to be connected to other Macs and the Internet. Additionally, the AppleShare File Protocol (AFP) client or the SMB client programs can be used to connect to Windows machines for file sharing on a network. [2]

NetWare: Novell NetWare has been used for basic file/print serving for many years; NetWare today also includes Web-based networking capabilities. [3]

IBM: For several years IBM published an OS/2 Strategy, however as of December 2006, IBM's intention was to reduce OS/2 support and ask customers to implement a phased transition from client-server environments to the WebSphere software platform. [4] z/OS is a 64-bit mainframe operating system from IBM. It is the successor to the operating system OS/390, which in turn was based on the OpenMVS. IBM System z servers are supported by a number of operating systems, such as z/OS, z/OSe, z/VSE, Linux on System z and the z/VM hypervisor. [5] It needs to be said that IBM are not in the business of providing general purpose O/Ss but rather they provide business networking solutions that are tailored to the clients' needs.

Special-Purpose Operating Systems: These operating systems appeal to specialised or 'niche' audiences. Some servers and routers use this type of operating systems, for example: Cisco IOS (originally Internetwork Operating System). [6]

It is worth mentioning that most desktop operating systems have network client side software built in and therefore they support networking. For example, Linux can be configured as a network client or a server depending on the requirements. Many IBM business solutions of today support a version of Linux configured as a server. As an example, table 1.1 indicates the network operating systems versions that the IBM System x™ and BladeCenter® servers support. [7]

Table 1.1

OS manufacturer	Version
IBM	4690 Operating System V4
Microsoft	Microsoft Windows Server 2003 R2, Enterprise
Novell NetWare	NetWare 6.5
Novell SUSE LINUX	SUSE LINUX Enterprise Server 9 for x86
Red Hat	Red Hat Enterprise Linux 5 Server x64 Edition
The SCO Group	SCO OpenServer 6.0.0 (Unix base)
Sun Microsystems	Solaris 10 Operating System
Vmware	VMware ESX Server 3.0

1.3 Computer software

Computer software provides a degree of flexibility that cannot be easily provided by the hardware. By software programming, the hardware can be made to function in different ways. Figure 1.4 provides a simplified view of the computer programming hierarchy. Here the levels of programming are split into a number of categories at different levels of the hierarchy. Hierarchical decomposition is used to show that every level depends on the one below it for operation.

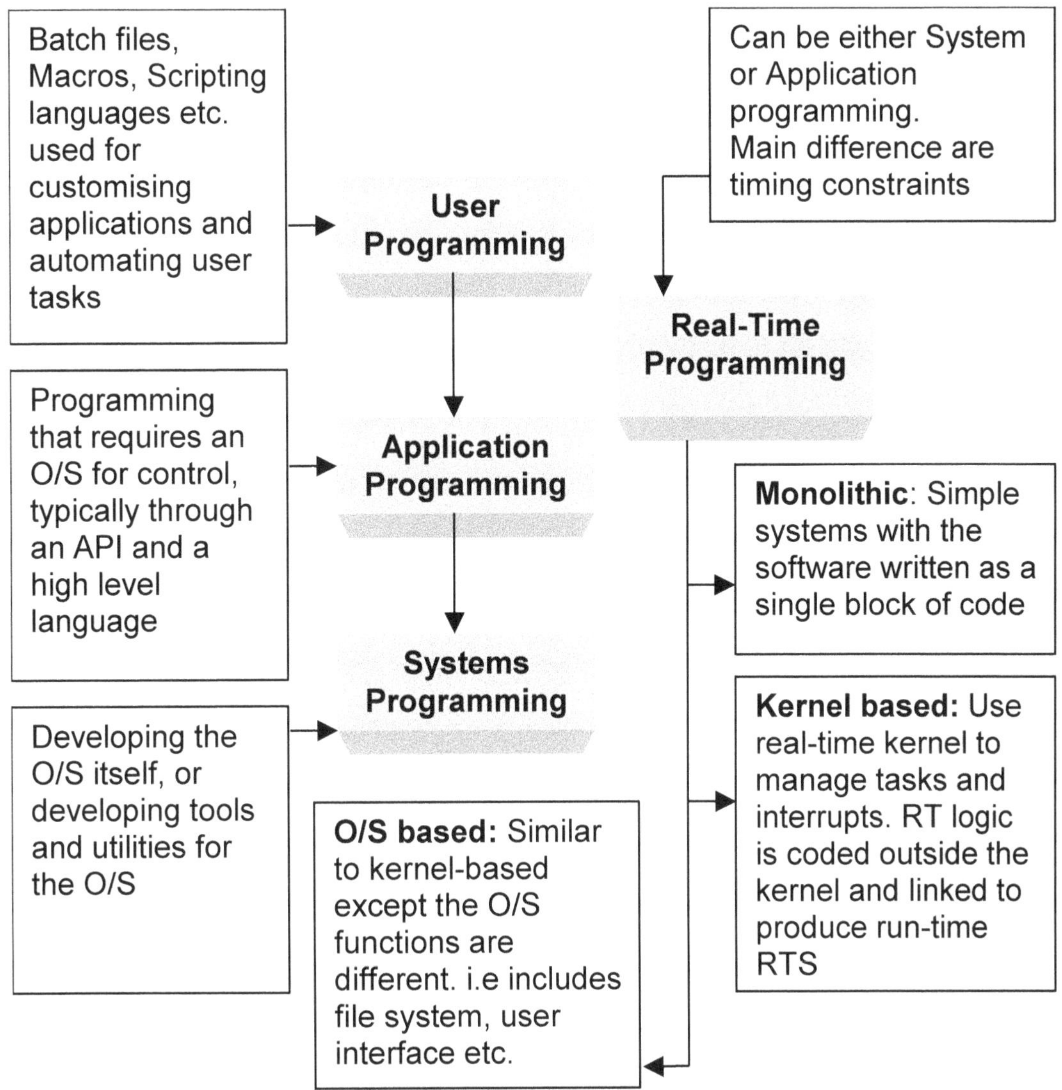

Figure 1.4. Computer programming hierarchy

Software programming at high and low level includes system software, application software, program loader, I/O control system etc. The development tools that are used include compilers, linkers, loaders and debugging tools. Application programming usually requires a run-time library to enable portability. Operational users typically use scripting tools to write programs. Some visual programming tools include a GUI, to simplify the programming task (i.e. Visual Basic). With reference to figure 1.4 a brief explanation of some software components is given next.

User programming

This type of programming refers to general users who have not been formally taught how to program in a conventional high level programming language (i.e. C++, VBasic, Java etc). User programming languages enable users to change the actions and/or user interface of a system. For example, AutoCad has an embedded Lisp language for extensions, and Microsoft Office applications have an embedded Basic language. End-user programmers also include self-taught Webmasters writing Javascript; network administrators writing logon scripts and script to configure routers; as well as experts in complex business automation tools like SAP (Systems, Applications, Products). [8]

Application programming

This type of programming utilises an Application Programming Interface (API) to develop programs that run on the platform for which the API has been developed. [9] In computer program development, APIs are a set of routines, protocols, and tools for building software applications. A good API makes it easier to develop a program by providing all the building blocks, which can be easily put together by a programmer. Most operating environments, such as Windows, provide an API so that programmers can write applications that are consistent with the operating system. Although APIs are designed for programmers, they are also good for users because they guarantee that all programs using a common API will have similar interfaces. This makes it easier for users to learn new programs.

Systems programming

Systems programming produces software, which provides services to the computer hardware. Examples include implementing certain parts in the O/S such as, for example, a paging system (Virtual Memory) a disk defragmenter or a device driver for a network operating system. This level of programming requires a greater degree of hardware understanding by the programmer. More specifically, the programmer will utilise the properties of the hardware in order to write efficient code to perform system functions. Originally systems programmers wrote in assembly language, which is made up of an instruction set that is supported by the CPU and this provides a low-level programming language. With the growth of UNIX operating system, C language emerged as a viable and efficient systems programming language (i.e. UNIX was written in C). An object-oriented variant of C, namely C++, was used for O/S development such as the Windows NT, and embedded C++ is used to write the I/O Kit drivers of Mac OS X. As an example of a typical architecture of a popular O/S, figure 1.5 shows the Windows 2000 architecture. Here it is seen that the architecture is divided into two parts, the User mode and the Kernel mode. User mode refers to all the applications, services, system processes and the environment subsystem, all of which use the dynamic-link library (DLL) in order to access the kernel mode. The kernel is part of the operating system that provides the very basic services for all other parts of the operating system.

Typically, a kernel includes an interrupt handler that looks after all requests for completed I/O operations that compete for the kernel's services. It will also have a scheduler that determines which programs share the kernel's processing time and in what order. With reference to figure 1.5, all the processor services are performed in kernel mode and before accessing the hardware these services need to pass through a hardware abstraction layer (HAL). The Windows HAL provides a link to the hardware interfaces such as buses, I/O devices, interrupts, interval timers, DMA, memory cache control etc. In the Windows O/S the HAL layer was first introduced with Windows 2000 O/S and for this reason drivers for devices pre-Windows 2000 are different to post-Windows 2000. The introduction of the HAL layer implies that the O/S does not have direct access to the hardware and also, by suitably replacing the HAL, the O/S could potentially run on different hardware platforms.

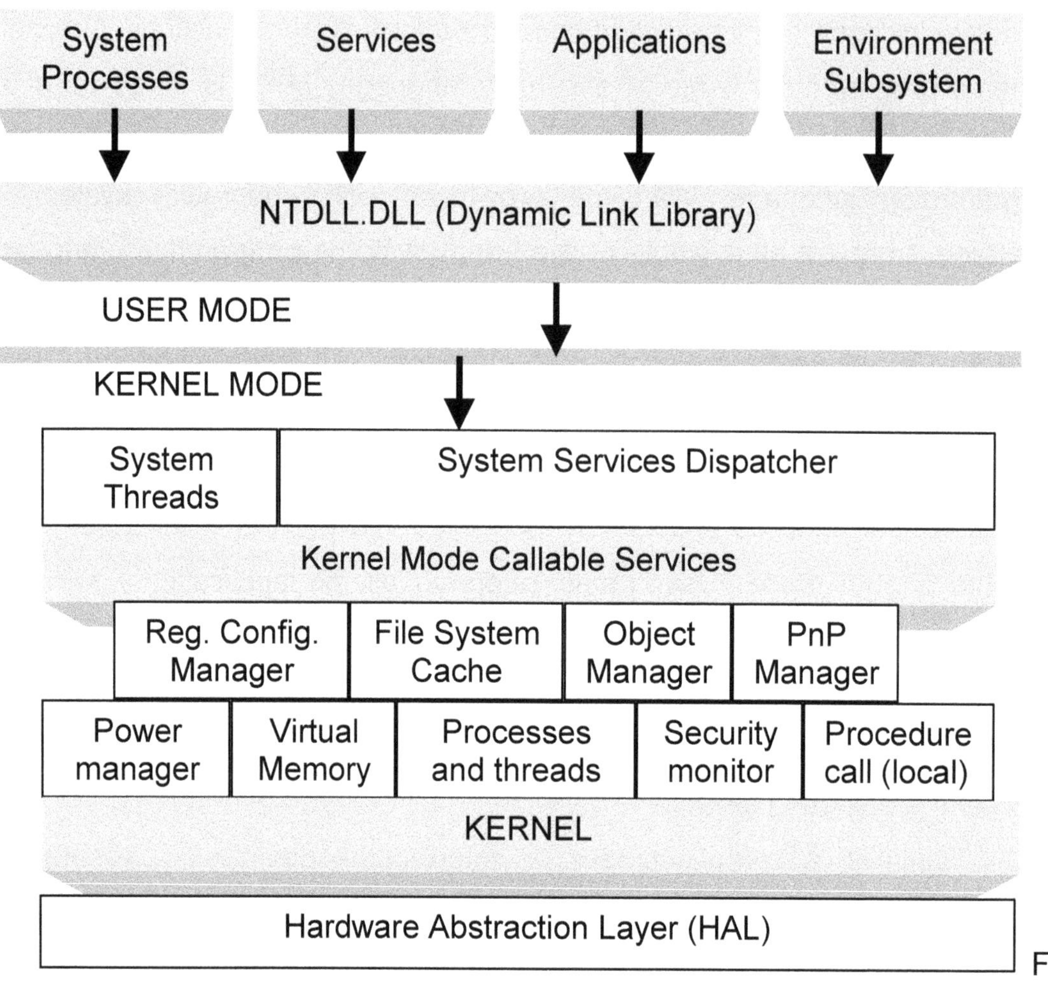

Figure 1.5. Simplified Windows NT 2000 Kernel Architecture [10]

1.4 Windows NT memory model

As part of its 32-bit design, Windows NT contains two separate and distinct components that together comprise the core services of the NT operating system. [10] These are the Windows NT Kernel and Executive. As mentioned earlier the Kernel works in conjunction with the Hardware Abstraction Layer (see figure 1.5), which gains its name from the fact that it provides a middle layer (i.e., it abstracts) between Windows NT's core operating system services and the actual hardware in use on the system (e.g., Intel versus Alpha-based, uni-processor versus multi-processor, etc.). Listed below are three main components, which support the processing and memory management features provided by Windows NT operating system.

- **Virtual Memory Manager:** This is part of the Windows NT Executive, which is responsible for mapping virtual addresses in the process's address space to physical pages in the computer's memory. Note that virtual memory is not the same as physical memory. Physical memory is RAM and virtual memory is typically an area within secondary storage, which is used to store pages from processes that are executing. The virtual memory manager hides the physical organisation of memory from the process's threads to ensure that threads can access their own memory but not the memory of other processes.

- **Process Manager:** This is part of the Windows NT Executive. It is that part of the O/S, which creates and deletes processes and manages process and thread objects. It also provides a standard set of services for creating and using threads and processes in a particular subsystem environment.
- **Thread Dispatcher:** This is part of the Windows NT Kernel, which is responsible for scheduling the execution of threads. Threads can also be executed in a uniform way across all available processors, and this feature is supported by NT's Symmetric Multi-processing (SMP) architecture.

1.5 Microprocessor hardware

A microprocessor is a highly integrated chip that contains components like the CPU, memory, I/O ports, timers etc as shown in figure 1.6. Buses carry digital signals and are used to interconnect the various components. All computer operation is based on processing digital signals that have their values represented by a series of binary bits. Each bit is represented by one of two possible voltage levels, typically 0V and 5V d.c. (Transistor-Transistor Logic-TTL). [11] For example, a voltage of around 5V can be used to represent a binary value of '1' and a voltage of 0V is used to represent a binary value of '0'. Placing these values on the bus a binary value can be used to represent data.

These binary values are processed by an arrangement of Boolean arithmetic operators. A series of these operations constitutes a computation.

Thus, a microprocessor is an integrated circuit that contains all the digital circuits that are needed to perform the required data processing.

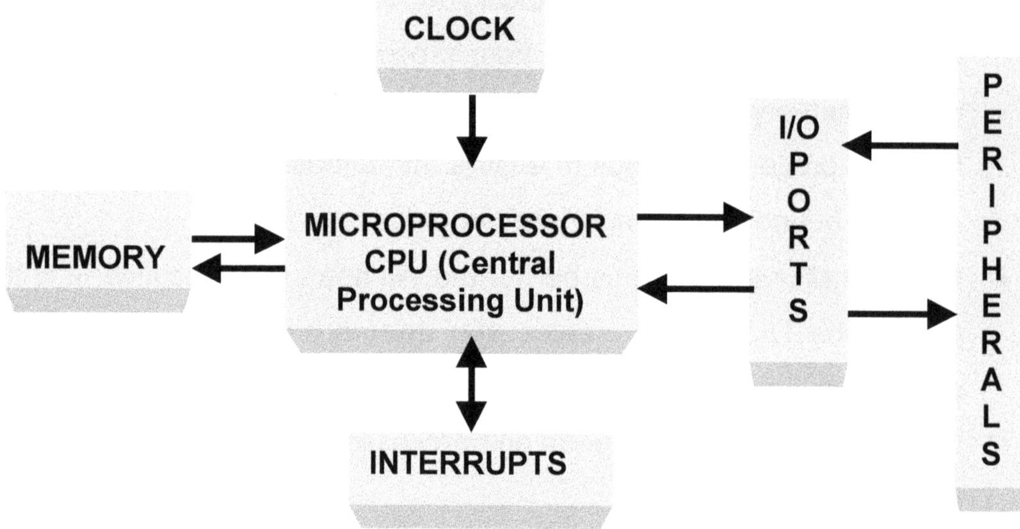

Figure 1.6. Standard computer components.

In order for a microprocessor to be useful it needs to connect to other digital components such as memory, input/output, clock etc. A typical arrangement of components as shown in figure 1.6 would use a central clock that determines the standard clock rate for all CPU activity. For example, all instructions executed by the CPU are timed in terms of the number of clock cycles that they consume.

An interrupt system allows the microprocessor to be programmed to respond to external or internal events. Typically interrupts are vectored so that when they are triggered, an Interrupt Service Routine (ISR) is automatically executed. Typically the ISR contains a sequence of instructions which instructions, which are executed in order to service the interrupt request.

Buses connect the CPU to memory and input/output so that data can be processed and transmitted to and from peripheral devices.

Computer hardware architecture

In computer systems the term architecture can refer to either hardware or software, or a combination of these. Hardware computer architecture generally consists of components such as the CPU, memory and Input/Output devices. These hardware architecture components are interconnected by a number of single line sets, called buses as shown in figure 1.7. Buses are electrical conductors that can carry electronic signals between the interconnected components. Typically in any computer architecture three buses are present and these are the Data, Control and Address buses. The data bus is used to transfer data between the connected units. The width of the data bus is typically 32 or 64 bits, which at any instant, represents a 32 or 64 bit binary value. A wider bus can transfer data faster and this is desirable in the interests of overall speed of processing. The address bus is used to specify the source or destination of data. The control bus is used to transmit timing and control signals between devices.

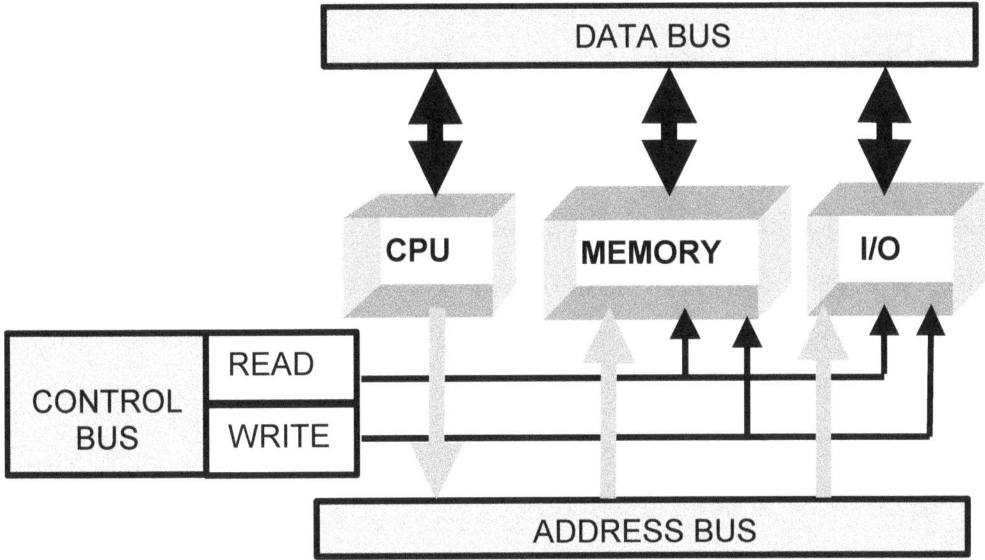

Figure 1.7. Essential hardware of the computer system

Computer Buses

Buses are essentially a group of conductors, which carry electrical signals between components. The internal architecture of the CPU includes buses that interconnect registers and other components inside the CPU. Outside the CPU, devices on the motherboard connected to the CPU will also have buses that interconnect them. Thus it is seen that buses can be implemented at different hardware levels. In a very simplified sense however the CPU controls all the activity of a computer system. Much of this activity concerns the movement of data. For example, instructions and data travel back and forth from the CPU to memory over the data bus and the I/O ports enable communications with the outside world.

Before the CPU can access memory, register or an I/O device, the address of this component must be known. Therefore, the address bus is used to identify the source and destination addresses of components participating in any given connection. Once a connection is established between components the control bus is needed to tell these components what to do. Typically at any given time the CPU will communicate with a single device. In order for this to happen data must be present on the data bus and the address of the device must be placed on the address bus. At the same time control signals for the device need to be present on the control bus.

Address bus: Address bus is a collection of conductors connecting the CPU with main memory and I/O space. Specific values placed on the address bus are used to identify particular address locations within the memory or I/O space. Looking at the printed circuit board of a typical motherboard, the bus can be seen as a collection of thin copper strips running in parallel between components. The width of the address bus determines the number of unique location that can be addressed.

- 8 bit => 2^8 = 256 addresses.
- 16 bit => 2^{16} = 64k addresses.
- 32 bit => 2^{32} = 4G addresses.

Data bus: A data bus is used to transmit data from one part of a computer to another. It can be visualised as a highway on which data travels within a computer. While the address bus locates the source and destination addresses, the data bus carries the data between them.

Control bus: A control bus enables correct exchange of information between components. The control bus carries information such as READ, WRITE, RESET etc between the CPU and other devices within the computer. While the data bus carries actual data being processed and the address bus determines the location of this data, the control bus carries signals that report the status of the various devices.

Input/Output communications

A major requirement of all computer systems is to communicate with other computers and peripheral devices. Therefore a brief description of some of the input/output standards and systems is given next.

I/O bus

This is used to facilitate communication between the CPU and the I/O peripheral device. Peripheral device speeds are considerably slower than CPU speeds and the I/O bus takes care of synchronisation during communication. This avoids data corruption. There are a variety of I/O buses available, for example, Industry Standard Architecture (ISA) has a 16 bit data flow and was a standard for many years although it has now been virtually phased out.

Peripheral Component Interconnect (PCI) bus and the expanded PCI-e are now the standards used in PCs. For example a network interface card (NIC) will have a PCI interface to connect to the PCI slot on the motherboard. This will enable the computer to connect to other computers on the network.

Small Computer System Interface (SCSI)

SCSI is a parallel interface standard used by Apple Macintosh computers, PCs, and many UNIX systems for attaching peripheral devices to computers. SCSI interfaces provide faster data transmission rates (up to 80 megabytes per second) than standard serial and parallel ports. In addition, many devices can be attached to a single SCSI port, so that SCSI is essentially an I/O bus rather than simply an interface. While SCSI has been the standard interface for Macintoshes, the iMac and all PCs come with IDE/ATA, a less expensive interface, in which the controller is integrated into the disk or CD-ROM drive.

Universal Serial Bus (USB)

USB was introduced in 1998 as a new standard for connecting external peripherals to a PC without the use of expansion cards. It allows up to 127 devices to be connected through one port at speeds of up to 480Mbps (USB 2.0 – high speed). A standard serial port in comparison can receive data from only one device at a time at rates of up to 115Kbps. As a result the USB has become the de-facto industry standard for modern peripheral communications.

USB 2.0 is suitable for high-performance devices such as high-quality video conferencing cameras, high-resolution scanners, and high-density storage devices.

Firewire

Also known as IEEE-1394 or i.Link, is a high-speed serial interface that was originally developed by Apple, who called it FireWire; this name became popular, but Apple owns the rights to it, and many companies refused to pay to license the name. The IEEE-1394 is licence free and therefore is often used to refer to this standard. It is a serial interface that supports,

- Dozens of daisy-chained devices.
- Speeds of up to 400Mbps.
- Hot swapping, and plug-and-play.

1.6 Bandwidth

All communication between the hardware architecture components is done by placing binary numbers onto buses. The number of bits, which are used, indicates the size (width) of the bus. Thus, for example, an 8-bit bus consists of 8 bits (one byte), which in decimal can uniquely identify 256 numbers, in the range 0-255 (i.e. 28=256). In other words, if a byte is placed onto the address bus then this value is used to uniquely identify a location in the address space, which in this case has 256 possible locations. If the address bus were 32 bits wide, then 232=4Giga locations can be uniquely identified. Evidently, the wider the address bus, the larger the address space that can be accessed.

If the bus is used for moving data, then the wider the bus, the more data can be transmitted simultaneously. For example, a 16-bit bus will transfer a data size of 1KBytes in $\frac{1024}{2}=\frac{2^{10}}{2^{1}}=2^{9}=512$ units of time. A 64-bit data bus will transfer the same size of data in $\frac{1024}{64}=\frac{2^{10}}{2^{3}}=2^{7}=128$ units of time. Therefore in general, it can be said that wider data buses mean higher data throughput performance. The speed of the bus is dictated by the system clock speed, which is the other main driver of bus performance. The term bandwidth of the data bus is often used to describe how much information can flow through it. Thus the bandwidth is a function of the bus width (in bits) and its speed (in MHz) such that, the bandwidth in bits per second (bps) is given by,

$$bandwidth = bus\_width \times frequency \quad (1.1)$$

Clearly from equation 1.1, the higher the speed in MHz and the wider the bus in bits, the higher the bandwidth.

Hardware modules that facilitate communication with I/O space are usually plugged into slots within the computer frame, and use a slower, peripheral bus to connect to devices. The reason for this is that peripherals do not often support large bandwidths. For example consider an 8-bit ISA I/O bus, running at the speed of 8.3MHz. Using equation (1.1), the bandwidth can be calculated as,

$$\frac{8}{8} \times (8.3 \times 10^6) = 8.3 \times 10^6\, Bps \Rightarrow \frac{8.3 \times 10^6}{2^{20}} = 7.9\ MBps.$$

(Note: Equation is divided by 8 to give result in Bytes, also 2^{20}=1M to give MBps)

Internal data buses connecting CPU to memory are much faster with for example, the Pentium II 64-bit data bus running at 66MHz. Once again, the bandwidth can be calculated as,

$$\frac{64}{8} \times (66 \times 10^6) = 528 \times 10^6\, bps \Rightarrow \frac{528 \times 10^6}{2^{20}} = 508.6\ MBps.$$

For processors that have front side buses (FSB), linked to cache memory the speeds are even faster. For example, 1333MHz (Pentium 4/LGA775) has a 64-bit, FSB running at 333MHz. The bandwidth for this bus is,

$$\frac{64}{8} \times (333 \times 10^6) = 2664 \times 10^6\, bps \Rightarrow \frac{2664 \times 10^6}{2^{20}} = 2540\ MBps.$$

Processors are sometimes referred to as being 16, 32 or 64 bit processors. Basically these numbers designate the number of bits that each of the processor's general-purpose registers (GPR)s can hold. This also means that data transfer can occur 64-bits at a time and that the processor can process an instruction that operates on 64-bit numbers. As a result of this the data and the address buses are also 64-bit wide. For example, Intel EM64T provides support for,

- 64-bit flat virtual address space.
- 64-bit pointers.
- 64-bit wide general purpose registers.
- 64-bit integer support.
- Up to 1 terabyte (TB=2^{64}) of platform address space.

1.7 CISC and RISC Processors

The first computers that came into general use had very simple set of instructions such as add, subtract, increment, decrement, shift left and right etc. (i.e. Intel 8080). Later version such as the Intel 8088 had more instructions that could multiply, divide, decimal adjust etc. As the instruction set became more complex these computers became known as, CISC (Complex Instruction Set Computers) and they were the first type of CPUs used in personal computers. Every CISC instruction given to the CPU is individually decoded by the control unit and executed by the CPU.

At some stage in development, computer designers considered the idea of reducing the instruction set to a set of primitives and arranging a number of these to work in parallel. These CPUs were called Reduced Instruction Set Computers (RISC). In this way the instructions were made simple and they executed quickly. Provided that a large number of CPUs were available to execute instructions in parallel the result would provide fast computational speeds.

Consider for example the multiplication of two integers. i.e. $5 \times 4 = 20$. Assume that the instruction to ADD two numbers takes 10 CPU clock cycles to execute. If the multiplication instruction is not supported in the CPU instruction set, then the multiplication can be performed by repetitive additions. For example to multiply 5×4 starting from result=0; perform addition of 5 to the result, four times. Each addition takes 10 clocks and so after four of these the time taken to execute the sum will be 40 clocks. This is shown in table 1.2.

Table 1.2

Clocks	0	10	10	10	10
Instruction	-	ADD 5	ADD 5	ADD 5	ADD 5
Result	0	5	10	15	20

Thus, ignoring any time lost to for example, jumps in a software loop, the multiplication takes 40 clock cycles to complete. If on the other hand four separate processors were used in parallel to execute the same arithmetic, then each would perform the addition in 10 clocks. Consequently, and assuming that data dependencies are neglected the multiplication instruction could complete in approximately 10 clock cycles, which is four times faster. (See figure 1.8).

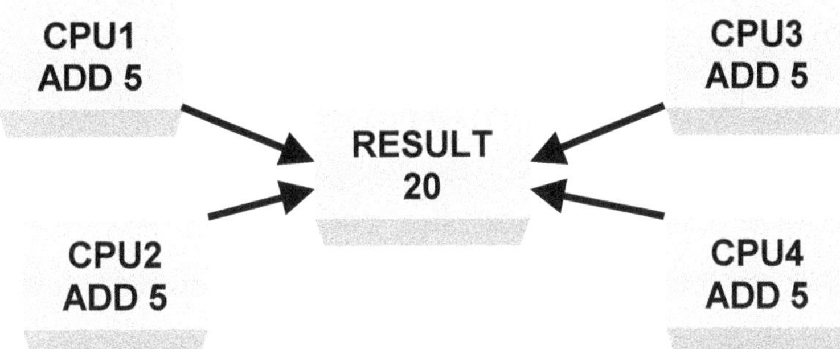

Figure 1.8. RISC execution by parallel processors

The Advent of RISC

As computers quickly evolved, changes were in the favour of RISC. These included the following improvements,

- Caches to speed instruction fetches.
- Large increases in capacity of RAM chips and price reduction.
- Better pipelining.
- Advanced optimising compilers.

Cache memory is RAM that a CPU can access more quickly than it can access regular RAM because it is located in the vicinity of the CPU and it also uses a high-speed data bus. As the CPU executes instructions, it searches through the cache memory first and if it finds the data, (from a previous reading of data), it does not have to do the more time-consuming reading of data from larger memory. Cache memory is categorised according to the levels of accessibility to the CPU. A level-one (L1) or primary cache is the closest to the CPU and in fact it is on the same chip as the microprocessor. For example, the PowerPC 601 processor has a 32-Kbyte level-1 cache built into its chip. [12]

Note that this size of memory is considerably smaller than the typical size of a conventional RAM chip. The reason for this is the limited space that is available on the CPU chip. To help improve performance a secondary, level-two cache (L2) is usually added to work in conjunction with the L1 cache. This is a separate static RAM (SRAM) chip that works in conjunction with L1 cache. L2 cache on computers can range from 64KB to 2MB in size. Some new processors are including L2 cache in the CPU architecture and in this case they also provide a Level-three (L3) cache.

Main RAM is usually a dynamic RAM (DRAM) chip. The pace of computer technology has resulted in cheaper production methods, falling component prices and increasing demand for RAM. Advanced RAM architectures have also increased the speed of RAM. For example, the Rambus XDR™ is a memory architecture that reportedly achieves an order of magnitude performance improvement over standard memories. [13]

1.8 Pipelining

All computers follow the basic fetch-execute cycle in order to process the instructions of a computer program. This makes sense, because it would be impossible to execute something that has not been made available, i.e. fetched. Pipelining refers to the principle of splitting the fetch-execute cycle of an instruction into smaller sections that can be processed independently. In this manner, a pre-processor can process a particular stage while at the same time the CPU can be executing another stage. Simply put, if there was one pre-processor doing the fetching, and at the same time the CPU is executing an instruction, then the speed of processing instructions could be improved significantly. In fact the original Intel 8086 family of processors, used the internal architecture which split the fetch and the execute stages between the bus interface unit (BIU) and the execution unit (EU). Typically in modern computer architectures, pipelines are split in the following stages,

1. Fetch instructions from memory.
2. Read registers and decode the instruction.
3. Execute the instruction or calculate an address.
4. Access an operand in data memory.
5. Write the result into a register.

The above 5 stages of processing can be performed by individual processing units, and so at any one time 5 separate instructions are being processed in a particular stage. For the simple pipeline shown in figure 1.9 to work, the various stages (1-5) need to complete in the same amount of time. Thus, the length of the longest stage determines the length of the pipeline. For this reason, CISC processors have difficulties with pipelining because of differing lengths of instructions. Pipelining is therefore more common with RISC processors where instruction set is reduced, and all instructions are the same length. In an ideal situation, each stage in a RISC processor pipeline should complete in 1 clock cycle. This would mean that the processor finishes an instruction every clock cycle and averages one cycle per instruction (CPI).

Instruction 1	**Stage 1**	**Stage 2**	**Stage 3**	**Stage 4**	**Stage 5**
Instruction 2	**Stage 2**	**Stage 3**	**Stage 4**	**Stage 5**	**Stage 1**
Instruction 3	**Stage 3**	**Stage 4**	**Stage 5**	**Stage 1**	**Stage 2**
Instruction 4	**Stage 4**	**Stage 5**	**Stage 1**	**Stage 2**	**Stage 3**
Instruction 5	**Stage 5**	**Stage 1**	**Stage 2**	**Stage 3**	**Stage 4**
Time units	1	2	3	4	5

Figure 1.9. Simplified instruction pipelining stages

Figure 1.10 shows a simplified diagram of the Intel dual pipeline architecture as used in Pentium processors.[14]

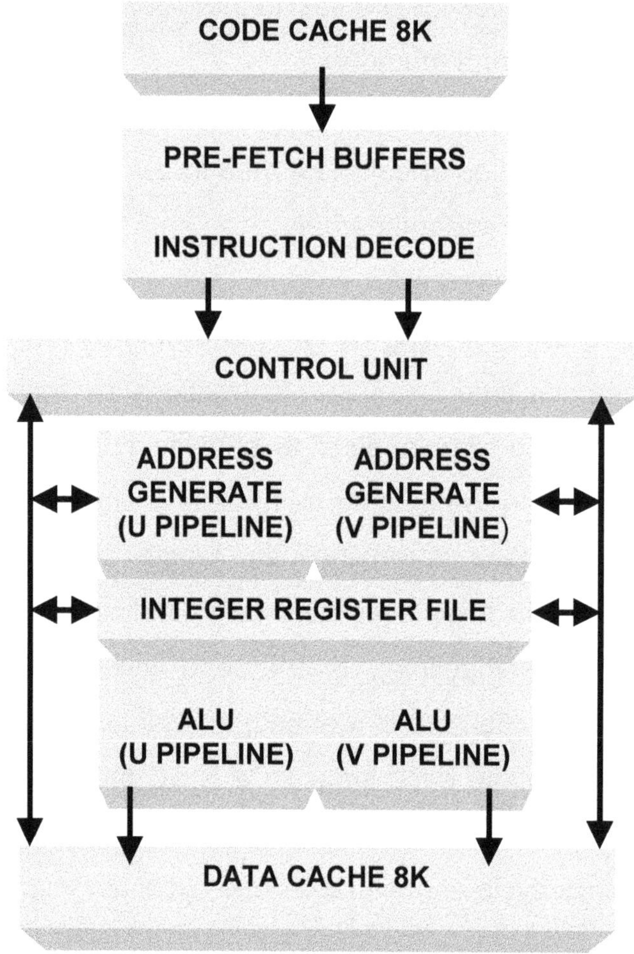

Figure 1.10. Intel dual pipeline architecture

Here the control unit comprises two separate pipelines (U and V), which can process instructions in parallel. The pre-fetch buffers and instruction decode blocks ensure that instruction level parallelism is possible. Parallelism here refers to the ability for instructions to execute in parallel. For example, when instructions of different lengths are being moved along several pipelines, each will complete at different times. On a CISC processor this will lead to instructions completing out of sequence. To some extent RISC avoids this by keeping instructions the same length and making it easier for instructions to be pipelined in parallel. This does not reduce the problem of procedural or data dependency, but it does at least mean that completion of instructions in parallel will not cause out of sequence execution. [15]

This instruction level parallelism that is supported by RISC processors is a very strong argument for their use. While CISC processors still exist, they are increasingly being improved to look more like RISC.

Exercises

1.1 Explain the essential functions of a computer operating system.

1.2 Discuss the different levels of programming that an O/S typically supports.

1.1 What are the main features of a real-time RTO/S?

1.2 Give examples of typical Network Operating Systems and discuss their basic features.

1.3 Explain the Windows NT internal Kernel architecture.

1.4 Within the NT kernel architecture, explain the memory management component.

1.5 Explain the buses that are typically used to connect devices on the motherboard. How does the CPU use these buses?

1.6 What is the bandwidth of a bus?

1.7 All the buses in a computer system including the I/O bus are 16-bit wide. The I/O bus operates at 66MHz.

a) What is the maximum size of the address space that the bus can address?

b) Calculate the maximum bandwidth for this bus.

c) If you were transferring a 4Gbyte multi-media file through this bus, how much time would it take to complete?

d) How much time would you need if the same file was transferred via the a) USB 2.0 bus, b) IEEE-1394?

1.8 Explain the essential features of CISC and RISC processors.

1.9 An integer multiply instruction on a CISC CPU takes 1

1.10 10 clock cycles. An alternative RISC processor does not support multiply but does support loop and ADD instructions. The loop instruction takes 5 clock cycles, and the ADD instruction takes 10 clock cycles. Assume that both machines are 16 bit, that they run at 100MHz clock speed, and that the RISC processor has 20 CPUs running in parallel. Calculate the time that it would take each machine to perform the following multiplications, and compare all the results that are possible: a) 50x4, b) 25x1000, c) 165,000x20.

1.11 Explain how the pipelined architecture can improve performance.

1.12 For a CICSCISC processor, the pipelined architecture is configured into 2 stages, namely stage 1 is Fetch, and Stage 2 is Execute. The longest execute instruction supported by the CPU is 120 clock cycles, and the shortest is 5 cycles. A fetch is 20 cycles at all times. What are the quickest and the longest times that an instruction can be processed on this processor?

2. PROCESS MANAGEMENT

2.1. Introduction

In computer processing terms a process refers to an execution of a program and is used as a unit of measure of CPU activity. In a multi-tasking operating system, the CPU has to manage several processes simultaneously. In reality a single CISC processor can only execute one instruction at a time. Nevertheless, a number of processes can be loaded into memory, and the CPU can switch between them and execute each of these for a short amount of time. The actual length of time spent on each process is determined by the O/S specifications, and the term that is often used to describe it is the 'quantum'. The actual changeover of the CPU executing one process and changing over to another is generally referred to as context switch.

With modern CPUs running at clock speeds of above 1GHz, these context switches can occur very frequently, and are transparent to the user. Thus, by switching rapidly between processes a CPU can multi-task, even if it is only capable of executing one instruction at a time. Related to multi-tasking is the unit of measure for the clock speeds of computer microprocessors (for example, 1GHz). The clock period at this frequency is,

$$\frac{1}{1\times10^{9}} = 1nS \qquad (2.1)$$

For example, if a task is allocated 10ms of CPU time (i.e. quantum) the number of CPU clock cycles that will be allocated to this task is one million clocks, which is calculated as follows,

$$\frac{1\times10^{-3}}{1\times10^{-9}} = 1\times10^{6}\ \textit{clock cycles}$$

In order to give a measure of the relative processing potential it is useful to note that the Intel x86 family of CPUs will perform a simple integer addition in approximately 10 clock cycles. Which means that at 1GHz clock speeds, 100,000 of these can be performed in 10ms? i.e,

$$\frac{1\times10^6}{10}=1\times10^5\,ADD\ operations$$

This means that the task execution time is unnoticeable to human reflexes and therefore the multi-tasking is transparent to the human operator.

2.2. Time-sharing operation

A time-shared operating system uses CPU scheduling to provide each user with a small portion of a time-shared computer. Since all programs that are executing need to reside in RAM, each user has a separate program in memory. When a program executes, it typically runs for only a short time before it either finishes or needs to perform I/O. I/O may also be interactive; that is, output to a display, or input from a keyboard, which in real terms can take a large number of CPU clocks to wait for. For example the speed of a human operator typing a character on a keyboard may be in the region of five characters per second. In other words it takes a human operator 200ms to type each character on the keyboard.

To accept a character from the keyboard, the CPU will execute an interrupt and do some processing. Let us assume that this takes the CPU 50µs to service the interrupt. This means that the CPU will work for 50µs and then wait for 200ms until the next character is received from the keyboard. In other words the CPU is working $\frac{50\times10^{-6}}{200\times10^{-3}}\times100=0.025\%$ of time and wasting 99.975% of its available processing time. Rather than let the CPU wait idle when this happens, the operating system will rapidly switch the CPU to another process. A software program called the scheduler performs this task.

Time-sharing operating systems provide a mechanism for concurrent execution of several processes, which must be simultaneously present in memory. In order to facilitate this some form of memory management is required for memory protection, and also to assist with CPU scheduling. So that a reasonable response time can be obtained, jobs may have to be swapped in and out of main memory. Hence, disk management must also be provided. Time-sharing systems must also provide an on-line file system and memory protection mechanisms.

This is particularly important in situations when several copies of the same program are in the memory (RAM) at the same time. This can occur when one program may be under execution more than once or several users may be running the same program simultaneously. An example of this could be a compiler, which would appear to be compiling several different programs simultaneously. A program executing in this manner is called re-entrant. Machine code of the program that is in memory must not be altered during execution and therefore separate memory must be maintained for each execution. In this manner, each copy of the program that is executing is a unique process.

2.3. Multi-threading

The basic principle of program execution is the fetch-execute cycle, where the CPU reads (fetches) the machine instruction from memory and executes it. This is repeated for every instruction in sequence until the program completes. When execution of a process begins the O/S creates a data structure called Process Control Block (PCB), which is used to control the process. Within the PCB is a process identification number that is used as an identifier during scheduling.

A thread, also called a lightweight process, is a sub-process that behaves as a stand-alone subsection of the process. A simple way to view a thread is as an independent program counter within a process, indicating the position of the instruction that the thread is working on. Almost all modern operating systems support the concept of threads by allowing multiple threads in a single process, which is referred to as multi-threading. Older operating systems were not designed to support multi-threading. For example,

- MS-DOS supports a single user process and a single thread.
- Some traditional UNIX systems are multi-programming systems, thus they support multiple user processes but only one execution path is allowed for each process.

- A Java Virtual Machine (JVM) is an example of a system of one process with multiple threads.
- Modern operating systems, such as Windows, Solaris and Linux, support multi-threading.

The advantage of using threads is that if the computer has many processors that support multi-threading, then threads can be distributed among different processors. In this case threads rather than processes form the basic unit of scheduling and execution. This makes the processing task more efficient in terms of system's overheads.

In multi-threading, the process which is executing would possess one or more threads. In this case each of these threads shares the same address space and as a result of this, communication between threads is simple and efficient. If the O/S does not support multi-threading then processes are executed in their own address space. Consequently, inter-process communications involves additional mechanisms such as sockets or pipes. Thus, it is seen that the benefits of a multi-threading derive from the conservation of resources. Since threads share the same code section, data section and O/S resources, less overall resources are used.

2.4. Clustering

In process execution terms, clustering can be considered the inverse of multi-tasking. A cluster is a group of independent processors that are used to execute portions of one common task. In other words a task that needs to be executed is distributed across the cluster of processors, each of which executes a section of the task concurrently. Executing a process in this way requires some additional processing. For example, a network is used to provide inter-processor communication. Applications that are distributed across the processors of the cluster use either message passing or network shared memory for communication. With the depreciating cost of Intel-based PCs, network clusters can be built relatively economically. Using PCs with large memories and connecting them into a high-performance network, with some additional clustering software, can provide significant computing power.

For example, Windows Computer Cluster Server 2003 [16] supports five different cluster topologies. These clusters can use Public, Private, and Message Passing Interface (MPI) networks.

Public network: Here cluster traffic is shared with other organisational functions. All intra-cluster management and deployment traffic is carried on the public network. Cluster performance is therefore degraded.

Private network: A dedicated network carries the required intra-cluster communication between nodes. This network, if it exists, carries management, deployment, and MPI traffic. This offers a significant improvement in cluster performance, but is more expensive than the public network option.

Message Passing Interface (MPI) network: Message passing interface networks are dedicated, high bandwidth and low latency networks that carry parallel MPI communication between cluster nodes. Of the three networks listed here, this is the highest bandwidth network. However, if the tasks submitted to the cluster do not use MPI libraries, no MPI traffic will be generated and an MPI network is not needed. Some examples of high-speed networks include,

- Gigabit Ethernet.
- 10 Gigabit Ethernet.
- Myrinet©. [18]

Clustering is most widely recognised as the ability to combine multiple systems in such a way that they provide services that a single system could not. Clustering is used to achieve higher availability, scalability (allows expansion of systems or geography) and easier management. Clusters are designed for improved performance by distributing demanding computations across an array of hosts. For the cluster to be effective, the hosts must communicate over high speed, low-latency networks. Another feature of clusters is their availability and clustering solutions are described according to their ability to withstand faults. That is to say, a high availability cluster would allow a computation to continue with a subset of the hosts. In this case the inter-processor communications architecture would detect and isolate faults by providing alternative communication paths.

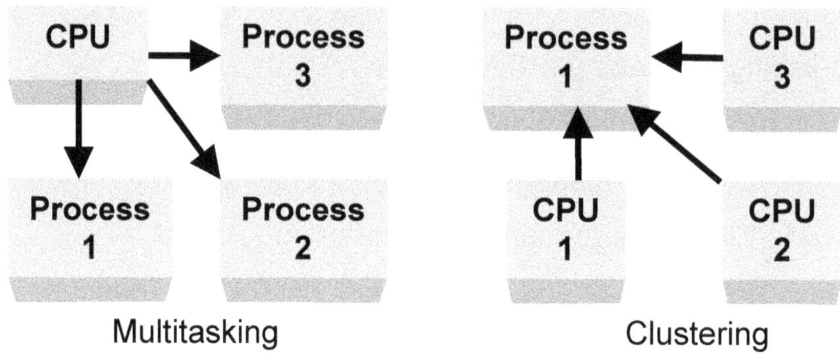

Figure 2.1. Simplified view of multi-tasking and clustering

2.5. Scheduling

In a multi-tasking environment, the operating system has the job of determining the sequence and timing of the execution of processes. Schedulers that adhere to prescribed scheduling policies do this. Process scheduling is divided into three levels,

- **High-Level:** This is also termed long term or job scheduling and at this level the scheduler deals with decisions whether to admit a new job to the system. All jobs that are admitted enter the system into the READY queue.
- **Medium-Level:** Decides whether to temporarily remove a process from the system or to re-introduce the process (for example, in order to balance processor loading).
- **Low-Level:** This is also termed short-term or processor scheduling and this level decides which READY process to assign to the CPU.

In order to maintain consistency schedulers work according to a prescribed policy, such as for example, First Come First Serve (FCFS), Shortest Job First (SJF) etc. Time slicing is often applied with scheduling policies in order to allocate a prescribed period of time to a task. For example, in a time-slicing environment the kernel may interrupt each process after a few milliseconds in order to switch control to another process. Schedulers that work at different levels have different tasks, but in a general sense, the objectives of scheduling are as follows,

- Provide maximum process throughput.
- Allocate jobs to the processor according to a scheduling policy. This way all the processes are treated consistently.
- During busy periods, in order to prevent CPU over-load, schedulers avoid further loading (e.g. inhibit any new job new users) or reduce level of service (i.e. response time).

Scheduling levels

In order to better describe the various levels of scheduling it is necessary to introduce the three-state and five-state process models. These models describe the states that a process can take during execution. The assumption here is that there is a single processor that executes all the tasks. In a multi-tasking environment, where more than one task is being processed by a single CPU, it follows that tasks need to be in different states of execution. The three-state diagram identifies the three states that a process can have as ready, running and blocked states. The five-state models allow the blocked and ready states to be suspended, and therefore these two suspended states are added to the basic three states.

Three-state process diagram

In a multi-tasking environment each of the many processes can be in one of three distinct states. These are the ready, blocked and running states as shown in figure 2.2. A process traverses between these states under the control of schedulers.

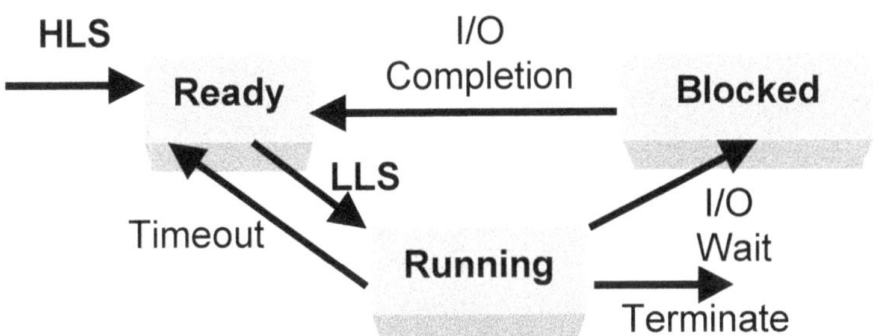

Figure 2.2. Three-state process diagram

With reference to figure 2.2, it is seen that a process enters the system via the High Level Scheduler (HLS) and enters the READY state. There may be a queue of processes in this state and in this case they are maintained in a linked list of their respective PCBs.

When the CPU is free to accept a process, it is the job of the Low Level Scheduler (LLS) to determine which of the processes that are in the READY queue, should be allocated to the CPU. The process that is in the running state can exit that state in one of three ways. Namely, it can terminate or the scheduler can time it out in which case it is returned to the READY queue. It can also leave the running state if it enters an I/O wait and in this case the LLS sends the process into the BLOCKED state. If the process goes into a BLOCKED state then the LLS will place the process, which is next in the READY queue into the RUNNING state. When the I/O wait for the BLOCKED process is complete, it is placed by the LLS into the READY state and its PCB joins the linked list queue.

Five-state process diagram

The five-state model arises from the operations of the Medium Level Scheduler (MLS) where a process that is in READY or BLOCKED or RUNNING state can be SUSPENDED. This gives rise to two more states namely, the READY SUSPENDED and BLOCKED SUSPENDED states. The reason to temporarily suspend a state can arise from a number of O/S related actions. For example, a Timer Interrupt would cause the CPU to suspend the currently executing process in order to pass control onto an interrupt service routine (ISR). When the ISR completes the process that was suspended can be resumed. However it has to be said that if the process was suspended form the running state, it cannot resume in that state and has to be returned to the READY queue. Therefore the transition from suspended state into running state is always through the READY state. This is because there is only one point of entry into the running state and this is from the READY queue.

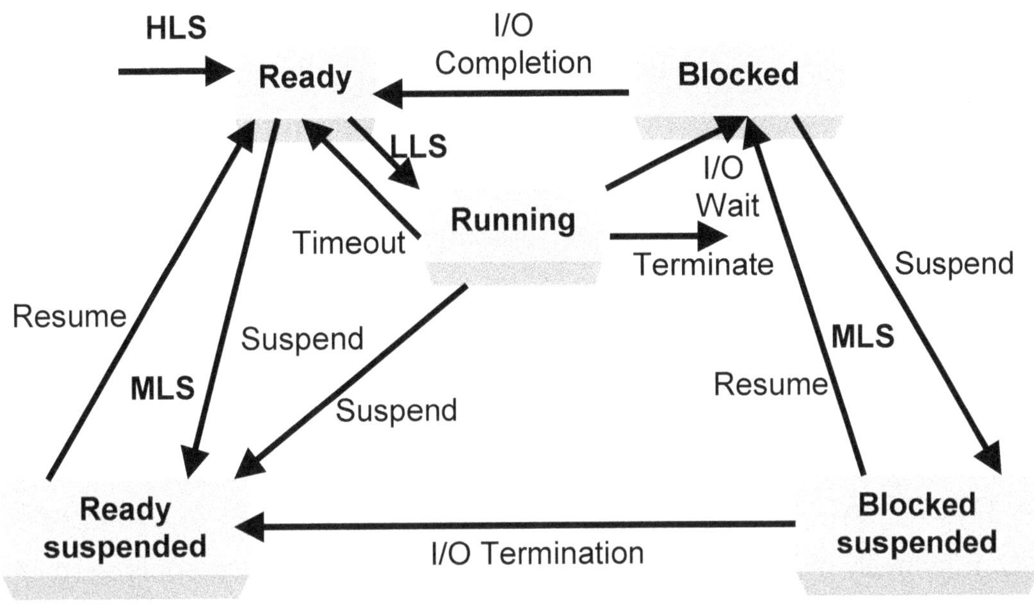

Figure 2.3. Five-state process diagram

A more detailed description of the three levels of scheduling is given next.

2.6. Scheduling Policies

Scheduling policies are rules governing decisions whether a particular action is taken. In process terminology actions are performed on processes, and can range from suspending, resuming, loading a process etc. Policies are used to decide how to schedule the activities of different tasks in a multi-tasking environment. Scheduling policies are divided in two major categories, namely pre-emptive and non-pre-emptive depending on whether the processes can be interrupted or not.

Pre-emptive

In the pre-emptive scheme LLS may remove a process from a RUNNING state in order to allocate another process to the CPU. The cost of this in processing time is the added overhead of the context switching. Nevertheless, this overhead may be justified in cases where a long process is in danger of monopolising the processor. Additionally, pre-emptive multi-tasking allows the computer system to more reliably guarantee each process a regular time-slice of CPU time.

Non-pre-emptive

A scheduling discipline is non-pre-emptive if, once a process has been allocated to the CPU; the CPU cannot be taken away from that process. In this case, the only time the process will relinquish the CPU is when it terminates, or when it enters the BLOCKED state. Another, more drastic way to leave the READY state is when a non-maskable interrupt (NMI) occurs. (i.e. power loss). In non-pre-emptive systems, response times are more predictable because incoming jobs cannot displace waiting jobs, even if they have higher priority.

Another type of policy, which incidentally is no longer very common, is the COOPERATIVE policy that was used in the Windows 3.1 multi-tasking O/S. Effectively this was cooperative multi-tasking since each application when running would periodically relinquish control back to Windows scheduler. The main disadvantage here is in that, if an error occurs and the application is unable to transfer control to the operating system, then the system may freeze. As mentioned earlier, schedulers work according to a prescribed scheduling policy. There are 6 Low level scheduling policies that are most commonly applied to process scheduling, these are as follows,

- (SJF) Shortest Job First.
- (FCFS) First Come First Serve.
- (RR) Round Robin.
- (SRT) Shortest Remaining Time.
- (HRN) Highest Response Ratio Next.
- (MFQ) Multi-level feedback queue.

FCFS-First Come First Serve

This is a non-pre-emptive policy and consequently it favours long jobs over short jobs. This is because the waiting time to run time ratio is smaller for long jobs than for short jobs. Table 2.1 shows the typical ratios that can be expected with this policy. Here it is seen that shortest job has the highest wait-to-run time ratio.

Table 2.1

Process	Estimated run-time (T_{ER})	Waiting time (T_W)	Ratio (T_W) /(T_{ER})
P1	10	0	0/10=0
P2	2	1	11/2=0.55
P3	1	13	13/1=13
P4	100	14	14/100=1.4

SJF – Shortest Job First

This is another non-pre-emptive policy and it works on the principle that it schedules the shortest jobs first, leaving the longer jobs for later. The assumption here is that once all short jobs have been completed, the longer jobs can proceed. This avoids delaying the short jobs by waiting for long ones to finish. With SJF if there are a large number of shorter job there is a risk that the longer job suffers longer waits, and therefore may result in job starvation. For SJF an estimated run time must be available for each process and could be supplied by Job control Language (JCL). Table 2.2 shows the typical ratios that can be expected with this policy. Here is seen that in comparison with the FCFS policy, all jobs have a lower wait-to-run-time ratio. However the highest ratio is for the longest job.

Table 2.2

Process	Order SJF	Estimated run-time (T_{ER})	Waiting time (T_W)	Ratio (T_W) /(T_{ER})
P1	P3	1	0	0/1=0
P2	P2	2	1	1/2=0.5
P3	P1	10	3	3/10=0.3
P4	P4	100	13	13/100=1.3

SRT-Shortest Running Time

This is a pre-emptive variation of SJF that uses a timeout to context switch between jobs. In fact it uses a time stamp to monitor the length of jobs and schedules these according to the principle of Shortest (Remaining) Running Time (SRT) policy. With this policy the job with the shortest time to completion is processed first. Each job runs for the duration of the timeout and then a new calculation is done to determine which of the remaining jobs are the shortest. Table 2.3 shows an example of the performance of this policy.

Although this policy has the overhead of keeping a time-stamp, it is seen to be fair to all jobs, and more importantly, it guarantees that jobs will not be starved of CPU time.

Table 2.3 SRT

			Units of time elapsed FROM START						
Process	**Time in Unit**	**Order of SJF**	**1**	**2**	**3**	**4**	**<--- >**	**10**	**11**
P1	10	3	10	10	10	9			0
P2	2	2	2	1	0	-			-
P3	1	1	0	-	-	-			-
P4	100	4	100	100	100	100			39

Highest Response Next (HRN)

HRN is also a pre-emptive policy derived from SJF, which has been modified to allow the longer jobs to have a better chance to complete. This is made possible by calculating a dynamic priority after each unit of execution time. It is based on a calculated priority value and the formula is as follows,

$$P = \frac{T_W + T_{RT}}{T_{RT}} \qquad (2.2)$$

Looking at equation 2.2 it is clear that P is never less than 1. For example, assume two processes P1 and P2 with run times of 5 and 10 units respectively have been waiting for 1 unit of time. Their priority values can be calculated from (2.2) as follows,

$$P_1 = \frac{T_W + T_{RT}}{T_{RT}} = \frac{1+5}{5} = 1.2 \ and \ P_2 = \frac{T_W + T_{RT}}{T_{RT}} = \frac{1+10}{10} = 1.1$$

From the result it is seen that process P1 has a higher priority value and therefore takes precedence over P2.

Consider another example. Assume that process P4 has a run time of 100 units and has been waiting for 12 units of time. At this time, another process P5, with a run time value of 10 units joins the queue. Another unit of time later, after P4 has waited for 13 units of time, P5 has been in the queue for 1 unit time and it has a running time of 10 units of time. The priority calculation for P4 and P5 would be,

$$P_4 = \frac{T_W + T_{ER}}{T_{ER}} = \frac{13+100}{100} = 1.13 \ and \ P_2 = \frac{T_W + T_{ER}}{T_{ER}} = \frac{1+10}{10} = 1.1$$

In this situation even though P4 is a long job the priority has moved up higher than P5, which has shorter running time but joins the queue later. Table 2.4 show the calculated priorities for a range of process lengths.

Table 2.4 HRN with the Priority calculated priority value

Process	Estimated run-time (T_{ER})	Waiting time (T_W)	Priority value (T_W+T_{ER}) /(T_{ER})
P1	10	0	10/10 =1
P2	2	10	12/2 =6
P3	1	12	13/1 =13
P4	100	13	113/100 =1.13

Round Robin

Round robin is a common scheduling scheme where processes are allocated to the CPU in a rotating fashion with a timeout signalling the change form one process to the next. A process is selected from the READY queue in the First In First Out (FIFO) sequence. Processes are assigned a quantum of time to run on the processor, which must not be exceeded. As soon as the time quantum has been reached, an interrupt occurs and the executing process is placed at the back of the FIFO queue. A hardware timer that generates an interrupt at pre-set intervals usually provides the time quantum. This policy is pre-emptive which only occurs at expiry of quantum time.

Perhaps the most significant feature of this policy is that it guarantees the completion of even the longest jobs. Since each process is allocated a quantum, and when this has expired, it moves to the back of the queue, every process remains in the queue until it has completed. Thus, for n processes in the queue and a fixed time quantum (Q), each process gets a proportion of CPU time given by,

$$P_{CPU} = \frac{1}{n}$$

If each of the n processes is allocated a quantum Q then it follows that no process waits longer than $T_W = (n-1) \times Q$ time units. The main disadvantage of this policy is the significant overheads because each quantum time generates a context switch.

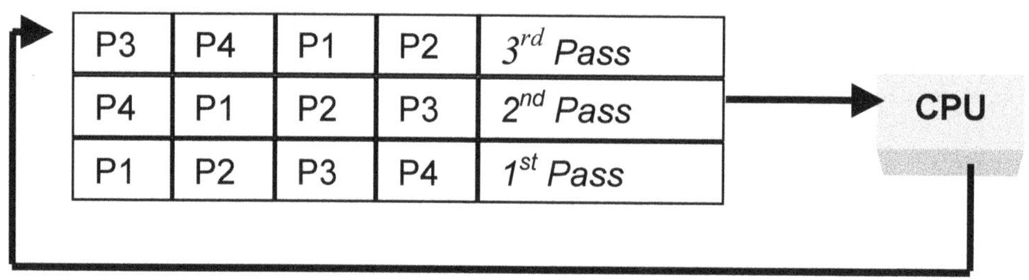

Figure 2.4. Round Robin Process Swapping

The choice of this time quantum is very important with the round robin scheduling policy. It should not be too short because this will increase the frequency of context switch. Every context switch consumes CPU time and this can lead to a condition called 'thrashing', where the CPU spends all its time context switching. On the other hand if the context switch is too long, that could introduce idle time, when the process has terminated and the quantum has not elapsed. (Typical quantum = 10-20ms). Figure 2.4 represents the round robin scheduling scheme.

Multi-level feedback queues (MFQ)

MFQs are a combination of FIFO queues arranged at different higherarchical levels in accordance with the level of CPU usage. It combines several levels of FIFO queues with a time quantum applied to limit processor time given to each process. As the process runs, if it uses up its quantum, it will return to the back of the queue at the lower level and work its way back again. The highest level is for processes with the shortest CPU time, and levels below this have progressively longer CPU time requirements. Transition from the higher level to the one below is achieved by providing a timeout (quantum Q). This is seen in figure 2.5 which shows that a new process enters at the highest level, and progresses down the levels for as long as it does not complete.

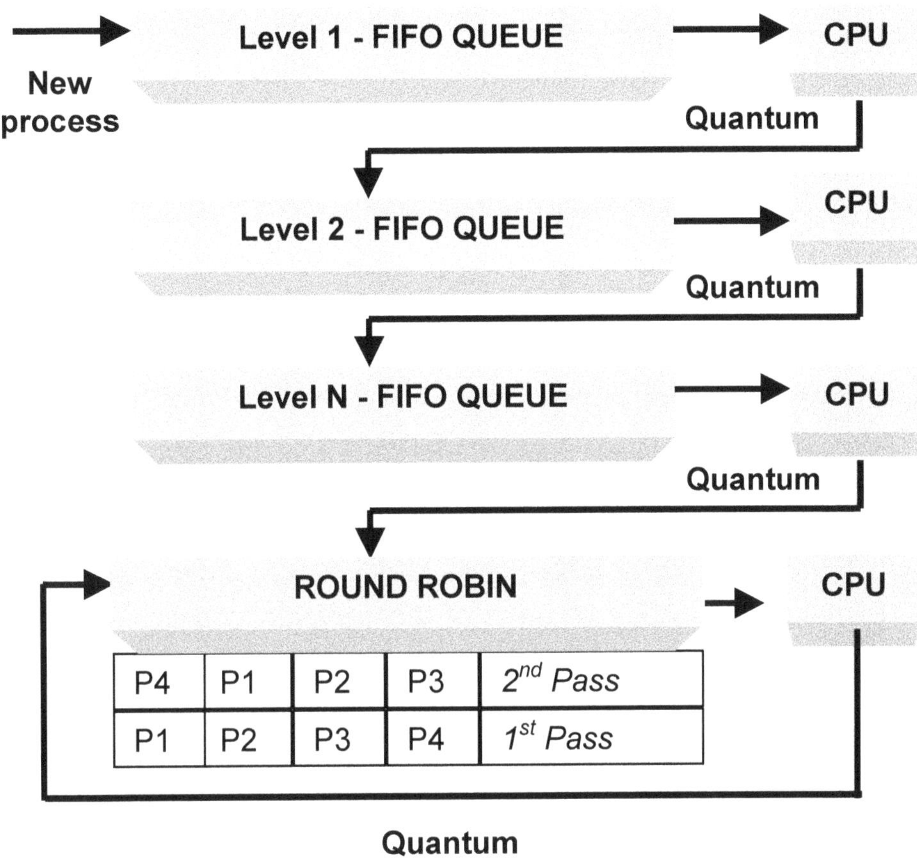

Figure 2.5. Multi-level feedback queues.

MFQs can be made adaptive by recording the level at which each process terminated when it was last in the queue. When the same process is next in the queue, instead of placing it at the highest level, it will be placed at the level that it exited. In this manner the process will not waste time in the higher levels where it will not complete. This is an attempt to provide an adaptive policy which treats processes on the basis of their past behaviour.

Exercises

2.1 A CPU clock speed is 1GHz; calculate the amount of time it will take the CPU to complete 1000 instructions, each using 100 clock cycles.

2.2 Explain the following in relation to process control,

a) Context switch.

b) Thrashing.

c) Multi-tasking.

d) Multi-threading.

e) Clustering.

2.3 Explain the 5-state process model and indicate how it is derived from the 3-state process model. Also explain the three levels of scheduling that apply to these states.

2.4 Explain the function of each of the 5 states and the rules governing state transitions.

2.5 Discuss the factors that influence the choice of the time quantum used to trigger the transition of a process from the running state to the ready state.

2.6 Describe the main features of the 6 scheduling policies given in this text.

2.7 Discuss how the following processes compare when used in a MFQ scheduling system.

- A short CPU-bound process.
- A long CPU-bound process.
- An I/O Bound process.

2.8 For the processes given in the table below compare the performance of the 6 scheduling policies.

Process	P1	P2	P3	P4	P5
Estimated run-time (T_{ER})	20	11	2	750	1

2.9 Explain the operation of the multi-level feedback queues (MFQ) scheduling system in a single processor computer. Include in your answer a clear description of the scheduling policies that can be used at these levels and suggest the possible modifications to MFQs that would enhance the performance of the process.

3 MEMORY MANAGEMENT

3.1. Introduction

During the time that they are executing all processes reside in the physical memory (RAM) of the computer at the same time. As the processes are running the schedulers decide what to run next, and at the same time the memory management system needs to ensure that the correct process is loaded. Thus, the memory management subsystem is one of the most important parts of the operating system.

Since the early days of computing, there has been a need for more memory than exists physically in a system. Consequently managing the limited physical memory has become one of the most challenging and complex tasks for modern operating systems. This challenge is heightened by the fact that a multi-tasking O/S must divide physical memory among the many processes that are running simultaneously, giving each process an appropriate memory share. Furthermore, the O/S must be able to adjust its behaviour within a wide range of memory sizes, from as little as 16MB to as much as 1GB or more.

Strategies have been developed to overcome this limitation and the most successful of these is virtual memory. Virtual memory makes the system appear to have more memory than it actually has by sharing it between competing processes, as they need it.

3.2. Process loading and swapping

All CPUs operate on the basis of the fetch-execute cycle, which means that every instruction is fetched first and then executed. This is done for every instruction in the program until there are no more instructions to execute. In order for the CPU to be able to fetch the instructions quickly, the program has to reside in the main memory. That is to say, program code is transferred from secondary storage (hard disk) to main memory. This transfer of process code is referred to as process loading (see figure 3.1). When the program terminates, its code is transferred back (swapped) to the hard disk. In terms of the 5-state diagram of a process, access to the hard disk for loading and swapping implies that this is an I/O wait. All this data transfer between main memory and the hard disk takes time. Data transfer rates are a feature of the hardware architecture and the type of transfer taking place. Table 3.1 gives an example of transfer rates for PCI and SCSI adapters for 32-bit and 64-bit buses.

Table 3.1

Bus Type	**Clock Frequency**	**PCI Spec.**	**Transfer Rate**
32 bit	33MHz	PCI 2.1	132 MBps
64 bit	133MHz	PCI X	1066MBps
32 bit	33MHz	SCSI Ultra 2	80 MBps
64 bit	66MHz	SCSI Ultra 4	320 MBps

It is seen that 133MHz PCI X bus can transfer data at 1066MBps. Therefore, if the file size is 100KBytes, the amount of time it takes to transfer the file can be calculated as follows,

$$T_{TF} = \frac{100 \times 2^{10}}{1066 \times 2^{20}} = \frac{100}{1066 \times 2^{10}} = 91.6 \mu S$$

For the same file size on the 32 bit, 33MHz, SCSI Ultra 2 bus, with a rate of 80MBps, the transfer will take,

$$T_{TF} = \frac{100 \times 2^{10}}{80 \times 2^{20}} = \frac{100}{80 \times 2^{10}} = 1.2 mS$$

Typically with disk access, besides the actual transfer rates it is necessary to take into account disk related time delays. These include the average seek time (moving the read/write head to the required track) and the average latency (rotation of disk to the required sector). They also need to include controller overhead and queuing delay. On average hard disks have access times in the region of 10 milliseconds. [18] (note that Access Time = Command Overhead Time + Seek Time + Settle Time + Latency). By comparison, RAM access times are in the region of 70 nanoseconds. The speed differential between access to RAM and access to HD is given by,

$$S_D = \frac{10 \times 10^{-3}}{70 \times 10^{-9}} = 142857$$

This is useful as a comparison although it has to be said that overall HD performance is significantly influenced by channel speed (transfer rate), interleaving and caching.

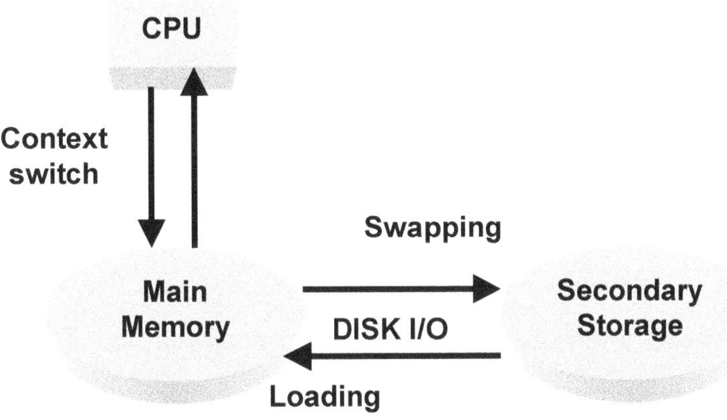

Figure 3.1. Process loading and swapping from secondary storage

For reference purposes, the most common type of RAM at present is the synchronous dynamic RAM (SDRAM). This has a peak transfer rate of around 800MBps. This converts to an equivalent bus frequency of,

$$f_{SDRAM} = \frac{1}{800 \times 2^{20}} = \frac{1.25 \times 10^{-3}}{2^{20}} = 1.192GHz$$

Newer DDR SDRAM (double-data-rate SDRAM) has a peak transfer rate of 2.1GBps.

3.3. Memory management

In computer systems the memory management subsystem is concerned with ensuring that all the processes, which are running have the necessary memory allocated to them. This task can be divided into three areas, [19]

1. Memory management hardware (Memory Management Units (MMUs), RAM, etc.). The MMU is a hardware device responsible for handling memory access by the CPU.
2. Operating system software for memory management (virtual memory, protection), (refer to Chapter 2 for Windows kernel memory management features). [10]

3. Application memory management (allocation, de-allocation, garbage collection).

Memory management hardware consists of the electronic devices that look after the physical connections and bits transfer. These devices include RAM, MMUs (memory management units), caches, disks, and processor registers.

Operating system memory management controls the way that the hardware works in order to provide memory resources to programs. The most significant part of this is virtual memory, which creates the illusion that every process has more memory than is actually available. The O/S memory management is also concerned with memory protection and security.

Application memory management is the actual process loading and swapping that was mentioned earlier. Most applications or processes that are running have dynamically changing memory requirements. The application memory manager must deal with this while at the same time optimising CPU and memory usage. To summarise therefore, memory management is concerned with providing the following,

1. Enable several processes to appear to execute at the same time (i.e. time share the CPU).
2. Enable processes to share physical memory.
3. Provide satisfactory program execution speeds.
4. Protect one process from another.

3.4. Memory allocation methods

Memory is allocated to processes according to the microprocessor architecture and the way that the memory manager is designed to operate. For example, the memory manager may allocate a fixed size partition to every process. This could be found in embedded microcontroller applications where the processes that need to run are lightweight and whose size is known. Since only one process can reside in memory at any one time, these would typically be single task systems. If multi-tasking is required, such as for example, in real-time systems, then there could be more than one fixed partition in memory. This arrangement was initially used in early IBM360s systems, and it is very useful for two main reasons namely,

1. It allows a number of processes to be stored in memory of different sizes.
2. Memory protection is derived from the fact that the size of a partition is known and wrong address generations are easily detected.

Single process system

In embedded computer applications where, it is common for the CPU to run only one process at a time, memory management is simple. The process to be executed is loaded into the free memory space and the rest of the memory space will be unused. Figure 3.2 represents a single process allocation. Such an arrangement is clearly limited in capability and is now found only in simple systems such as hand held games computers. Also early MS-DOS systems operated in this way. While it is still valid to have such a memory model in simple embedded systems, this arrangement is not applicable to multi-tasking applications.

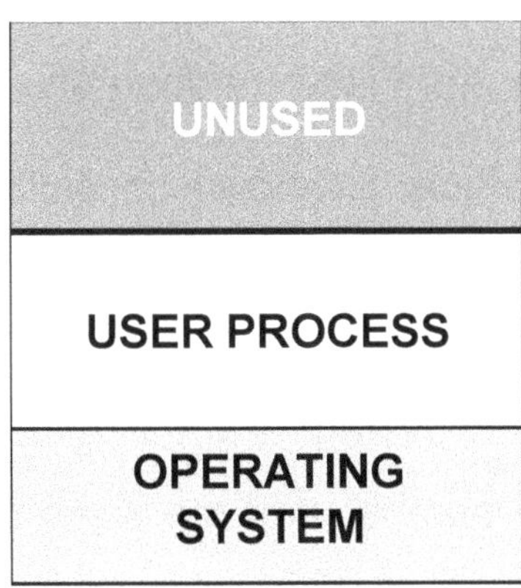

Figure 3.2. Single partition memory with single process allocation.

For multi-tasking, a necessary extension to this basic model is to permit the loading of more than one process into memory simultaneously, which leads on to alternative schemes considered next.

Fixed partition memory

This scheme follows on from the single partition above, by offering a number of partitions of fixed sizes. Each of these partitions can accommodate a separate process, and so multi-tasking is possible. The arrangement is shown in figure 3.3.

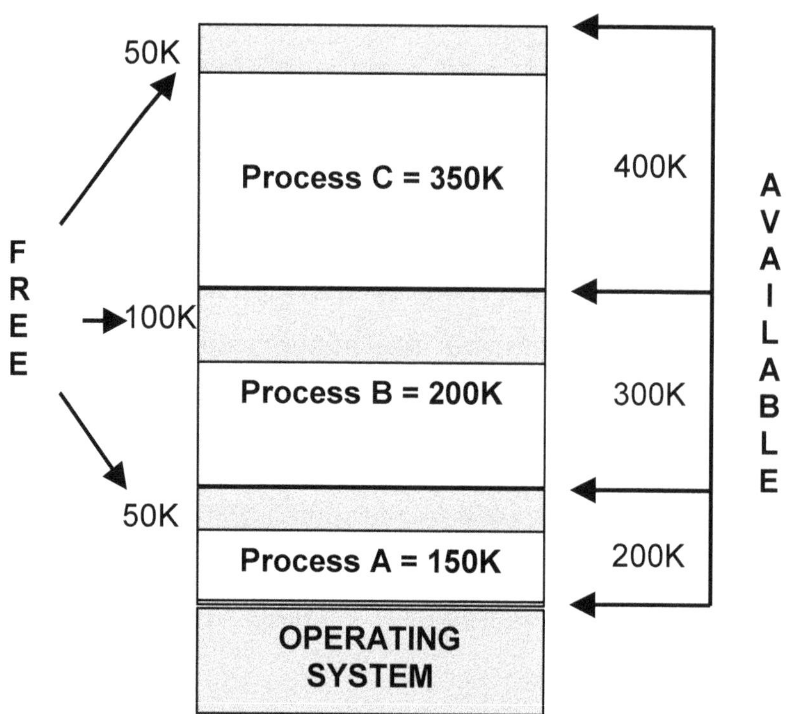

Figure 3.3. Fixed Partition Allocation

In figure 3.3 the memory is shown consisting of three areas, of size 200K, 300K and 400K respectively, each of which holds a process. If the operating system can support multi-tasking, all three processes can be active at any one time. In a practical system with this allocation method, the memory manager would control the number and the sizes of partitions. This would in turn depend on the amount of total memory available and the size of processes to run. Typically, a range of partition sizes would be set up, so that a mixture of large and small processes could be accommodated. Since there is no general way to prevent a process generating an invalid address, memory protection has to be implemented by the operating system and/or hardware. Since the partition sizes are fixed, it is relatively straightforward to implement basic memory protection by using limit registers.

Fixed partition systems are useful in embedded multi-tasking applications, but they do have limitations. The main problem is in the fact that the fixed size of memory limits the size of the program that can run, and also if a very small program needed to run, then the memory space would be under-utilised. Another major concern is internal fragmentation, which is explained next.

Internal fragmentation

During normal operation processes are loaded into memory and upon completion, swapped back to secondary storage. As processes are running, every partition will typically contain unused space, illustrated by the shaded areas in figure 3.3 and as a result the total unused space could be considerable. With reference to figure 3.3 the total combined unused space is 50K+100K+50K=200K.

This type of space distribution is referred to as internal fragmentation because the total available space is fragmented. Internal fragmentation wastes space within partitions which, if combined would provide sufficient memory to run another process. Another problem with fixed partitions is that large programs cannot fit into all the partitions, and therefore they have to wait for a large partition to be freed up.

Variable partition memory

One solution to the fixed partition problems is to allow partitions to be variable in size at load time. The variable partition method allocates to every process the exact amount of memory that it needs. Initially, processes are loaded into consecutive memory areas as shown in figure 3.4. When a process that is in a partition terminates, the space which it occupied, is freed up and this becomes available for the loading of a new process. After a number of processes have terminated the memory space appears as a series of 'holes' between the active memory areas. Fragmentation is obvious in this case and this can lead to a situation where, even though the total free space is adequate, a new process cannot be started because none of the available holes is large enough.

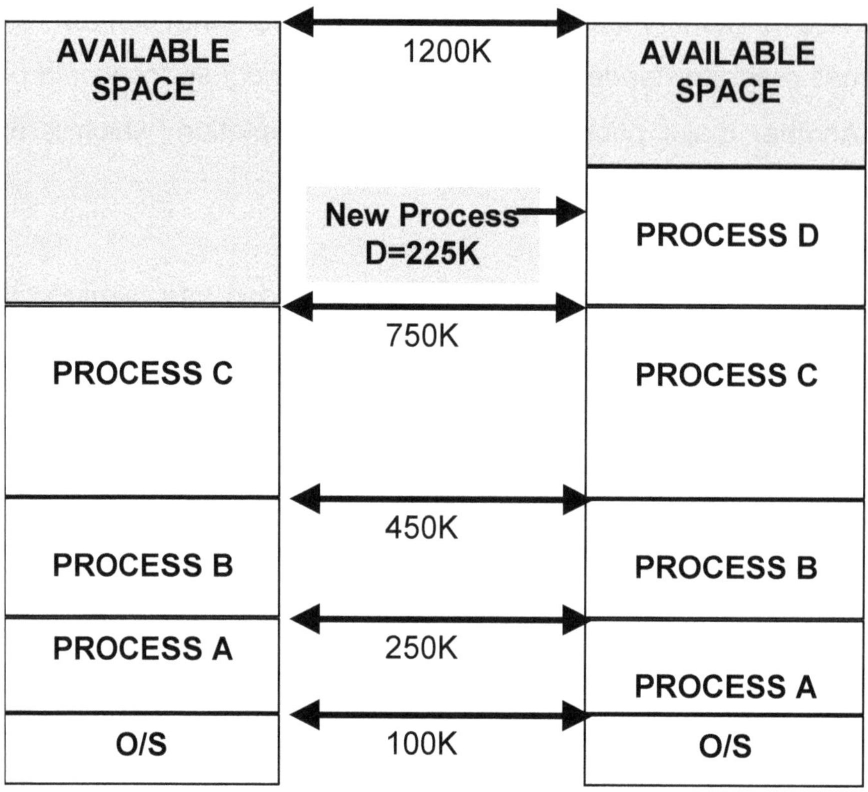

Figure 3.4. Variable partition allocation method

This situation is illustrated in figure 3.5 a) in which processes A and C have terminated. The total available space is 150+300+225=675K and yet the largest program that can be accommodated is 300K. Such distribution of free memory space is called external fragmentation where 'external' refers to space vacated by a process that has terminated. Note that internal fragmentation occurs in the fixed partition scheme where 'internal' implies 'within the space allocated to a process.

Coalescing of holes

It is frequently the case that a process adjacent to one or more holes will terminate and free its space. The result of this is the creation of two or more adjacent holes. These empty memory locations can then be merged together and utilised as a single hole, as shown in figure 3.5 b) in which Process B has terminated, linking up the holes created by previously running processes A and C. The combined effect is that the free space is now a contiguous space of 500K. This effect of combining adjacent empty memory locations is referred to as coalescing of holes, and is a significant factor in maintaining fragmentation within usable limits.

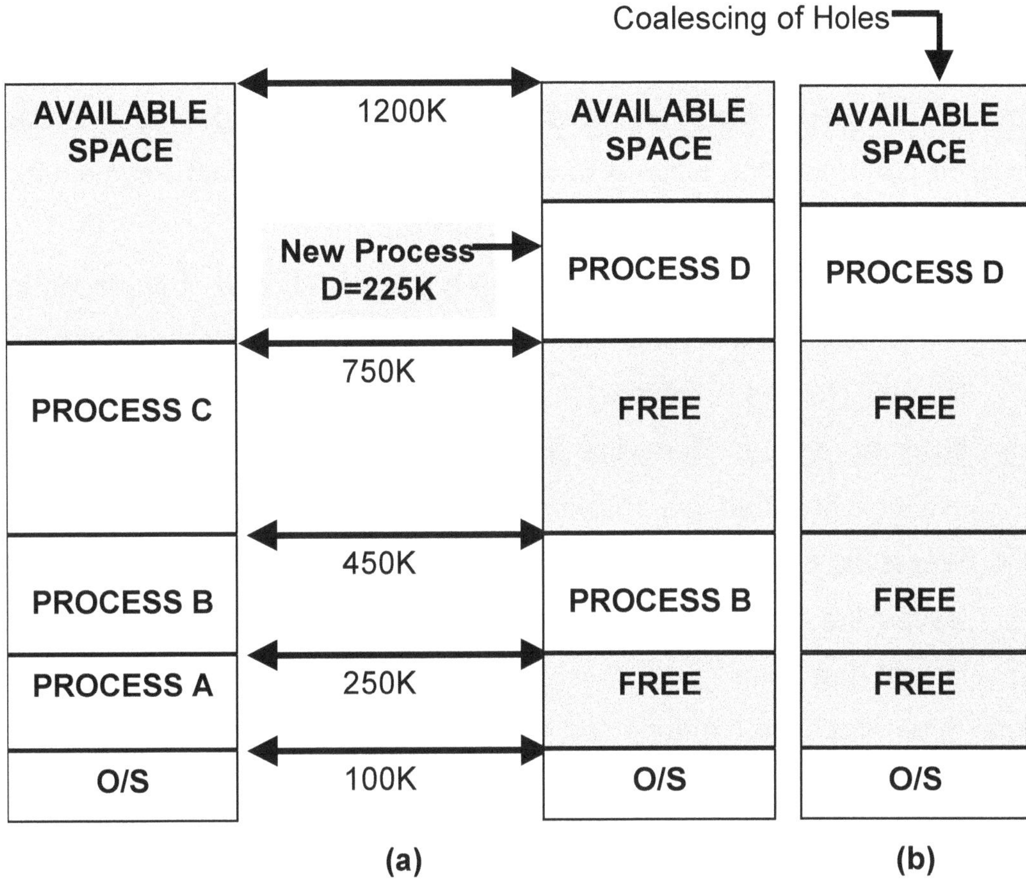

Figure 3.5. a) External fragmentation b) Coalescing of holes

It is also possible for the O/S to periodically flush the memory by rearranging the memory allocation to processes in order to eliminate external fragmentation. This process, referred to as compaction, physically moves resident processes in memory to produce the best general fit. The problem with this is that processes have to be suspended while they are being moved. This can produce heavy CPU overheads and therefore it is seldom used. However, when compaction is used, it can either be done at preset intervals, as soon as a process terminates or when a process does not have sufficient memory to load.

3.5. Storage placement policies

Processes that run in a multi-tasking system are usually of different sizes and therefore the allocation of memory to every process has to be governed by a placement policy. With the variable partition scheme it is necessary to select the 'best' location to load new processes. Inefficient allocation can delay the loading of a process due to external fragmentation. The following describes a number of such policies,

- **Best-fit policy:** In this policy when a process arrives, it is placed in a hole where the difference between the size of the hole and the size of the new process is the least.
- **First fit policy:** Here the incoming process is placed in the first available hole that can accommodate it.
- **Worst fit policy:** An incoming process is placed in the hole, which leaves the maximum amount of unused space, implying the current largest hole.

These three allocation methods can be illustrated with reference to figure 3.6. Here, a new process needs to be placed into one of the three available partitions, which are of different sizes. All partitions are large enough to accommodate the process, which is 150K bytes. However each partition will leave a different memory residue. For example,

Using the first fit policy: P1 (150K) fits into 300K leaving 150K free. Partitions 2 and 3 are still free and the three partitions can accommodate process ranging from 150K-400K. The smallest partition is 150K, which means that relatively large processes can be loaded.

Using the best fit policy: P1 (150K) the least amount of residue is obtained when P1 is placed into 200K leaving 50K free. Partitions 1 and 3 are still free and the three partitions can now accommodate any process ranging from 50K-400K, where the smallest partition can hold only 50K. Thus, if a process larger than 50K arrives, it can only fit into larger partitions. In the event that all processes arriving are greater than 50K, the smallest partition will remain unused.

Using the worst fit policy: P1 (150K) the most residue is obtained when P1 is placed into 400K leaving 250K free. Partitions 1 and 2 are still free and the three partitions can now accommodate any process ranging from 250K-400K, where the smallest partition can hold 250K.

Thus, it is seen that if processes larger than 150K are likely to prevail, then it may be better to use the worst-fit policy than the best-fit policy. This is because the residue that is left in this case can accommodate larger processes.

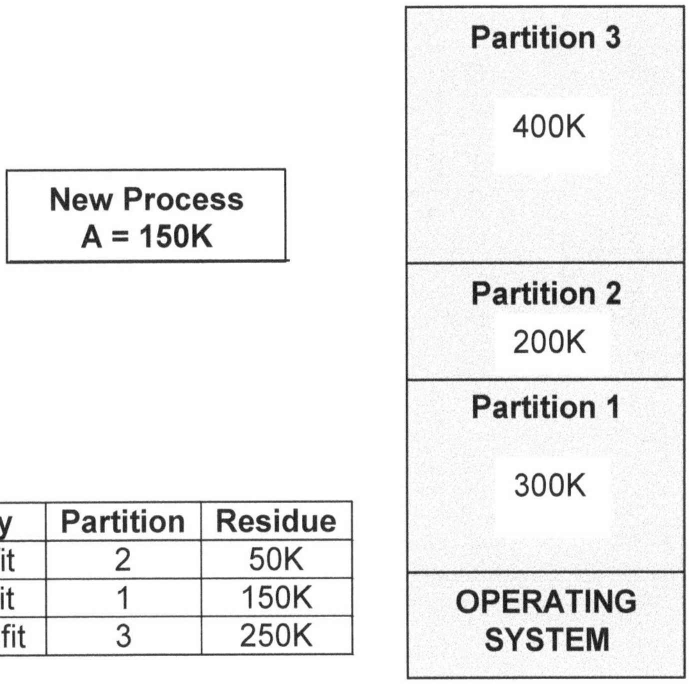

New Process
A = 150K

Partition 3
400K
Partition 2 200K
Partition 1 300K
OPERATING SYSTEM

Policy	**Partition**	**Residue**
Best fit	2	50K
First fit	1	150K
Worst fit	3	250K

Figure 3.6. Placement policies with a table of memory residues

In order to facilitate placement policies and to monitor the size of the memory residue, linked lists are used to describe each partition. Linked lists contain pointers to the size of each hole and its start address.

3.6. Paging

Paging is a very valuable feature of memory management. By dividing memory into equal size pages, any process can be loaded into a number of these pages. Additionally, when a page from one process completes, a page from another process can easily replace it because all the pages are of the same size. Therefore, paged memory divides all memory in equal size pages, each with a page number and a displacement contained in the 'Page Table'. Process pages do not need to be contiguous since allocation is done on a page-by-page basis. Furthermore, it is possible to relocate processes by only changing the reference in the page table.

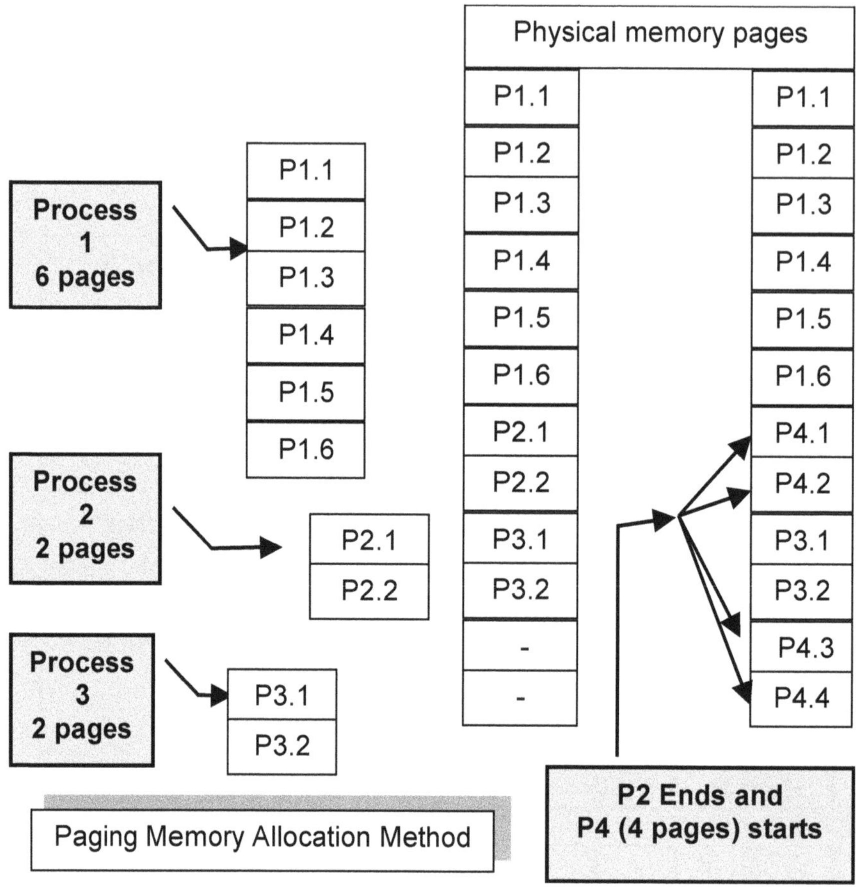

Figure 3.7. Paged memory system

With reference to figure 3.7, when the processes P1, P2 and P3 are first loaded, the memory pages are filled in a sequential manner. As these processes run and pages terminate, some pages leave physical memory. For example, figure 3.7 shows that P2 finishes and vacates two pages that it occupied. Another process P4, which is four pages long, subsequently enters, and occupies the four pages that are free. It is seen that when P4 enters, it occupies pages that are not contiguous. This is perfectly acceptable because process pages do not need to be contiguous since allocation is done on a page-by-page basis. A paging table takes care of locating pages for every process and keeping track of where pages are.

Implementation of paging

Paging is a very useful feature of memory management and in particular when it is used in a multi-tasking environment with virtual memory. Allocating the pages of memory to processes is a very complex task if the overall performance needs to be optimised. Splitting a process into a number of pages implies that when the process runs, the paging system must monitor and schedule multiple parts of each process. The solution to this problem lies in the way a specific memory location is addressed in a paging environment.

A page address is made up of two components a page number (*p*) and a displacement (*d*) within that page that identifies a particular memory location. In this manner, and in the knowledge that all pages are of the same size, it is relatively easy to locate a desired physical address using the equation,

$$P_{address} = p \times size \times +d \qquad (3.2)$$

For example, assume that all pages are 4K and that we want to find the location of a byte in memory with page *p=4* and offset *d=32*. According to equation 3.2, the location is given as follows,

$$P_{address} = 4 \times (4 \times 2^{10}) + 32 = 16{,}416$$

The form (*p, d*) used to locate a physical memory location is easy to represent using binary representation. For example if the page size is 2K then the displacement value is made up of 11 bits (i.e. 2^{11}=2K). If a 16-bit address bus is used, this means that 5 bits remain for the representation of the page number. In other words, there are 2^5=32 page numbers. Figure 3.8 shows an example of how a 16-bit address can be divided into the *p* and *d* fields. Here, the page number uses the high 5 bits and therefore has a value range of 0 to 31, which gives 32 pages. The displacement value uses 11 bits and therefore has a range of 0 to 2023. This means a system based on this scheme would have 32 pages each of 2024 locations. Increasing the page size to 4K would reduce the number of pages to 16, since the total address space is still 16–bits.

Figure 3.8. 16 bit address example

Consider an example, using a 16-bit address 0010 1000 0010 1010. This can be divided into page and displacement values as follows,

	Page	Displacement
Binary	00101	00000101010
Decimal	5	42

Hence this location can be expressed as the paging address of (5, 42).

Example

A computer uses a 20-bit address system, with 6 bits used as a page address and 14 bits used as a displacement. Given that a paging address is 00111100000011100010, calculate the total number of pages.

Solution

Page number (6 bits)   001111= 15 decimal

Displacement (14 bits)   00000011100010= 226 decimal

Hence the paging address of (15,226).

As mentioned earlier, a page can be relocated by simply changing an entry in the page table. This is shown in figure 3.9 where the converted address to the right is made up of the 5-bit page number and in this case an 11-bit displacement. The displacement remains the same, but the page number changes according to the pointer p in the page table. If for example, p changed to 0010, then location 2, i.e. (10111) in the page table would be used to reference the page.

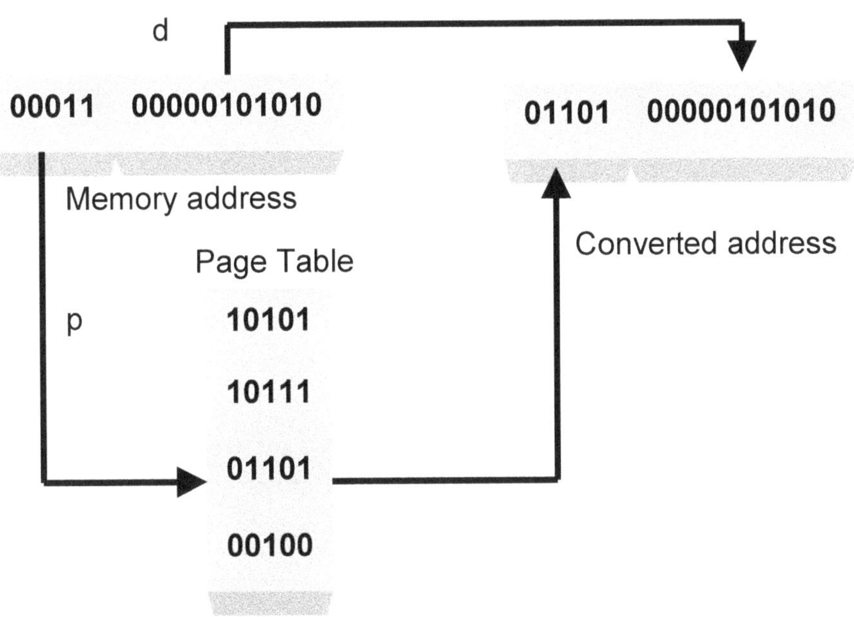

Figure 3.9 Relocation using page table

3.7. Simple segmentation

Segmentation is the principle of dividing memory into segments. Segments are larger than pages and the main reason to use them is to provide additional control over the addressing and the allocation of memory. Segments can be configured to be variable in length, or as in the case of the Intel 80x86 microprocessor, all segments have the same length of 64K. Figure 3.10 can be used to explain the principle of simple segmentation. Here, two separate processes are loaded into memory. They are dispersed in the main memory into segments that are of different sizes. The reason for this is that different processes are themselves of a different size, and segments are allocated to reflect this. Once again, as in paging, segments belonging to a process do not need to be contiguous because the address of every segment is stored in a segment table. It is also possible to have overlapping segments and this happens when the start address of the segment is within another segment. In these situations there is a strong possibility of data corruption since the code in one segment may be corrupted by data of another segment. In all cases it is the responsibility of the programmer to ensure that code is designed in such a way that segments are protected from interference by programs.

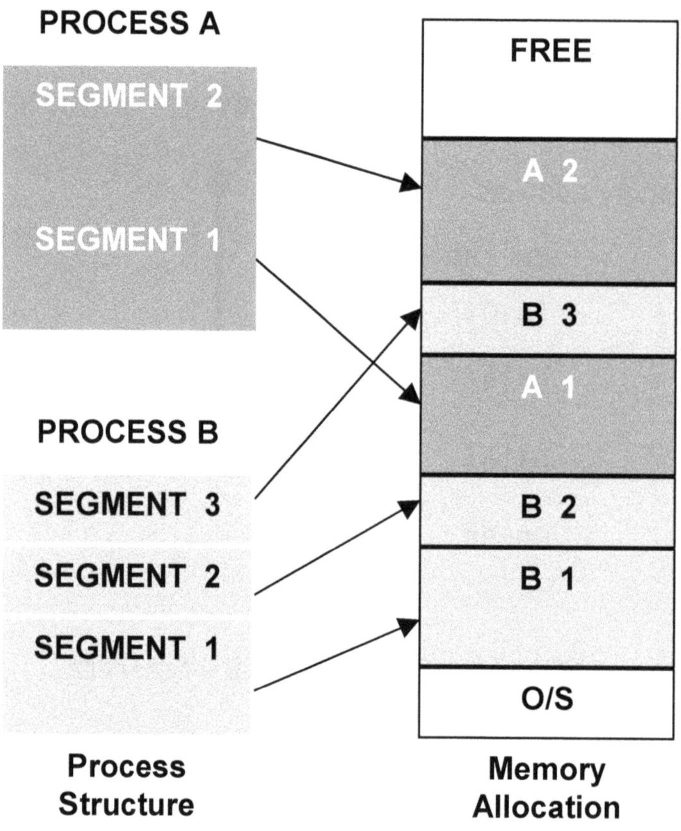

Figure 3.10. Simple segmentation

Segment addressing

Conversion of a logical address into a physical address is similar to the paging system in so far as two parameters are used to locate a memory address. Namely, the segment reference *s*, and the displacement *d*, within that segment are used to locate an address. Note that physical address is the actual address in memory. The logical address is what the program uses while executing.

A process segment table, as shown in figure 3.11 contains the size and the base address of each segment. The logical address contains a reference to the segment and the offset address. The physical address is obtained by locating the base address of the segment and adding to this the displacement. Thus, for example a logical address given in figure 3.11 is made up of the LHS five bits that point to the segment; the other bits contain the offset. The segment pointer *s*, points to the segment with the base address of 0110 1110

1110 0000. The physical address of the memory location is obtained by adding this base address to the displacement. This is shown in table 3.2.

Table 3.2

Logical address	0	0	0	1	1	0	0	0	0	0	1	0	1	0	1	0
Base address	0	1	1	0	1	1	1	0	1	1	1	0	1	0	1	0
Physical address	0	1	1	0	1	1	1	1	0	0	0	0	1	0	1	0

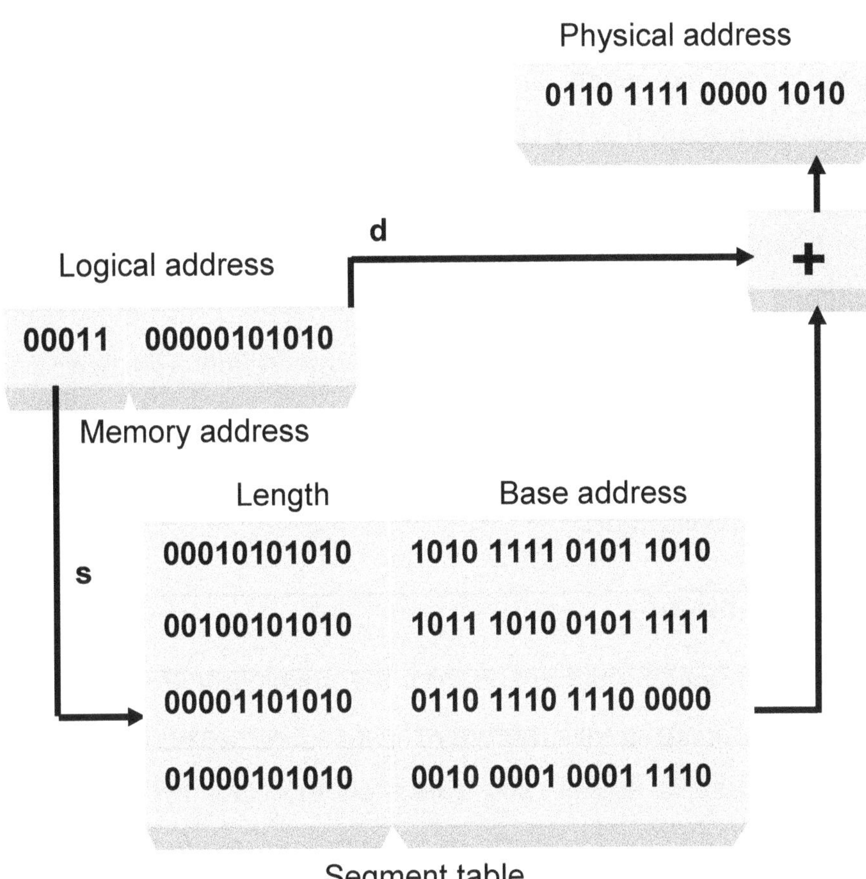

Figure 3.11. Addressing using a segment table

In general therefore, a segmented address reference requires the following steps,

- Separate the segment number and the displacement from the logical address.
- Use the segment number to index the segment table and obtain the segment base address and length.
- Check that the offset does not exceed segment length; if it does then an invalid address error is generated.

- Calculate the required physical address by adding offset to the base address.

In a shared-memory environment segmentation can be used to protect one process from another. Since the CPU is not able to distinguish between instructions and simply executes the bytes that have been fetched, if there is a memory error, and the instruction that has been fetched is not the correct one, the program will fail. Thus, it is necessary to protect memory space allocated to a program during execution. Segmentation provides the size of the segment that is being referenced; this can be used to check for any addressing errors.

For example, on the Intel x86 architecture, the Global Descriptor Table (GDT) and Local Descriptor Tables (LDT) are used to reference segments in the computer's memory. Together these are used to protect memory by performing checks on address limits, privilege levels etc. Every memory reference is checked before the memory cycle begins and any violation results in an exception. Detailed explanation of the Intel memory management system can be found in Intel literature. [10]

3.8. Virtual memory

Virtual memory concept arises from the principle that it is not necessary to load the entire process into memory for it to begin execution. Rather, if a portion of a process is loaded and executed then the rest of the available memory can be used to load portions of other processes. In this manner, many large processes can run in physical memory, which is significantly smaller than the sum-total of the memory requirements of all these processes. Furthermore, if small sections of processes are loaded into memory it is logical to assume that they will terminate sooner than full program code. Replacing a section of the process that has terminated with another one incurs a context switch overhead, as would a normal process termination. Therefore, it makes complete sense for these sections to be of equal size, so that they can be interchanged without the worry of fragmentation. Consequently, if each process is divided into pages of equal size then some, rather than all, of the pages belonging to a process can be loaded into memory for the CPU to execute. In this manner the CPU can execute the code for each page and call on new pages, as the code that it is executing requires.

For example, looking at figure 3.12 the total available physical RAM is 20K and the total size of all the executing processes is 48K. Therefore the system appears to have 28K of virtual memory.

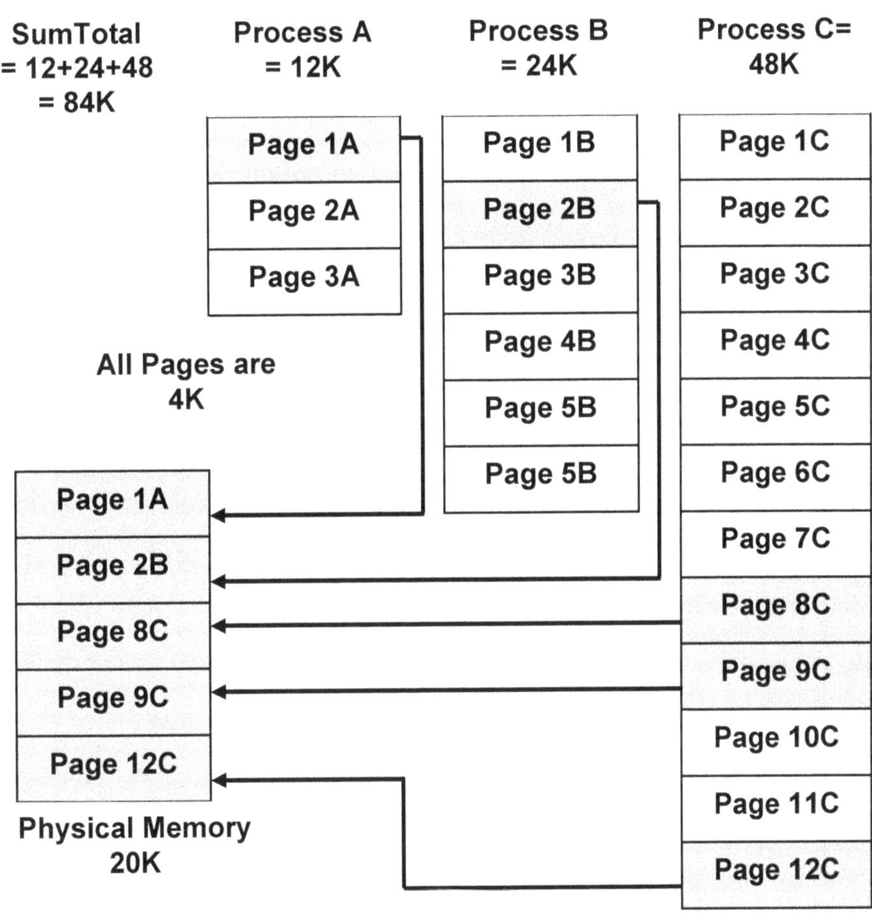

Figure 3.12. Virtual memory

Thus, it is seen that virtual memory is not physical RAM; rather it is the memory address space that a process would occupy if it were loaded in full. To speed things up a section of the hard disk is delegated as the virtual memory space and it is here that the virtual pages are stored. Nevertheless, when these pages need to be transferred to physical memory, this is a disk I/O. Figure 3.12 shows that only five virtual memory pages are mapped onto physical memory. (Which means that these pages are in RAM). When a page that is required cannot be found in physical memory a page fault occurs. For example, with reference to figure 3.12, if page 2 of process A needs to be loaded into physical memory this is called a 'page fault'. Table 3.3 show the sequence of events that occur following a page fault. Here, the executing program is interrupted and control is transferred to the O/S. The memory management system decides which page to replace and this is followed by a page replacement, which involves a disk I/O. When the replacement is complete, the page table is updated and control returned to the interrupted program.

Table 3.3

	Sequence of operations on a page fault
1	Page fault
2	User program interrupted, OS takes control
3	OS identifies page to overwrite/replace (page replacement)
4	Disk I/O, page replacement, update page table
5	Restart interrupted program

When a page fault occurs, the memory manager needs to make space available for the new page and if the physical memory is full, it needs to decide which of the pages to evict. Thus, a page that is already executing and is present in physical memory must be evicted and the term used for this is 'demand paging'. The decision as to which page to evict relies on a page replacement policy and this will be covered later in this chapter.

Resident set

When a new program needs to run, the loader must load at least one page from this process. As the page code is executed, there may be a need to load another page from the same process. When more then one page from the same process is present in physical memory then this forms the so-called 'resident set' for the process.

Once again referring to figure 3.12 pages 8C, 9C and 12C are the resident set for process C. Clearly, the larger the resident set for any process, the sooner it will complete, because the process as a whole is receiving a higher proportion of CPU time. It has to be said however that, when too many processes are running at the same time their resident sets will change quickly causing frequent page faults. In this event the processor spends most of its time swapping pages rather than executing program code, and this situation is called 'thrashing'. On the other hand if the page size is large, fewer pages can reside in physical RAM and therefore fewer processes will be able to run. This means that a compromise is needed between page size and the number of processes that are running at the same time. This compromise is based on the reasoning that small page sizes and many processes leads to thrashing and large page sizes with a few processes leads to idle processor time.

Working set

Another useful measure of memory and process performance is the so-called 'working set'. This is a set of pages belonging to a process that have been used during an observation period, called the 'working set window'. Furthermore, it is likely that during the observation window, these pages also constituted the resident set. In fact, the execution of a process is most efficient when the resident set and the working set have the same pages.

Locality of reference

Most of the programming effort to produce computer programs has been done by human programmers. The rules of programming that are taught in schools and colleges govern the general approaches to programming. For example function oriented programming and object oriented programming are distinctive and programmers will adhere to the general principles of the paradigm that they are working with. As a result the executable code that the programmers produce tends to have a pattern so that most processes while executing tend to linger within a narrow range of addresses. This in turn leads to a reduced number of page faults due to the so-called 'locality of reference'.

3.9. Page replacement

In terms of the amount of time that it takes to complete, page replacement is very costly. Typically the ratio between access to a page in the physical memory and to a page in the hard disk is 1:1000 time units. Hit ratio is defined as a measure of paging system performance as follows,

$$HR = \frac{Hits\_Time}{Total\_Page\_Calls\_Time} \times 100\% \quad (3.1)$$

A high hit ratio is desirable because of the very large speed differential between access to main memory and access to the hard disk. (i.e. at least 1:1000) For example, assume that after 100 page calls there is 1 miss, and 99 hits, which gives a 99% hit rate. Assuming that a page hit consumes 1 unit of time, and a page miss consumes 1000 units of time, then the cost in time of 99 hits is 99 units of time. Similarly, the cost in time of 1 miss is 1000 units of time.

Therefore the Hit Ratio is $HR = \frac{99}{1000} \times 100\% = 9.9\%$

Thus, a single miss in 100 calls results in only approximately 10% of maximum performance. This simple observation suggests that much effort needs to be directed toward reducing the number of page faults during program execution. Perhaps the most obvious way to deal with this is to define the policies that will govern the replacement of pages. Some of the common page replacement policies are given next.

Page replacement policies

When a page fault occurs the memory manager needs to have well defined rules that will govern page replacement. These rules are called page replacement policies and they are used to decide which of the pages in memory should be evicted. In order to demonstrate the replacement process it is common to use a simulated table of pages as they are called, and then to apply a page replacement policy in order to decide which page to evict. An example of this simulated table is shown in table 3.4.

Table 3.4 Example of simulation with 3 physical page frames

Page call sequence	2	3	2	1	5	2	4	5	3	5	3	2
Page frame 0												
Page frame 1												
Page frame 2												

Here the page call sequence is 2,3,2,1,5,2,4,5,3,5,3,2 refers to the pages that the memory manager calls as a result of the execution of the process. Thus starting from left to right, page 2 is called, and then some arbitrary time later, page 3 is called etc. These pages can belong to different processes and are used here only to simulate the page replacement policy.

LRU:- least recently used: This replacement policy looks at the previous page calls to identify the page whose last call happened the longest time ago. i.e. least recently. To illustrate this, the simulation is shown below.

Page call sequence	2	3	2	1	5	2	4	5	3	5	3	2
Page frame 0	2	2	2	2	2	2	2	2	3	3	3	3
Page frame 1	-	3	3	3	5	5	5	5	5	5	5	5
Page frame 2	-	-	-	1	1	1	4	4	4	4	4	2

From the simulation the misses are highlighted in grey and we note that there are 4 misses out of a total of 12 calls. This means that there were 8 hits. Assuming a time differential of a 1000:1 for (miss: hit), the hit ratio can be calculated from equation 3.1.

$$HR = \frac{Hits\_Time}{Total\_Page\_Calls\_Time} \times 100\% = \frac{(8 \times 1) \times 100}{(8 \times 1) + (4 \times 1000)} = \frac{800}{4008} = 0.199\%$$

FIFO- first in first out: The first page to enter the main memory is also the first to be replaced. This policy is based on the notion that the page you replace has been in memory the longest, and so it should be safe to remove it. To illustrate this, the simulation is shown below.

Page call sequence	2	3	2	1	5	2	4	5	3	5	3	2
Page frame 0	2	2	2	2	5	5	5	5	3	3	3	3
Page frame 1	-	3	3	3	3	2	2	2	2	5	5	5
Page frame 2	-	-	-	1	1	1	4	4	4	4	4	2

From the simulation the misses are highlighted in grey and we note that there are 6 misses out of a total of 12 calls. This means that there were 6 hits. Assuming a time differential of a 1000:1 for (miss: hit), the hit ratio can be calculated from equation 3.1.

$$HR = \frac{Hits\_Time}{Total\_Page\_Calls\_Time} \times 100\% = \frac{(6 \times 1) \times 100}{(6 \times 1) + (6 \times 1000)} = \frac{600}{6006} = 0.999\%$$

Optimal policy: Selects page for which the time for next reference is the greatest. This means that the policy relies on being able to predict the future page calls. This can be done in software by looking at past trends in page calls in order to identify patterns. There is a probability calculation overhead, but when it is considered that single miss costs 1000 units of time, this overhead can be justified. To illustrate this, the simulation is shown below.

Page call sequence	2	3	2	1	5	2	4	5	3	5	3	2
Page frame 0	2	2	2	2	2	2	2	2	3	3	3	3
Page frame 1	-	3	3	3	3	3	4	4	4	4	4	4
Page frame 2	-	-	-	1	5	5	5	5	5	5	5	2

From the simulation the misses are highlighted in grey and we note that there are 4 misses out of a total of 12 calls. This means that there were 8 hits. Assuming a time differential of a 1000:1 for (miss: hit), the hit ratio can be calculated from equation 3.1.

$$HR = \frac{Hits\_Time}{Total\_Page\_Calls\_Time} \times 100\% = \frac{(8 \times 1) \times 100}{(8 \times 1) + (4 \times 1000)} = \frac{800}{4008} = 0.199\%$$

This happens to be the same value as the LRU policy above, but the two policies would normally give different results for the hit ratio.

Clock policy: This policy is difficult to simulate and therefore only an explanation is offered. The policy arranges pages in a circular list. Each page that is in this list has a run bit R, which can take a value of 0 or 1, depending if it has been used or not. The clock goes around the circle and checks to see if a page has the R-bit set to one so that it can be evicted, i.e. R=1. If the bit is not set to 1 it has to be 0 and the page is passed but at the same time its R-bit is set to 1. In this manner, it is guaranteed that after a full circle, even if all the R-bits are zero, there will be a one on the next cycle. Thus, if R=1 the page is evicted, if R=0 clock sets this R=1 and continues to make a circle. For example, in figure 3.13, when R=1 is reached, that page will be replaces and its R-bit set to zero.

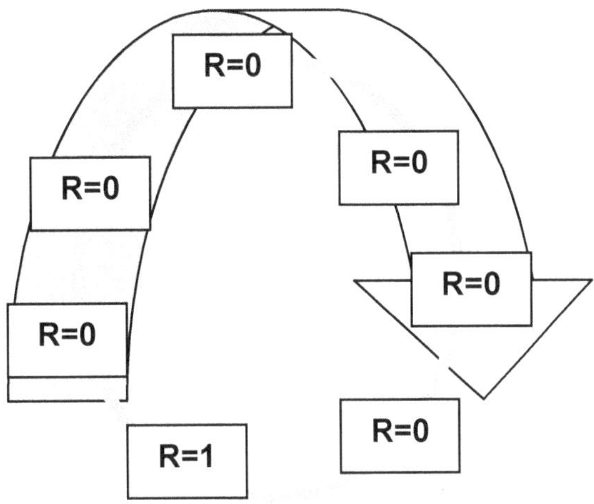

Figure 3.13 Clock page replacement policy

Exercises

3.1 Explain what is meant by the following terms in memory management; coalescing of holes, internal and external fragmentation, and compaction.

3.2 Explain how a logical address consisting of 18 bits could be converted to a paging address where each page was 1K. How many pages would be available?

3.3 In a segmented memory system an address of 24 bits is used to support up to 256 segments. Describe this system and how it could be implemented. What would be the maximum size of each segment?

3.4 For a Pentium processor with 32-bit addressing the maximum addressable space is 4Gigabytes ($4.3x10^9$). If page size=4K. How many virtual pages can be addressed? If each table entry is 5 bytes how much memory space is required for the whole table?

3.5 Explain the following terms; virtual paging, page fault, resident page set, working set, thrashing, locality of reference, hit ratio.

3.6 Assume a virtual paging system has 3 real page frames. Simulate the effect of LRU, FIFO and optimal policies for page replacement for the following sequence of virtual page references:

Sequence 1332545414225

(Assume that all page frames are initially empty).

For each replacement policy calculate the hit-ratio and compare these.

3.7 A computer uses an 18-bit address system with 6 bits used as a page address and 12 bits used as a displacement. Calculate the page size, the total number of pages and express the following address as a paging address; 001110000000111000 .

3.8 In a paged-segmented system, a virtual address consists of 32 bits of which 12 are a displacement, 11 bits are a segment number and 9 bits are a page number. Calculate: page size, maximum segment size, maximum number of pages, and maximum number of segments.

4 COMPUTER NETWORKS

4.1. Introduction

A computer network is obtained when two or more computers are connected together and are able to exchange information. The hardware, including computers, communication links, the location of the devices etc is described by the 'physical design' of these networks. The IEEE provides the operational standards for a wide range of networks and devices. For example, the IEEE 802 LAN/MAN Standards Committee develops Local Area Network (LAN) standards and Metropolitan Area Network (MAN) standards. The most widely used standards are for the Ethernet family including, Token Ring, Wireless LAN, Bridging and Virtual Bridged LANs. An individual Working Group within the IEEE provides the focus for each area. The logical network design describes the domain architecture, the server arrangement and the roles of computers on the network.

All networks rely on communications that link the participants in the network together and enable them to share resources. In computer networks data travels as digital signals and therefore the data communications element is a significant component of network design. By design, the central processing unit (CPU) works with digital data and it cannot process analogue signals. However, digital signals are generally low power and they cannot travel very far. For long distances these digital signals are modulated onto an analogue carrier at the sending end, and de-modulated at the receiving end. This has led to the term Modem (i.e. MODulator DEModulator). Some basic techniques will be discussed next.

Signal transmission

Signalling refers to the manner in which a signal moves through a medium. Computers process data in digital format and this is how data must be presented to them. Digital signals that are presented to the CPU are at Transistor-Transistor Logic (TTL) voltage levels of either 5V or 1V representing a logical '1' or a '0'. As mentioned earlier, these signals are not powerful enough to travel long distances so they need to be modulated onto an analogue carrier that has sufficient power to travel through the medium. However, data can travel through different media types and also a digital signal can be modulated onto a range of analogue carriers. When these signals reach their destination they must be demodulated so that they can be processed. An electronic device called a Modem performs this signal conditioning, where modulation and de-modulation takes place.

Modulation tends to deform the analogue carrier signal in a manner that is related to the digital signal and consequently, the modulated signal appears distorted. There are many different modulation techniques that can be utilised in a modem some of these are as follows,

- Amplitude shift key modulation (ASK).
- Frequency shift key modulation (FSK).
- Binary-phase shift key modulation (BPSK).
- Quadrature-phase shift key modulation (QPSK).
- Quadrature amplitude modulation (QAM).

The description of the above is beyond the scope of this text, but as a brief example figure 4.1 shows the manner in which Quadrature Amplitude Modulation (QAM) can be performed. QAM is used to modulate each of the two digital input digital signals with a sinusoidal analogue carrier, and the two carriers are 90° out of phase (i.e. in quadrature). Each digital signal feeds into an electronic multiplier circuit where it is modulated with the appropriate carrier. The two signals, thus modulated, are electronically summed to produce a modulated signal. The multipliers and summers are electronic circuits that are based on operational amplifier circuits. In order that the digital signals may be retrieved, the modulated signal has to be de-modulated. Demodulation occurs in reverse to modulation and the modulated signal is fed into circuits that filter out the carries and leave only the digital signals.

In order to illustrate what a modulated signal may look like figure 4.2 shows a simple encoding of a digital signal onto a plain sine-wave carrier. This technique is known as binary phase-shift keying.

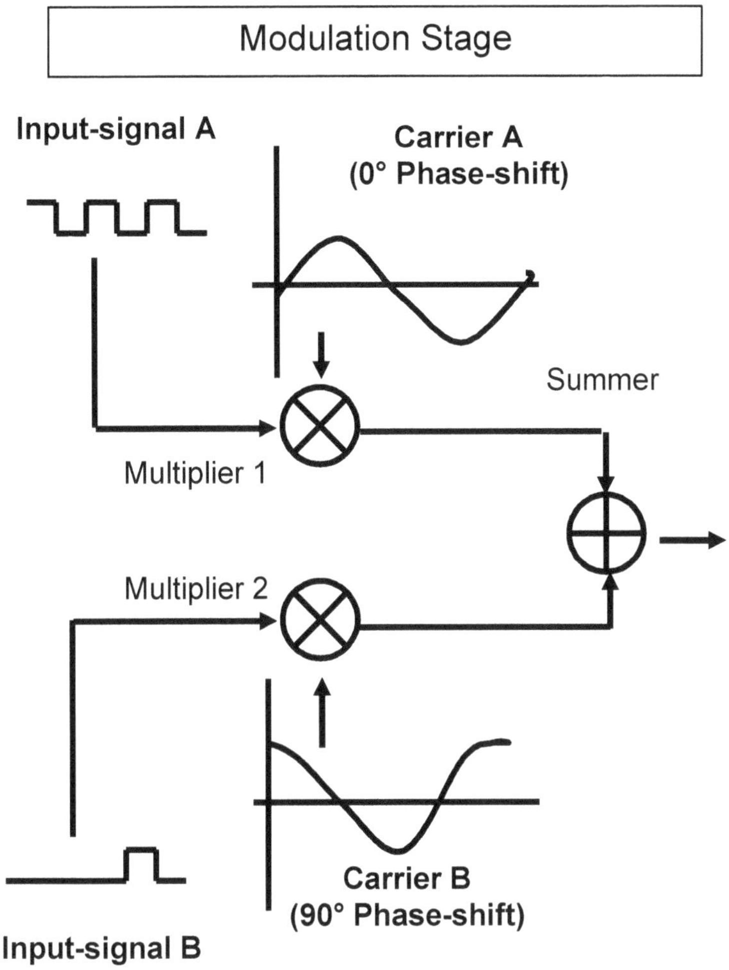

Figure 4.1. Basic principle of quadrature amplitude modulation (QAM)

At the top-left of figure 4.2 is an analogue signal that can be used as a carrier, while to the right is a digital signal representing a value as a series of bits (i.e. 0,1,1,0,1,1). The two signals can be combined together using the principle of modulation, so that the sine wave is the carrier, and the digital signal is the modulating wave. In the case shown in figure 4.2, the modulation is based on the principle that when the digital bit changes, the phase of the analogue signal is shifted by π. This way of representing a bit stream is known as binary phase-shift keying and abbreviated BPSK.

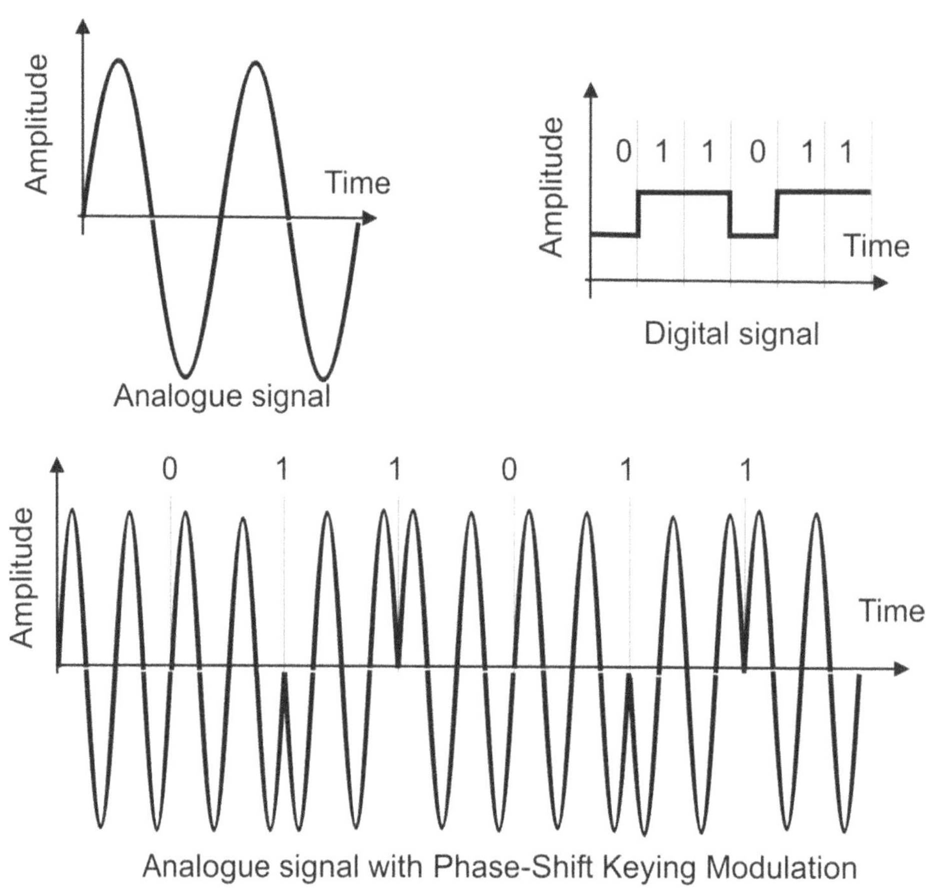

Figure 4.2. Digital signal modulation with a sine-wave carrier

4.2. Bandwidth

For analogue signals, bandwidth describes the range of frequencies that a communications channel can carry. It is usually measured in hertz as a frequency band between two frequencies i.e. *bandwidth=* (f_2-f_1). It can also be used to describe a signal, in which case the meaning is the width of the smallest frequency band within which the signal can fit. In a general sense, the higher the frequency, the higher is the bandwidth and the greater is the capacity of a channel, which carries the signal.

In computer networks, bandwidth is often used as a synonym for data transfer rate, which is the amount of data that can be carried from one point to another in a given period of time (usually per second). This kind of bandwidth is usually expressed in bits (of data) per second (bps) or as bytes per second (Bps). For example, a modem that works at 57,600 bps has twice the bandwidth of a modem that works at 28,800 bps. In terms of computer networks, higher bandwidth means a higher capacity to transmit and receive data.

4.3. Baseband and broadband transmission

Using analogue carriers in a given frequency band (i.e. channel) means that different signals can be sent at the same time through different channels. The general term for this type of transmission is broadband. Broadband can carry multiple signals by dividing the total bandwidth into multiple, independent channels, where each channel operates only on a specific range of frequencies. Broadband transmission can be used over long distances.

On the other hand baseband refers to a transmission medium through which digital signals are sent without being modulated. Baseband is therefore only used in short distance networks. Baseband transmission cannot be split into channels and the entire bandwidth is dedicated to sending data.

In baseband transmission, Time Division Multiplexing (TDM), is used to combine multiple data streams into a single signal by separating the signal into many segments, each having a very short duration. Each individual data stream is reassembled at the receiving end based on timing information. TDM repeatedly transmits a fixed sequence of time slots over a single transmission channel. Within T-Carrier systems, such as T-1 and T-3, TDM combines Pulse Code Modulated (PCM) streams created for each conversation or data stream. For example, A T1 line between two locations can be leased from the telecommunications company provider (BT in U.K.). At the physical layer this will comprise two twisted pair lines, one for transmitting and the other for receiving. Where necessary repeaters are placed along the cable at in order to regenerate the signals. Typically repeaters are needed every 2km of cable.

Baseband is generally applied in an environment with requirements for high bandwidth over a short distance. Most communications between computers, including the majority of local-area networks, use baseband communications. An exception is B-ISDN networks, which employ broadband transmission. Ethernet, token ring, FDDI, and ATM generally use baseband. [20]

Note that broadband is commonly used when referring to purchasing Internet connection from a communications company provider. In these applications Asymmetric Digital Subscriber (ADSL) modems are used as gateways between the computer and the provider. For business Internet solutions T1 lines can provide reliable Internet connection for up to 50 users. Note that T1 is a point-to-point link, which was developed, in the late early 1960's to carry 24 digitised phone calls between telephone switching offices. Therefore 24 channel circuit which provide a broadband internet connection straight from the provider backbone. As such, a T1 line can provide stable and reliable broadband connection. I say this because I mentioned earlier that T1 lines used baseband and yet we also talk about broadband Internet through T1. Thus we need to be clear about the distinction, which is that T1 is a copper cable connected point to point. It can be used to carry baseband or broadband signals. How it is used depends on the technology.

4.4. Benefits of networking

Connecting computers in a network can be a cost effective way of sharing resources. For example, everyone connected to the network can share files, peripherals, printers, and Internet connection etc, all at the same time. However, probably the most significant benefit of networks is the ability to communicate with other users. In the world of business, timely communication is paramount and the significance of networks is evident across the globe. In large corporate networks shared resources such as a data warehouse for example can store data in a central location on the network where it can be accessed by any connected computer. It is possible to store, retrieve, and modify textual information such as letters and contracts, audio information, visual images and even video segments. In organisations that use licensed software applications, a network can reduce the cost of software. Instead of buying separate licences of the same application for various machines, it is often much more economical to purchase a single network license for multiple users. In large businesses the amount of money saved on software can be substantial.

But even on a smaller scale, in small offices and educational establishments, computer networks can reduce cost of hardware by sharing components and peripherals and at the same time reducing the amount of time spent on administering and managing the network. An illustration of this is shown in figure 4.3. A properly designed network can reduce equipment costs and increase productivity. Additionally, connecting users over a computer network provides a collaborative medium to combine the power and capabilities of diverse equipment and the skills of different people, regardless of their physical location.

A well-designed computer network produces benefits on several fronts, within the company, between companies, and between companies and their customers. Within the company, networks enable businesses to streamline their internal business processes. Common tasks such as employee collaboration on projects, holding meetings etc. can take less time and reduce cost. For example, editors, writers, and artists may need to work together on a publication. With a computer network they can work on the same electronic files, each from their own computers. They can open, view, or print the same files simultaneously. [21]

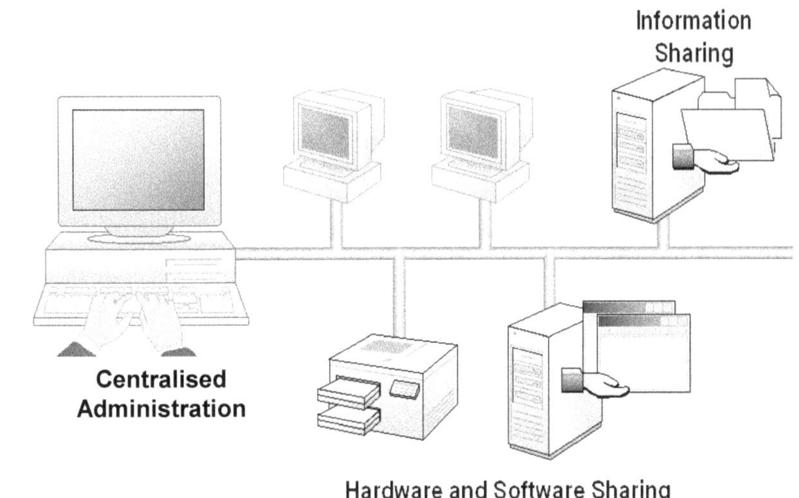

Figure 4.3. Benefits of networking

4.5. LANs and WANs

Depending on the physical location of computers networks can be local area (LANs) or Wide Area (WANs), as shown in figure 4.4. In general, LANs are used where the network is in a single location, such as a building, or a number of buildings in close proximity, for example a university campus. It is quite common for LANs to expand as the corporate network requirements increase. Expansion components such as repeaters, bridges, routers and gateways enable LAN growth. For example it is relatively easy to add workstations to remote parts of the building and to connect separate LANs to the local physical media in order to create a larger integrated local network.

Communications between LANs often includes analogue lines, digital lines and packet-switching technologies on both analogue and digital lines. These transmission methods are implemented across private or public networks (i.e. the Internet).

Local Area Network - LAN

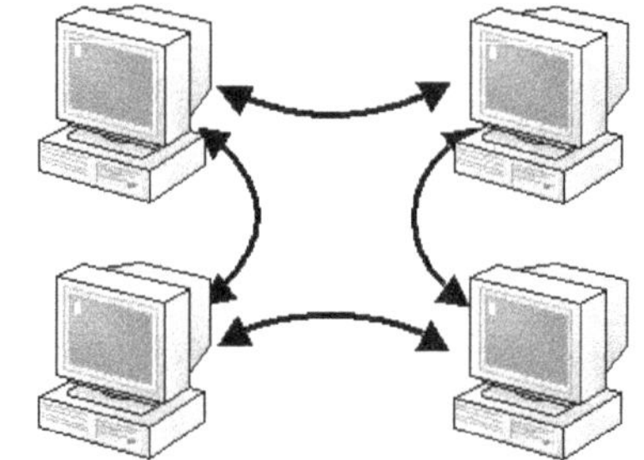

Wide Area Network - WAN

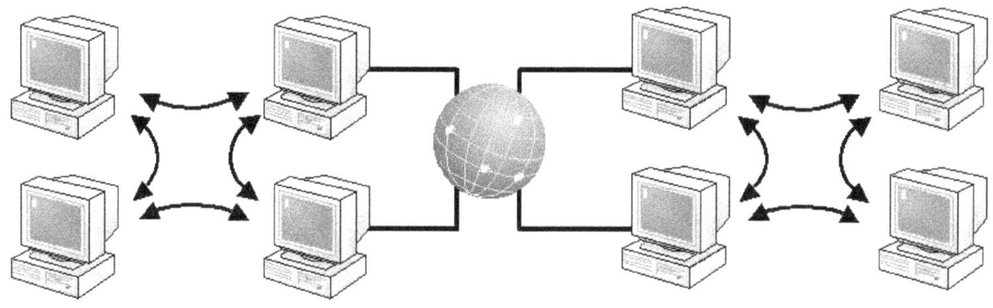

Figure 4.4. LANs and WANs

Generally, WANs spread over larger distances such as for example, inter-city or international and intercontinental networks. WANs are usually required for high-volume, long distance data traffic and as a result of this WANs tend to use different transmission media than do LANs. WAN connection services include ADSL (broadband), X.25, ISDN, Frame Relay, ATM and the transmission media can include the following,

- Public Switched Telephone Network (PSTN).
- High speed dedicated leased lines.
- Fibre optic cable.
- Wireless communications.

A brief description of these is presented next.

Public Switched Telephone Network (PSTN)

These rely on the standard telephone networks that have been used for a long time for analogue communications. (i.e. Plain Old Telephone Service – POTS). All of these are interconnected and the network facilitates long-distance telephone communications. Although PSTN have originally been designed to carry analogue signals, over the years they have become very sophisticated and are now able to handle digital data with high frequency carriers. Table 4.1 shows some of the services available on PSTN and their corresponding transmission rates. The technology available with POTS tends to use copper as the transmission medium and therefore the services listed in table 4.1 are primarily copper based.

X.25

This is an International Telecommunication Union-Telecommunication Standardisation Sector (ITU-T) protocol standard for WAN communications, which is capable of providing connectivity across public networks. It is typically used in the packet-switched networks (PSNs) of common carriers, such as the telephone companies. Subscribers are charged a fee, which is based on their use of the network. With data rates of 56 kbps it has now been superseded by faster technologies. [22]

Table 4.1

Service	Transmission Rate
X.25	56 Kbps
T1	1.544 Mbps
ISDN	1.544 Mbps
T3	44.736 Mbps
ATM	44.736 Mbps

Integrated Services Digital Network (ISDN)

This is a service offered by regional telephone carriers, which integrates digital telephony, and data-transport services. ISDN involves the digitisation of the telephone network, which permits voice, data, text, graphics, music, video, and other source material to be transmitted over existing telephone wires. In its basic form it provides two 64 kbps B channels. It is possible to aggregate both lines into a single high-speed 128 kbps link. [23]

A variation on the basic service is the Level 3 ISDN-PRI (Primary Rate Interface) service, which provides local access service for private branch exchanges (PBXs) and may be customised to meet specific subscriber requirements. ISDN PRI, also referred to as 23B+D, provides 23 B (bearer) channels, each operating at 64 Kbps for voice and data transmission, and a single D (signalling) channel. The Level 3 ISDN PRI service is delivered on a T-1 facility and has a total throughput of 1.54Mbps. [24]

B-ISDN and ATM

B-ISDN is a broadband communication network developed by International Telegraph And Telephone Consultative Committee (CCITT) that enables the transmission of design simulations and other multi-media transmission that include text, voice, video and graphics in one network. B-ISDN is able to provide end-users with increased transmission rate up to 155.54Mbits/s on a switching basis. [25]

A very clear explanation of the status of BISDN and ATM is given by Wikipedia and follows; “In the 1980s the telecommunications industry expected that digital services would follow much the same pattern as voice services did on the public switched telephone network, and conceived a grandiose vision of end-to-end circuit switched services, known as the Broadband Integrated Services Digital Network (B-ISDN). This was designed in the 1990s as a logical extension of the end-to-end circuit switched data service, ISDN.

The technology for B-ISDN was going to be Asynchronous Transfer Mode (ATM), which was intended to carry both synchronous voice and asynchronous data services on the same transport.

The B-ISDN vision has been overtaken by the disruptive technology of the Internet. The ATM technology survives as a low-level layer in most DSL technologies, and as a payload type in some wireless technologies such as WiMAX." From http://en.wikipedia.org/wiki/Broadband_ISDN accessed 30/5/09.

Asynchronous Transfer Mode (ATM)

ATM is an ITU-T standard, which is designed for the high-speed transfer of voice, video, and data through public and private networks using cell relay technology. It is a cell switching and multiplexing technology that combines the benefits of circuit switching (constant transmission delay, guaranteed capacity) with those of packet switching (flexibility, efficiency for intermittent traffic). [26]

High speed dedicated leased lines

These lines are leased from the telecommunications company and are available to the organisation as direct connections between two points. They are high-speed T1 lines that provide direct links between remote network sites. T1 bandwidth is 1.554 Mbps, divisible into 24 channels of 64kbps each. These lines can be quite expensive, and therefore service providers often allow customers to lease individual 64kbps channels. This is usually referred to as a fractional T line. For higher traffic loads, the T-carrier service uses multiplexing of the basic T1 carrier so that larger bandwidth can be made available on the line. Multiplexing provides multiples of T1 channels as given in table 4.2.

Table 4.2

T-carrier	Number of Channels	Transmission Rate
T1	24	1.544 Mbps
T2	96	6.312 Mbps
T3	672	44.736 Mbps
T4	4032	274.176 Mbps

Fibre optic cable

Fibre-optics use light pulses to transmit information down optical fibre lines. Light pulses move down the fibre-optic line using the principle of total internal reflection, which states that when the angle of incidence exceeds a critical value, light cannot get out of the glass; instead, the light bounces back in. When this principle is applied to the construction of the optic-fibre strand, it is possible to transmit information down fibre lines in the form of light pulses. Fibre optic cables can span long distances between local phone systems as well as providing the backbone for many network systems. Other system users include cable television services, university campuses, office buildings, industrial plants, and electric utility companies. Networks use Fibre Distributed Data Interface (FDDI) that has a potential bandwidth of 250Gbps. High bandwidth allows for high network speeds and most FDDI networks can handle data rates of 100Mbps. Another fibre optic transmission system is the Synchronous Optical Network (SONET). [27]

SONET data rates begin at 51.84 Mbps, and higher rates come in multiples of this. Rates are calculated in terms of optical carrier (OC) speed (see Table 4.3). SONET defines a technology for carrying many signals of different capacities through a synchronous, flexible, optical hierarchy.

Table 4.3. SONET Hierarchy

Signal	Capacity (Mbps)
OC-1	51.840
OC-3	155.520
OC-12	622.080
OC-48	2488.320
OC-192	9953.280
OC-768	39813.12

As a result of the high bandwidth potential, SONET systems are used in applications that require high speeds such as, Video-on-demand, high-speed LAN interconnections, full-motion catalogues, movies etc.

Wireless network communications

In wireless communications, data are sent along analogue frequency channels supported by the receiver and the transmitter. There are three types of wireless media namely, radio wave, microwave and infrared. Radio waves are most common in wireless LANs that use transmitters and receivers in-house for data communications. The frequency range for signal transmission is between 10kHz and 1 GHz. The IEEE 802.11b standard defines a total of 14 frequency channels within this range (see table 4.4). [28]

For communications in computer networks, radio wave transmission is further subdivided into the following categories,

- Low Power Single Frequency (LPSF).
- High Power Single Frequency (HPSF).
- Spread spectrum.

These are classified according to the distance that the signals can travel. For example, LPSF is used in wireless communications over 20-30m range while in HPSF signal bounce off atmosphere so range determined by earth's curvature.

Spread-spectrum signals are distributed over a wide range of frequencies and then collected onto their original frequency at the receiver. This means that they are unlikely to interfere with other signals even those that are transmitted on the same frequencies. This is major advantage which has opened up crowded frequency spectra to hugely expanded use.

Table 4.4 IEEE 802.11b

Channel Number	Centre Frequency (MHz)	Usage specification for
1	2412	US, Canada, Europe and Japan
2	2417	US, Canada, Europe and Japan
3	2422	US, Canada, Europe and Japan
4	2427	US, Canada, Europe and Japan
5	2432	US, Canada, Europe and Japan
6	2437	US, Canada, Europe and Japan
7	2442	US, Canada, Europe and Japan
8	2447	US, Canada, Europe and Japan
9	2452	US, Canada, Europe and Japan
10	2457	US, Canada, Europe and Japan, Spain, France
11	2462	US, Canada, Europe and Japan, Spain, France
12	2467	Europe and France
13	2472	Europe and France
14	2484	Japan

Transmitting at radio frequencies is licensed and regulated by national authorities. For example with reference to Table 4.4, in the USA channels 1 through 11 are available. Most of Europe and Japan can use channels 1 through 13 and Japan also has channel 14. A channel represents the centre frequency that the transmitter-receiver pair uses to communicate (e.g., 2.412 GHz for channel 1 and 2.417 GHz for channel 2). Table 4.4 gives the list of the available channels, their centre frequencies and usage specification.

In practical networks, with reference to table 4.4 it is worth bearing in mind that there is only a 5MHz separation between the centre frequencies. For example, channel 1 and 2 centre frequencies in table 4.4 are separated by 5MHz. Also, by definition the 802.11b signal occupies approximately 30MHz of the frequency spectrum. In other words the signal falls within about 15MHz of each side of the centre frequency. As a result, an 802.11b signal overlaps with several adjacent channel frequencies. This can be explained with reference to table 4.5.

Table 4.5

Channel Number	Centre Frequency (MHz)
1	2412
2	2417
3	2422
4	2427
5	2432
6	2437
7	2442
8	2447
9	2452
10	2457
11	2462
12	2467
13	2472
	2484

If a number of channels are used at the same time, then they must be separated by at least 15MHz from their centre frequencies. This means that if for example, channel 1 is selected with centre frequency of 2412MHz, then the next channel that is available must have a centre frequency of at least 2412+15=2427MHz. If channel 6 with centre frequency of 2437MHz is used at the same time, then the channels that are available for use are 2437-15=

2422MHz and 2437+15=2452MHz. This shows that there exists a frequency overlap between channels 1 and 6, which can cause interference around the centre frequency of 2422MHz.

Selecting channels 1 and 7 would solve this problem. Thus, if channel 7 with centre frequency of 2442MHz is used at the same time, then those channels that are available without interference are between the frequency ranges of 2442-15= 2427MHz and 2442+15=2457MHz. In this case there is no overlap with channel 1. The next channel that is available has a centre frequency of 2457+15= 2472MHZ, which is channel 13.

Table 4.6

	Sub-division	Comments	Bandwidth
Radio Wave (10kHz-1GHz)	LPSF (Low power single frequency)	Wireless communications over 20-30m range.	1-10Mbps
	HPSF (High power single frequency)	Signal bounce off atmosphere so range determined by earth's curvature.	1-10Mbps
	Spread-Spectrum	Same as HPSF but uses multiple frequencies, Bandwidth can be increased by simultaneous transmission on several frequencies.	2-6 Mbps
Micro wave	Terrestrial	(4-6GHz and 21-23GHz). Used where buildings are separated buy roads for example, and permission to dig-up roads is required.	1-10Mbps
	Satellite	(11-14GHz) Used to access remote sites on the globe by connecting to a satellite to receive and transmit signals.	1-10Mbps
Infra red	100GHz –1 1000THz. Either line of sight or point-to-point pure light transmission. Infrared technology used in local networks exists in three different forms: IrDA-SIR (slow speed) - data rates up to 115 Kbps IrDA-MIR (medium speed) - rates up to 1.15 Mbps IrDA-FIR (fast speed) infrared - rates up to 4 Mbps Very Fast Infrared, (VFIR) which support speeds up to 16 Mbps. The UFIR (Ultra Fast Infrared) protocol is in development. It will support speeds up to 100Mbit/s.		100Kbps-16 Mbps (at 1km)

Therefore, from table 4.5 it is seen that only three channels are available for concurrent use without causing interference. The way to mitigate this is to ensure that all access points within range of each other (i.e. about

100m or so apart) are set to channels that do not overlap (i.e., 1, 7 and 13). The same principle applies to networks on adjacent floors, i.e. they must not overlap since RF signals will pass through ceilings and floors.

The various wireless technologies are summarised in table 4.6. The table is divided between radio waves, microwave and infrared wireless technologies. For each of these a brief comment and the available bandwidth are given for reference purposes.

4.6. Network Topologies

The physical layout of computers and cables is generally referred to as network topology. Some of the standard topologies include Bus, Star and Ring topologies. All network design arrangements stem from the Bus, Star and Ring topologies.

For all topologies of computer networks data travel in packets. When a network computer wishes to send data, it uses the client network software to enclose the data into a 'packet' containing data as well as a 'header' and a 'trailer'. The header and trailer contain information, which is intended for the destination computer. For example, in the packet structure shown in figure 4.5, the header contains the address of the destination computer and the trailer contains an error-checking component called the Cyclic Redundancy Check (CRC). The exact form the packets take is determined by the protocol that the network uses. Therefore it is necessary that every computer on a network segment must have a unique address so that it can to communicate with other computers on the segment.

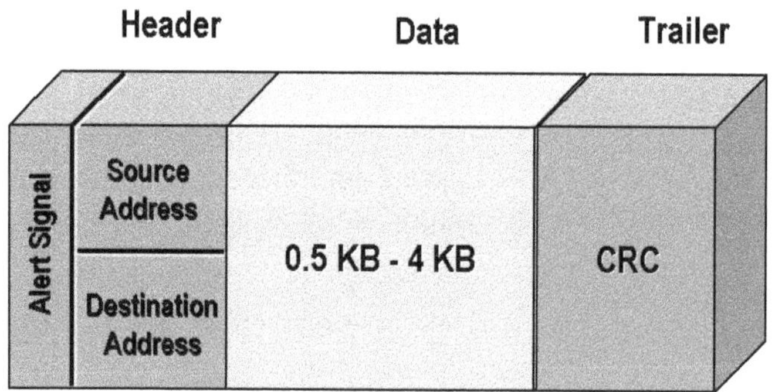

Figure 4.5. Packet structure

Packets can be routed to their destination either by packet switching or circuit switching. With packet switching the source and destination addresses are encapsulated with the data in the packet. Consequently, all the packets are routed across the network over data links shared with other traffic. In each network node, packets are queued or buffered, resulting in variable delay for packet delivery.

By contrast, in circuit switching networks, virtual circuits are set-up to provide a connection-oriented communication for packet transfer. These virtual circuits can be either Switched Virtual Circuits (SVCs) or Permanent Virtual Circuits (PVCs). Switched virtual circuits are temporary connections used in situations requiring only sporadic data transfer between devices across the network. Permanent virtual circuits are permanently established connections that are used for frequent and consistent data transfers between devices across the network.

Bus topology

In Bus topology only one computer can send information at any one time. The source and destination computer identifiers are packaged with the data. A computer that wishes to send data will place the signal containing the data packet and all computers connected on the network are able to process it, however only the computer designated as the destination can retrieve the data. Bus network topology is referred to as a passive network topology because, computers only listen to data on the network and do not process this data unless it is destined for them. Figure 4.6 shows the basic connection of a Bus network where computers listen to the data on the bus. Being as computers do not process the signal unless it is destined for them, the failure of any single computer on the network does not affect the rest of the network.

With reference to figure 4.6, it is worth noting that a Bus network segment has a terminator at each end. The reason for this is that when a signal is sent on the network, it will keep bouncing back and forth unless it is terminated after reaching its destination. The terminator is a resistor, which is placed at cable ends in order to absorb free signals and prevent them from bouncing back along the cable.

In a Bus topology, if a cable is cut or disconnected, the two free ends will not have a terminator and signals will bounce. The network is down and although individual computers will work, no network communications can take place.

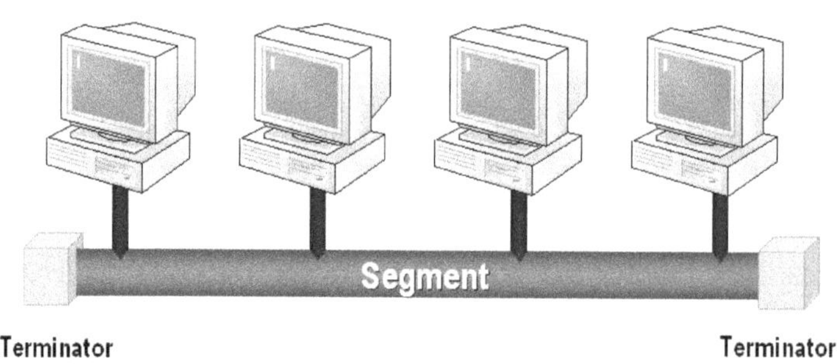

Figure 4.6. Bus network topology

From the aforesaid, it is intuitive; that the total number of computers connected together affects the speed of the network. Computer hardware, types of cable, distance of data travel, the number of times computers on the network transmit data and types of applications running, will also affect speed.

Bus topologies use coaxial cables and BNC connectors. Using a BNC barrel connector can lengthen the cable. These connectors weaken the signals and should be used sparingly. A repeater can be used to boost the signal at the point of connection and although more expensive it is much better than BNC extension or even a longer continuous cable.

Star Topology

A star uses a central hub, which connects to each computer on the network as shown in figure 4.7. Each computer communicates with the hub that resends the message onto the rest of the network. Star networks can be broadcast type, where the signal received by the hub is broadcast to all other computers on the networks. If the hub acts as switch, then the signal is switched to the destination computer rather than broadcast on the network. Switches are active devices however broadcast type networks can use active or passive topologies depending on whether or not the hub regenerates the signal. A passive hub does not need a power supply because it merely acts as a connection point. Active hubs and switches regenerate the signal and therefore require a separate power supply. These hubs are often called multi-port repeaters.

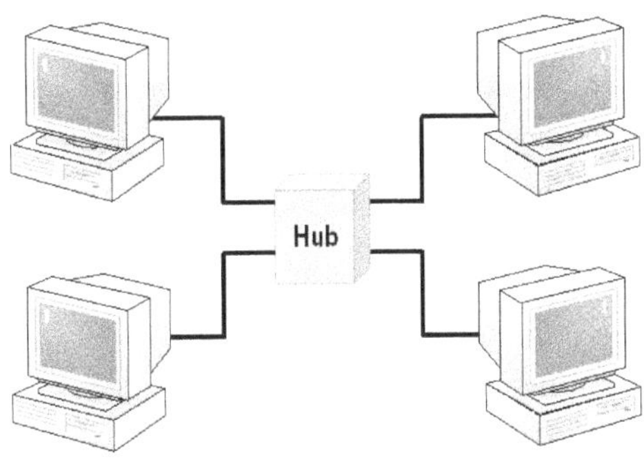

Figure 4.7. Star topology

The star topology is used in networks where end-points are directly reachable from the central location where the hub is situated. They are also useful in situations where expansion is expected because it is relatively easy to add computers to the hub. However with this arrangement, if the hub fails there is no connectivity on the network. Star networks are very common in small to medium type networks and they tend to use shielded twisted pair (STP) cabling with RG45 type connectors.

Ring Topology

In a ring topology each computer is connected to the next and the last computer is connected to the first to form a closed ring as shown in figure 4.8. The principle of operation is that each computer in the ring receives data and re-transmits it onto the ring. This is an active topology since each computer in a ring acts as a repeater to process the signal, boost it and send it on. In this manner signals can be made to travel longer distances but failure of a single computer will mean that data will not be able to travel beyond that point on the network. Active hubs are more common and they have multiple ports i.e. 8,12, 24 etc they are sometimes called multi-port repeaters.

The method used to transmit data around a ring is token passing. The basic principle here is as follows,

- A Token is created by a computer and released on the network. This token is available to any computer on the network wishing to send data.

- The sending computer modifies the token, puts an electronic address on the data and sends it around the ring.
- Token is passed from one computer to the next on the ring until it reaches the destination computer. In other words, data passes each computer until it finds the one with the address that matches the data.
- The receiving computer signals a message to the sender that data has been received.
- The sending computer verifies this and releases a New Token on the network.

Thus, the Token has one life cycle created by the sending computer after the completed transfer.

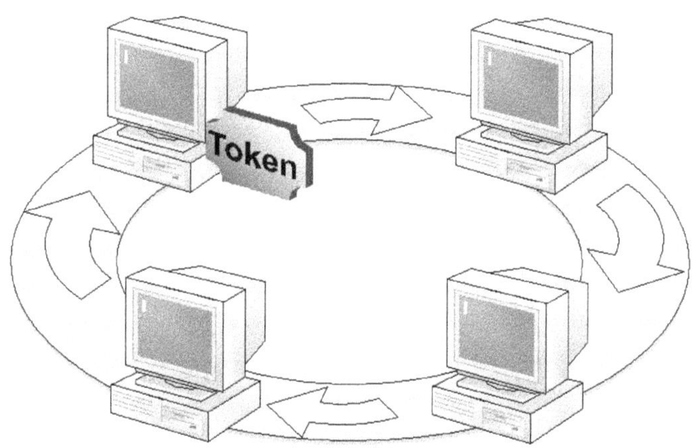

Figure 4.8. Ring topology

A token can circle a ring 200 meters in diameter at about 10,000 times a second. A fibre optic based ring topology FDDI uses two counter-rotating rings in order to help them recover from network faults.

Hybrid topologies

Popular variations of the basic topologies include star-bus and star-ring where hubs are used to connect different topology segments. These are illustrated in figure 4.9. In a star-bus topology there are several star topology networks linked together with linear bus hubs. The star-bus and the star-ring both connect computers through hubs.

A mesh topology has redundant links between devices. A true mesh configuration has a link between each device on the network. This is very expensive from the cabling viewpoint but it does have the advantage of fault tolerance. Most mesh topology networks are hybrid mesh, which contain some redundant links. These are needed in networks where connectivity is paramount. A summary of the advantages and disadvantages of each is given in table 4.7.

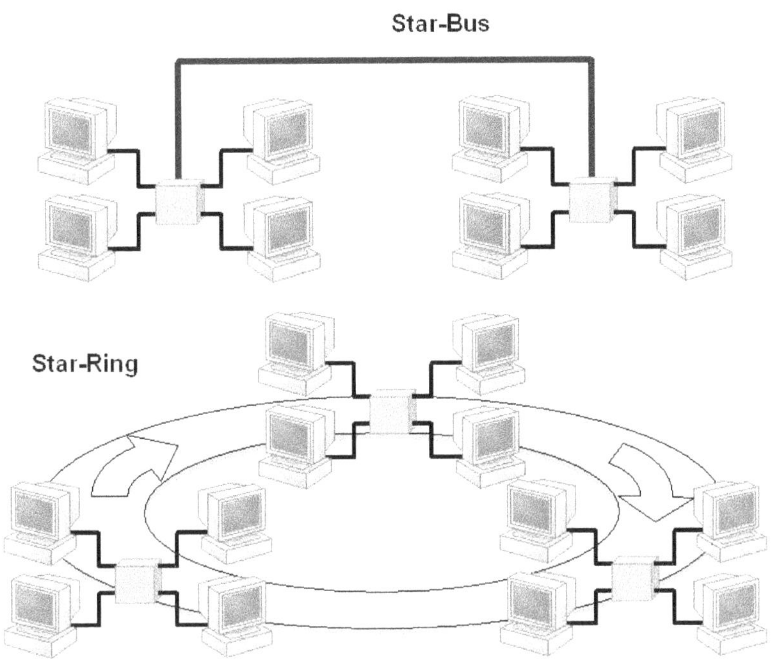

Figure 4.9 Network expansion using hubs

Table 4.7

	Advantages	**Disadvantages**
Bus	Economical cable usage, simple, cheap and reliable, easy to expand.	Slow in heavy traffic, cable break can affect many users, problems can be difficult to isolate.
Ring	Equal access for all computers. Even performance despite many users.	Single failure impacts on the whole ring, problems are hard to isolate, network reconfiguration disrupts operation.
Star	Easy to modify and add computers, centralised monitoring and management, failure of any number of computers on the network does not affect other computers.	If hub fails the network is disabled.
Mesh	Fault tolerance. Redundant data transfer links.	Expensive, difficult to reconfigure and maintain. For example a true mesh topology of 5 devices requires 4+3+3+1= 11 connections.

Most commonly installed networks currently are star-bus and bus topologies. A hub centred star-bus seems to be the best choice because of the ease of troubleshooting and reconfiguration. In practice approximately 90% of the cost of installing a LAN is in labour costs. On new installations a star-bus is less expensive than a bus.

4.7. Connecting network components

The media that connects the components on a physical network can be either a cable or wireless media types. Cable media normally transmit signals at the lower end of the electromagnetic spectrum whereas wireless uses the higher end frequencies. Networks that cover multiple sites usually use a combination of cable and wireless media types. The choice is governed by a number of factors including,

- **Cost:** For example, fibre-optic is fast but expensive and it is quite possible that your network does not require fibre-optic speeds to function well.
- **Installation:** How difficult the media is to install, depends on each individual installation. Nevertheless is accepted that for example, unshielded twisted pair (UTP) is easy to install whereas fibre-optic cable requires specialised tools and training. To connect two lengths of fibre together requires electric fusion or a chemical epoxy process.
- **Capacity:** This usually refers to the bandwidth. In the field of communications, bandwidth refers to the range of frequencies that a medium can accommodate. In networking it is usually measured in bits per second.
- **Attenuation:** This is the weakening of signals as they pass through a medium. It is common in copper media and also in wireless media. Optical media generally are less susceptible to signal attenuation.
- **Immunity from electromagnetic interference (EMI):** Electromagnetic signals interfere with the desired signal making it more difficult for the receiving computer to decode and process data. Some media are more susceptible to interference than other. Another concern is security and how easy it is for someone to tap into the media and pick-up the signal.

Once again copper and wireless are susceptible whereas fibre-optic is relatively immune to EMI.

Cables

Cables vary in terms of cost, speed and useable length for data transmission. Briefly speaking there are three main types. These are,

- **Twisted pair:** Copper cables with signal pairs twisted to reduce signal interference between them. Unshielded (UTP) and Shielded (STP) differ depending on whether a foil component is included to shield the data from unwanted electromagnetic interference.
- **Coaxial:** ThinNet for shorter distances (up to 180m) and ThickNet for longer distances (500m) usually as backbone.
- **Fibre Optic:** Using optical fibre to carry light signals over long distances.

Typical characteristics of each cable type are briefly listed in table 4.8

Table 4.8

<table>
<tr><td colspan="2">Coaxial
Central conductor core that carries data. It is surrounded by a dielectric insulating layer, which separates it from the braided wire mesh (ground), which also provides shielding. Shielding absorbs stray electronic signals and reduces signal interference.
One layer of foil and braided metal does dual shielding. Quad shielding is an arrangement with two layers of foil and two-braided metal.</td></tr>
<tr><td>ThinNet is a name often given to thin flexible Coax cable used for old style 10Base2 networking. It is also called Ethernet II cable. It has BNC style connectors at each end and requires T connectors and terminators to attach to PC's.
ThinNet is around 4-5mm in diameter and can carry signals in the range of 180m.</td><td>ThickNet 10Base5
Is between 8-10mm in diameter and as a result it is more difficult to install than ThinNet. It has a range of 500m. It is sometimes used as a backbone to connect several smaller ThinNet networks.</td></tr>
<tr><td colspan="2">Twisted pair
By twisting adjacent pairs of wires that carry the signal, the electrical noise between them is cancelled. A number of twisted pairs are made into cable with different number of pairs.</td></tr>
<tr><td colspan="2">Unshielded (UTP)
There is no additional shielding and consequently it is particularly susceptible to crosstalk. It has a maximum segment length is 100m.
UTP is the most popular cabling type - used with most of the major networking architectures and available in several categories- Cat-1, Cat-2, Cat-3, Cat-4, Cat-5, Cat-5e and Cat-6e and the augmented Cat6A. Cat-5 is still used today as it delivers up to 100Mbps. Cat-6 is the latest type of UTP cabling and is the fastest standard. Cat 6A is specified for both UTP and STP cables. . Cat-1, Cat-2, Cat-3 and Cat-4 are rarely used today as they have limited transmission speeds, up to a maximum of 16 Mbps.</td></tr>
</table>

Shielded (STP)

Has a higher quality copper braided jacket than UTP and also has a foil wrap around the wire pairs. This provides shielding to the pairs and supports higher transmission rates over longer distances than UTP.

STP prevents interference better than UTP, because the cabling is 'shielded'. This provides higher protection against electrical interference, however it is more costly. STP only supports transmissions speeds of up to 100Mbps and each cable length is also limited to 100 meters before requiring a signal boost.

At the time of writing there is general consensus that category 5e this is no longer an option for modern networking installations. Cat-6 features more stringent specifications for crosstalk and system noise. The cable standard provides performance of up to 250MHz and is suitable for 10BASE-T / 100BASE-TX and 1000BASE-T / 1000BASE-TX (Gigabit Ethernet). Therefore it is designed to allow users to specify a cabling system with enough performance for robust and reliable gigabit transmission. Augmented Category 6 (Cat 6A) specifies cable operating at minimum frequency of 500MHz, for both shielded and unshielded.

Type	Speed	Info
Cat. 5	10/100/1000MbE*	Category 5 cable is a currently outdated standard that provides a minimum of 100Mhz of bandwidth. It can be used for 10/100 Ethernet without worry, however for longer runs of 1000MbE it is recommended to use Cat. 5e or higher.
Cat. 5e	10/100/1000MbE	Category 5e cable provides a minimum of 100Mhz of bandwidth. Cat. 5e generally provides the best price for performance, however for future proofing Cat. 6 or Cat. 6a may be a better choice, as they usually do not cost that much more.
Cat. 6	10/100/1000MbE 10GbE*	Category 6 has a minimum of 250MHz of bandwidth. Allowing 10/100/1000 use with up to 100-meter cable length, along with 10GbE over shorter distances.
Cat. 6a	10/100/1000MbE 10GbE	Cat. 6a or Augmented Category 6 has a minimum of 500MHz of bandwidth. It is the newest standard and allows up to 10GbE with a length up to 100m.
Cat. 7	10/100/1000MbE 10GbE/100GbE	Cat. 7 is a future cabling standard that should allow for up to 100GbE over 100 meters of cable. Expected availability is in 2013. It has not been approved as a cable standard.

Fibre optic
Good for very high speeds, high capacity data transmission as there is very little attenuation and electrical interference. Optical fibres carry digital data signals in the form of modulated pulses of light. Consequently the cable cannot be tapped and data stolen. It is worth noting that fibre optic links are unidirectional and two cables are required for two-way communications. Fibre optic cables are used for high-speed communications over long distances. It is very expensive and needs careful installation for connectivity. Fibre Optic cabling supports transmission speeds of more than 1Gbps (Gigabit per second, alternatively known as 1000Mbps), making it the fastest cabling choice. It can also be run for longer distances than UTP, i.e. over 100 metres.

UTP and coaxial cabling use copper wire, which is susceptible to electrical interference. Fibre Optic works differently by converting data (bits) into beams of light, which do not carry electrical impulses. The major downside of Fibre Optic is the cost; it is more expensive than any other type of network cabling available. For this reason Fibre Optic cabling is often used selectively, alongside a cheaper form of cabling, to form the backbone of an organisations network to ensure the best data transmission between heavily utilised devices on the network.

4.8. Network components

Networks consist of computers, each of which must have a Network Interface Card (NIC) and a cable or other means of accessing other computers on the network. The main functions of NICs are,

- Receive data and convert it into electrical signals.
- Receive electrical signals and convert them into data.
- Determine if the data received is for a particular computer.
- Control the flow of data through the cable.

Components that are needed in order to expand the network include the following,

Repeaters

Function at the physical layer. They connect two segments of dissimilar or similar media. The signal is received and re-generated before it is sent on.

Bridges

Expand the distance on a segment by regenerating the signal at packet level. They operate at the data link layer and so they do not distinguish between protocols. For this reason they cannot be used between different networks i.e. Ethernet and token ring. Bridges work on the principle that each network node has its own address and all packets are forwarded to the destination address. They have some intelligence in that they learn where to forward data by storing a routing table in ROM so that like a CACHE, recent routes are easily retrieved. Multiple bridges can be used to combine several small networks into one large network.

Routers

Work at the Network layer. They contain a routing table with network numbers. They are slower than bridges because they are more complex. As packets pass from router to router, data link layer source and destination addresses are stripped off and then re-created. This enables communication between different networks such as for example Ethernet and Token-ring.

Gateways

Used for communications between different architectures and environments. They re-package and convert the data so they are able to connect different environments. They are used to link systems with different,

- Communications protocols.
- Data formatting structures.
- Languages.
- Architectures.

Gateways de-capsulate incoming data in a complete protocol stack of the sender, and then encapsulate the outgoing data in the complete protocol stack of the receiver. Some gateways use all the 7 layers of the OSI model, but typically they perform protocol conversion at the application layer.

4.9. Network Technologies

Ethernet

An Ethernet LAN typically uses coaxial cable or special grades of twisted pair wires, however it can also be used in wireless LANs. As mentioned earlier Ethernet uses baseband transmission. The most common Ethernet systems are called 10BASE-T and provide transmission speeds up to 10Mbps. The T here stands for twisted pair cabling. Fast Ethernet or 100BASE-T provides transmission speeds up to 100 megabits per second and is typically used for LAN backbone systems, supporting workstations with 10BASE-T cards. Gigabit Ethernet provides an even higher level of backbone support at 1000 megabits per second (1 gigabit or 1 billion bits per second). 10-Gigabit Ethernet provides up to 10 billion bits per second. [29] Full specification of the Ethernet characteristics can be obtained from the IEEE 802.x standard.

In networking terminology, the access method describes the mechanism that moves data between the computers in a network. In Ethernet networks computers use the Carrier Sense Multiple Access with Collision Detection (CSMA/CD) protocol as the access method. CSMA/CD is a protocol defined in the IEEE 802.3 standard. It describes how a device can access an Ethernet segment. Using this access method on the Ethernet, any device can try to send a frame at any time. Before sending the frame, each device senses whether the carrier is present on the line. If there is no carrier and the line is idle the device begins to transmit frames.

Figure 4.10 shows an Ethernet segment when a computer broadcasts a message on the network. If there are no other broadcasts, the network is accessed and communications can complete.

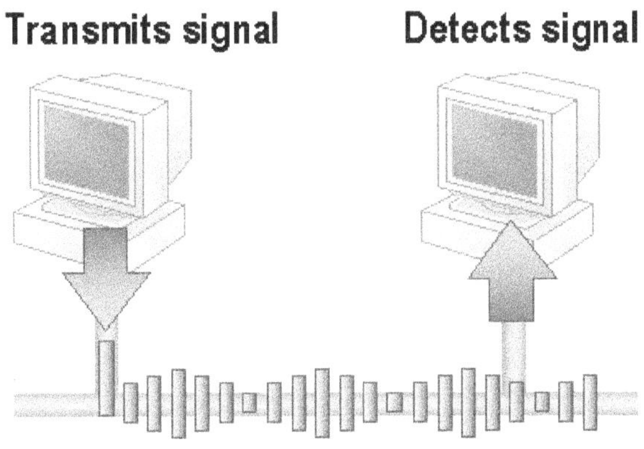

Access Method -	CSMA/CD
Transfer Speed -	Standard Ethernet – 10Mbps Fast Ethernet – 100Mbps Gigabit Ethernet – 1Gbps (1000Mbps)

Figure 4.10. Ethernet transmission using CSMA

If on the other hand a collision is detected as shown in figure 4.11, then access is not granted and re-transmission occurs after a suitable delay period.

Since multiple devices are allowed to access the network at the same time it is always possible that frames will collide on the segment. When a collision is detected all the frames are discarded and each device then waits a random amount of time and retries until successful in getting its transmission sent.

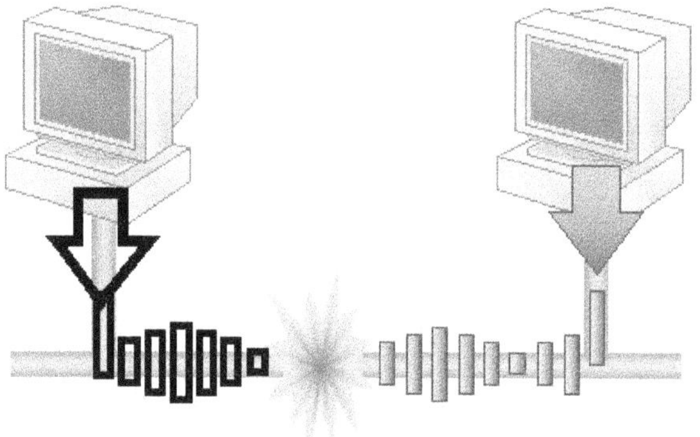

Figure 4.11. Collision detection in Ethernet networks

Token Ring

The token-ring topology was discussed earlier and a brief mention of the technology is given here. In a physical ring as shown in figure 4.12 a multi-station access unit (MSAU) is a central hub that connects a group of computers ('nodes') to a Token Ring local area network.

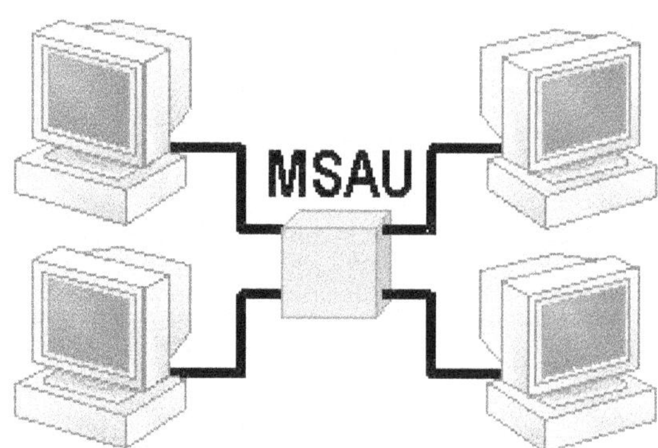

Access Method -	Token passing
Transfer Speed -	4 to 16 Mbps for all cable types

Figure 4.12. Physical ring

For example, eight computers might be connected to a MSAU in one office and that MSAU would be connected to a MSAU in another office that served eight other computers. In turn that MSAU could be connected to another MSAU in another office, which would be connected back to the first MSAU. Such a physical configuration is called a star topology. However, the logical configuration is a ring topology because every message passes through every computer one at a time, each passing it on to the next in a continuing circle. One significant advantage of an MSAU is that if one computer fails in the ring, the MSAU can bypass it and the ring will remain intact.

Control of the ring network is delegated to a computer on the ring with the highest MAC address. This is an arbitrary choice of selection but serves the purpose since MAC addresses are unique to each NIC. This computer then becomes the so-called 'active monitor' on the ring, whose job is to make sure that other computers in the ring are not causing problems.

The active monitor checks the ring by performing ring polling every 7 seconds to check if there are any problems. This enables computers in the ring to find out who is participating in the ring and to learn the address of their Nearest Active Upstream Neighbour (NAUN). Ring polling is also a way to see if there are any problems with any computers in the ring. It a problem is detected; the active monitor will perform a ring purge to isolate it. Ring purges are used to reset the ring after an interruption or loss of data is reported. Since each machine in a ring passes the token to the next machine, i.e. its NAUN, it is very important to monitor accurately when a computer enters or leaves a ring. For this reason, when a machine enters the ring it performs a lobe test to verify that its own connection is working properly. If the lobe test passes, the computer signals the hub to insert it into the ring.

When there is a problem in the ring, the computer, which is the NAUN after the fault, will stop receiving signals. The computer will consequently assume that its preceding neighbour is at fault and it will then send a signal to the active monitor and to the hub to invoke a recovery procedure

Fibre Distributed Data Interface (FDDI)

A fibre optic version of the token-ring implementation is the Fibre Distributed Data Interface (FDDI). [30] This is an ANSI LAN standard for a 100-Mbps token passing, dual-ring LAN using optic-fibre cable. As a topology FDDI is a token ring network, however it does not use the token ring access method, which is used in other token-ring networks and defined in IEEE 802.5. Instead FDDI uses a timed token protocol, which is somewhat different. This protocol is based on the IEEE 802.4 and unlike token ring; it allows several FDDI devices to transmit data simultaneously. Therefore, unlike token ring, FDDI may have several frames simultaneously circulating on the network. This is possible because the processor of the token may send multiple frames, without waiting for the first frame to circulate through the complete ring. The spin-off from this is that the next station may begin transmitting while the frames from the first are still circulating.

The timed-token protocol is a token-passing protocol in which each node receives a guaranteed share of the network bandwidth. In the timed-token protocol, access to the communication medium is controlled by a token that is passed among the nodes in a circular fashion. Messages are segregated into two separate classes: synchronous and asynchronous. Synchronous messages, used for real-time communication, can have deadline constraints and thus are given a guaranteed share of the network bandwidth.

FDDI uses dual-ring architecture with traffic on each ring flowing in opposite directions (called counter-rotating). The dual rings consist of a primary and a secondary ring. During normal operation, the primary ring is used for data transmission, and the secondary ring remains idle. The main purpose of the dual rings is to provide fault tolerance in case of ring failure. Figure 4.13 shows the primary ring and the counter-rotating secondary FDDI ring. FDDI rings can be implemented with stations that have the required interface cards linked with a fibre-optic cable. Alternatively, they can use concentrators and in this way the network can be constructed as a tree or a ring of trees.

It is worth noting that the same network architecture is available on a copper cable. The copper specification, called Copper Distributed Data Interface (CDDI), provides 100Mbps services over twisted-pair copper wire. Copper is significantly cheaper than fibre optic cable and it is also easier to install. With modern Cat 6A cabling standards CDDI offer 1GBps performance at a lower price than fibre.

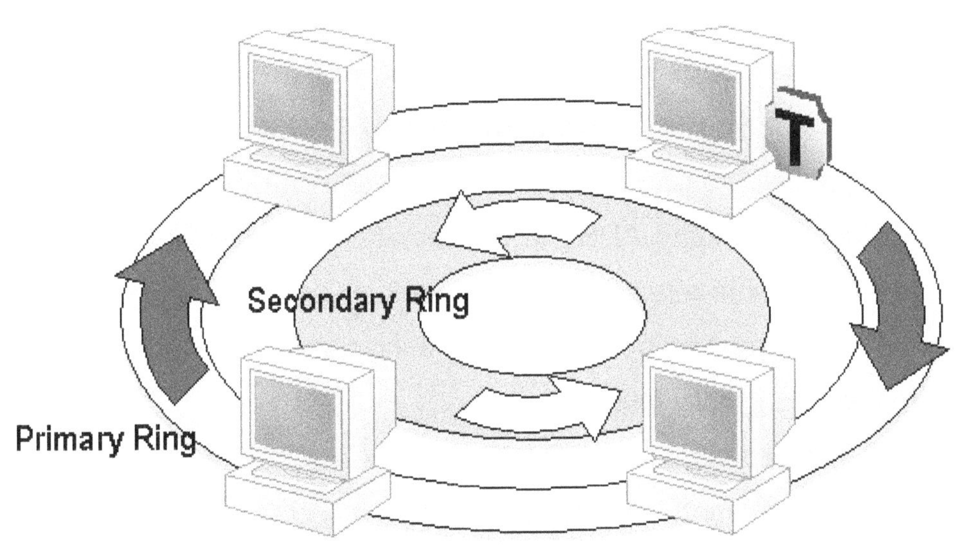

Figure 4.13. FDDI Uses Counter-Rotating Primary and Secondary Rings

Asynchronous Transfer Mode (ATM)

Network backbones are used to carry large amounts of data over long distances and consequently the technologies that are available rely on this long-haulage capability. Asynchronous Transfer Mode (ATM) is a high-speed network technology that uses fibre-optic cable or category 5e (and recently category 6a) to provide high bandwidth transfer of audio, visual and data traffic. Typical characteristics of ATM are given in figure 4.14. Rather than transmit data in frames, which can vary in size, ATM uses cells of a standard size (53 bytes) to package the data.

ATM does not specify the source and destination addresses rather it specifies the path that data will take from source to its destination. ATM uses a virtual circuit between the two devices to communicate on the network. These can be Permanent Virtual Circuits (PVC) or Switched Virtual Circuits (SVC), which are only active during the communication session that they have been created for. For this reason ATM is a connection-oriented technology, in which a logical connection is established between the two endpoints before the actual data exchange begins. Thus, ATM is a cell relay, packet switching network that encodes data traffic into small fixed-sized cells (53 bytes; 48 bytes of data and 5 bytes of header information). It provides data link layer services that run over Layer 1 links. This differs from other packet-switched networks (such as the Internet Protocol or Ethernet), in which variable sized packets (known as frames when referencing layer 2) are used.

ATM has proved very successful in the WAN scenario and numerous telecommunication providers have implemented ATM in their wide-area network cores. Also many ADSL implementations use ATM. However, ATM has failed to gain wide use as a LAN technology, and its complexity has held back its full deployment as the single integrating network technology in the way that its inventors originally intended.

Currently it appears likely that gigabit Ethernet implementations (10Gbit-Ethernet, Metro Ethernet) will replace ATM as a technology of choice in new WAN implementations. [31]

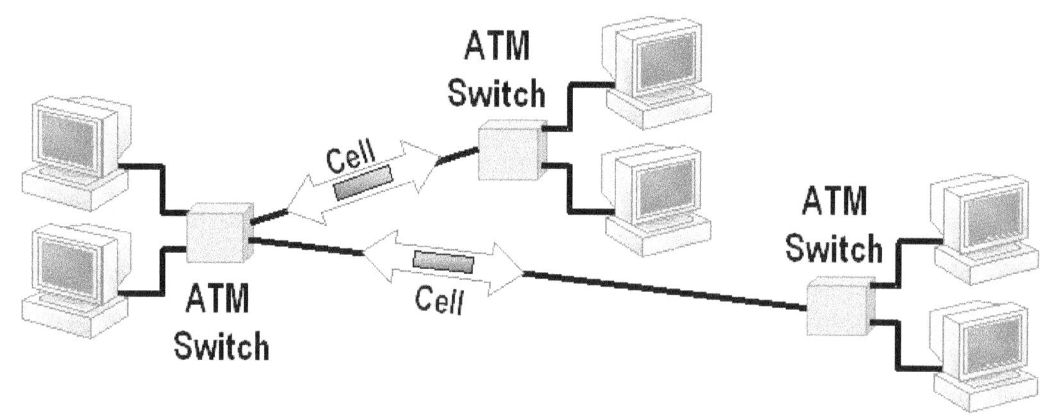

Access Method -	Point-to-point. Transfers fixed-sized
Transfer Speed -	Fibre-optic at 155 Mbps to 622 Mbps

Figure 4.14 Asynchronous Transfer Mode network

Several transmission speeds are available with ATM depending on the transmission medium used, i.e. copper or fibre-optic as shown in table 4.9.

Table 4.9

Signal	Capacity (Mbps)
T1	1.544 Mbps
T3	44.736 Mbps
ATM-25	25.6 Mbps
OC-1 SONET	51.840
OC-3 SONET	155.520
OC-12 SONET	622.080
OC-48 SONET	2488.320

Frame Relay

Frame relay is based on the older X.25 packet-switching technology. However unlike X.25, which was designed for analogue data such as voice conversations, frame relay is designed for digital data transfer. [32] Packets are relayed at the data link layer of the OSI model rather than at the Network layer. Consequently, a frame can incorporate packets from different protocols such as Ethernet and X.25. It is variable in size and can be as large as a thousand bytes or more.

The technology used in Frame relay is the so-called fast packet technology, which means that the protocol does not attempt to correct errors. When an error is detected in a frame, the frame is simply dropped. The end points are responsible for detecting and re-transmitting dropped frames. (However, the incidence of error in digital networks is extraordinarily small relative to analogue networks).

Frame Relay uses virtual circuits to establish stable end-to-end connections and therefore it is connection oriented. A basic arrangement and general characteristics are shown in figure 4.15. Virtual circuits fall into two categories, switched virtual circuits (SVCs) and permanent virtual circuits (PVCs). These circuits provide a bi-directional connection-oriented data link layer communication path from one device to another. A number of virtual circuits can be multiplexed into a single physical circuit for transmission across the network. This can often reduce the complexity of the network equipment required to connect multiple devices.

From a practical perspective, Frame Relay provides a cost-effective data transmission for intermittent traffic between local area networks (LANs) and between end-points in a wide area network (WAN). It is not ideally suited for voice or video transmission, which requires a steady flow of transmissions.

For most of its services, the network uses a permanent virtual circuit (PVC), which means that the customer has a dedicated connection without having to pay for a full-time leased line. The service is provided on fractional T-1 or full T-carrier system carriers.

The bandwidth offered by Frame Relay complements and provides a mid-range service between ISDN, which offers bandwidth at 128 Kbps, and Asynchronous Transfer Mode (ATM), which operates in somewhat similar fashion to frame relay but at speeds from 155.520Mbps or 622.080Mbps.

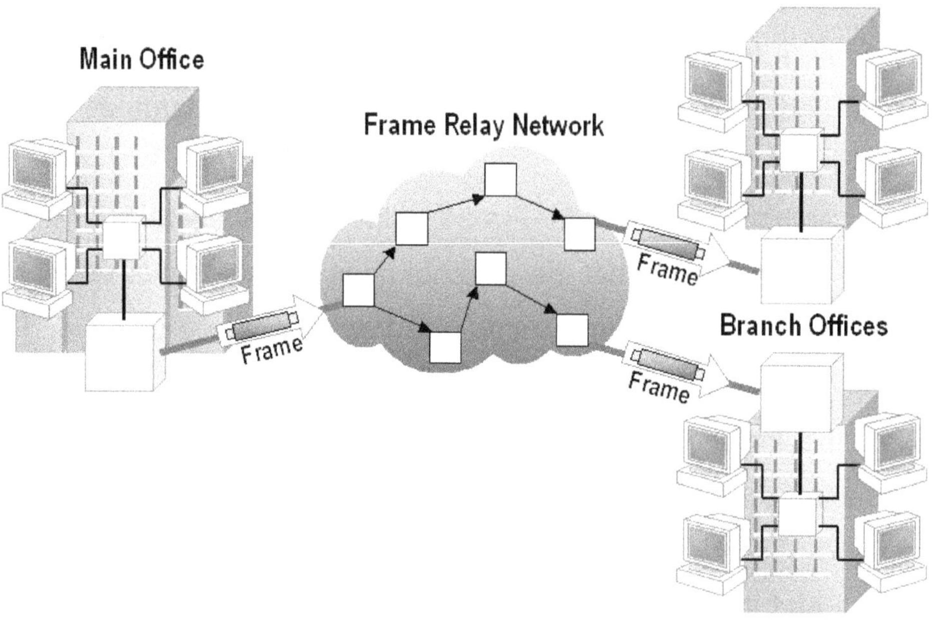

Access Method - Point-to-point
Transfer Speed - Dependent on digital leased lines

Figure 4.15 Frame Relay packet switched network

Exercises

4.1 The IEEE provides the operational standards of the various networks and devices briefly discuss the standards that apply to the following technologies- Ethernet, Token Ring, Wireless LAN

4.2 What is signal modulation?

4.3 Explain briefly QAM and PSK modulation techniques.

4.4 Describe what is meant by bandwidth.

4.5 Describe Baseband and Broadband signal transmission methods.

4.6 What are the major benefits of networking?

4.7 Describe the main differences between LANs and WANs.

4.8 What transmission media are available for data communications in modern networks?

4.9 What is SONET and what are its typical applications?

4.10 Explain the different wireless technologies for WANs and LANS

4.11 Explain why channel overlap is a problem in wireless networks.

4.12 Explain the difference between packet switching and circuit switching technologies.

4.13 What are the most common network topologies? Give their advantages and disadvantages.

4.14 Discuss the factors that affect the choice of cable types when specifying a computer network.

4.15 What are the main characteristics of the different cable types?

4.16 Discuss the various categories of UTP and STP Cabling.

4.17 Describe the networking components that can be used to expand the network.

4.18 Describe the main characteristics of the following network technologies,

a) Technologies.
b) Ethernet.
c) Token ring.
d) FDDI.
e) ATM.
f) Frame relay.

5 NETWORK PROTOCOLS

5.1. Introduction

For useful communications in a computer network it is necessary that each device follows a set of rules. These rules are contained in a number of different protocols. Protocols are distinguished according to the communications layer at which they operate. The Open System Interconnection (OSI) model defines a networking framework for implementing protocols in seven layers. In the context of this model, communication begins at the top layer of the sending end. Control is passed from this layer to one below it until the bottom layer is reached. This is the physical layer, which carries the raw signals to the receiving end. When these signals reach the destination they similarly move through the layers, starting at the bottom and working their way up. This is shown in a simplified diagram of figure 5.1.

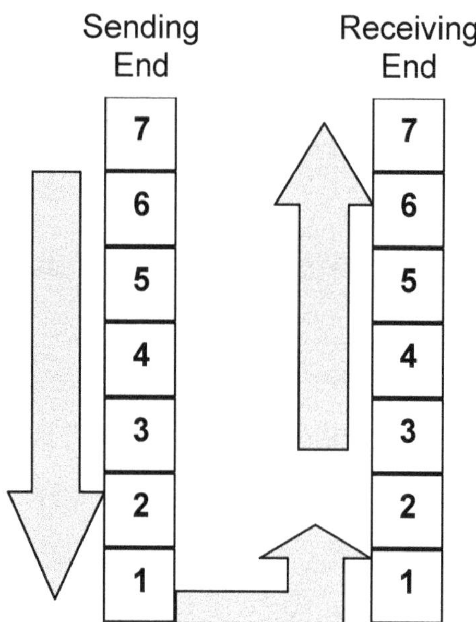

Figure 5.1. Data path through the 7-layer OSI model

As data travels through the layers, different protocols are used to ensure that the path that data is taking is correct. These protocols act as rules of engagement so to speak, and apply to different layers. Each layer at the sending end is communicating with the same layer at the receiving end. Some responsibilities of protocols are as follows,

- Detection of the physical connection.
- How network devices contact each other and communicate.
- How to ensure that network devices maintain a proper rate of data flow.
- Location of the other endpoint or node.
- Methods by which a device on the network knows how to transmit data.
- Handshaking negotiation of connection characteristics.
- How to format, start and end a message.
- How to deal with error correction and interruption of service.

The main aim of the protocol is to perform specific actions both at the sending and the receiving ends. For this reason both the sending and the receiving components must use the same protocol. An example of typical protocol actions is given in table 5.1.

Within the 7-layers of the OSI model, there exist a variety of protocols with different tasks and purposes. These protocols work within the different layers depending on their function and several layers may work together in a so-called 'Protocol Stack' or 'Suite'. Some standard protocol stacks include the following,

- **ISO/OSI protocol suite**. These protocols are defined by the International Organization for Standardization (ISO based on the Open Systems Interconnection (OSI) model. The OSI model defines the communications process into 7 layers, dividing the tasks involved in moving information between networked computers into seven smaller, more manageable task groups.
- **Internet Protocol Suite TCP/IP**. The TCP/IP protocol suite establishes the technical foundation of the Internet. Most of the protocols in the TCP/IP suite are developed by the Internet Engineering Task Force (IETF) under the Internet Architecture Board (IAB). The IAB provides the coordination for the R&D underlying the TCP/IP protocols and guides the evolution of the Internet. TCP/IP protocols are well documented in the Request For Comments (RFC), which are drafted, discussed, circulated and approved by the IETF committees. All

documents are open and free and can be found online on the IETF site listed in the reference.

- **IBM- System Network Architecture (SNA).** Although now considered a legacy-networking model, SNA is still widely deployed. SNA was designed around the host-to-terminal communication model that IBM's mainframes use.
- **Digital - DECNet**. Protocol suite developed by Digital Equipment Corporation (Digital or DEC, now part of HP). Several versions of DECnet have been released. Currently, two versions of DECnet are in wide use: DECnet Phase IV and DECnet plus (DECnet V). The DECnet now is part of the HP OpenVMS.
- **Novell- Netware**. This is Novell networks operating system (NOS) that provides transparent remote file access and numerous other distributed network services, including printer sharing and support for various applications, such as electronic mail transfer and database access. NetWare specifies the upper five layers of the OSI reference model and runs on any media access protocol (Layer 2). In addition, NetWare runs on virtually any kind of computer system, from PCs to mainframes. NetWare and its supporting protocols often coexist on the same physical channel with many other popular protocols, including TCP/IP, DECnet and AppleTalk
- **Apple-AppleTalk**. This is a multi-layered protocol suite of Apple Computers, providing internetwork routing, transaction and data stream service, naming service and comprehensive file and print sharing among Apple systems using the LocalTalk interface built into the Apple hardware. AppleTalk communicates with other network media such as Ethernet by the use of LocalTalk to Ethernet bridges or by Ethernet add-in boards for Apple machines. Many third-party applications exist for the AppleTalk protocols.

The increased popularity of the Internet has resulted in a more widespread use and expansion of communications protocols. Perhaps the most important of these are the Internet Protocol (IP) and Transmission Control Protocol (TCP). Together these two protocols make up the TCP/IP protocol stack.

Table 5.1

	Protocol Action
Sending Computer	Breaks data into smaller sections (packets) Adds addressing information to packets Prepares data for transmission
Receiving Computer	Takes packets off the cable Brings packets into computer through the NIC Strips transmission information from packets Copies data from packets to a buffer for re-assembly Passes the re-assembled data to the application in usable form

Request for comments (RFC) of the Internet Engineering Task Force (or IETF)[33] are a very useful reference source for anyone interested in detailed description of each protocol. It is worth noting that RFCs are continually evolving and new ones are introduced to reflect updates and changes to any preceding versions. Common Protocols along with the RFC, which describe them, are listed below.

- IP (Internet Protocol) RFC 791.
- UDP (User Datagram Protocol) RFC 768.
- TCP (Transmission Control Protocol) RFC 793.
- DHCP (Dynamic Host Configuration Protocol) RFC 1122.
- HTTP (Hypertext Transfer Protocol) RFC 2616, RFC 2818 with SSL.
- FTP (File Transfer Protocol) RFC 959.
- Telnet (Telnet Remote Protocol) RFC 854.
- SSH (SSH Remote Protocol) RFC 2246.
- POP3 (Post Office Protocol 3) RFC 1939.
- SMTP (Simple Mail Transfer Protocol) RFC 821.
- IMAP (Internet Message Access Protocol) RFC 3501.

For those interested in further reading, references [35-38] provide a useful direction towards additional information.

5.2. Network communications

In computer networks data travels in packets. For example, e-mail messages that are sent along the Internet are broken down into smaller packets of information. TCP protocol is responsible for breaking the messages into packets. Once the message is broken down into packets, each packet is transmitted to the destination computer individually. Packets are all made of equal size so that they can be managed more efficiently. Typically Internet packets contain around 1,000 or 1,500 bytes.

The TCP protocol header is added to the each packet at the sending end. It contains information such as the address of the source and destination computers, the amount of data in the packet and how the packets must be recombined to form the original message. The header also contains information known as the checksum, which is a numerical value related to the amount of information contained in the message. This is used to check if transmission was error-free.

Routers in the network will look at the destination address in the header and compare it to their lookup table to find out where to send the packet. The information contained in the header is used at the same layer (i.e. TCP) by the receiving end to gather the information about what needs to be done with the packet. This is to say that, once the packet arrives at its destination, the destination computer will remove the header and trailer from each packet and reassemble the message. At the same time another protocol, namely the Internet Protocol (IP), ensures that the information gets to the proper destination computer. When the destination computer receives the packets it uses TCP to recombine the packets into the original message. By comparing the amount of information indicated in the checksum with the amount of actual information in the message, the destination computer can check to ensure that no errors have occurred in the transmission of the message.

5.3. 7-Layer OSI model

Communication between computers on the network is best described by referring to the 7-layer OSI model. As mentioned earlier, the model is made up of seven layers and when two computers communicate, for each one, data begins in the top layer, which is layer 7 and goes down the layers to layer 1 sequentially. Briefly the 7-layers staring from top to bottom is described in table 5.2. [39]

Table 5.2

Layer	Description
7	**Application**- Includes services which directly support user applications i.e. file access, electronic mail, network access, flow control and error recovery
6	**Presentation**- Determines the format for data exchange between computers. For example, at the sending computer, this layer translates data from a format sent down from the application layer. This layer provides protocol conversion and data compression. Also, it contains the redirector, which enables access to resources on the server.
5	**Session**- Allows two applications on different computers to communicate during a session. It implements security, synchronises communications by using checkpoints and dialogue between processes.
4	**Transport**- Ensures that packets are delivered error-free, it re-packages messages at both receiving and sending ends and sends acknowledgement of receipt. It provides flow control, error handling and solving problems of sending and receiving packets.
3	**Network**- Addresses messages, translates logical into physical addresses. Decides on routing, packet switching and traffic problems.
2	**Data-Link**- Packages raw data into frames and sends it from the Network layer to the physical layer.
1	**Physical**- Transmits the raw data bit-stream over the network. It defines how the cable is attached to the network interface card (NIC) and relates electrical, optical, mechanical and functional interfaces to the cable or the transport medium. It defines data encoding and bit synchronisation as well as connector types and transmission techniques.

Each layer on one computer acts as though it is communicating with the same layer on another computer. The purpose of each layer is to provide services for the next higher layer and also to shield the upper layer from details of how these services are implemented. Additionally, at each layer the software adds some formatting or addressing to the data. A very good description of protocols and how they operate at different layers can be found on the Cisco website. [40,41]

5.4. TCP/IP Protocols

Note that the 7-layer OSI model is conceptual and different protocols operate at different layers. It is generally considered that TCP/IP is made up of four layers that correspond to the Application, Transport, Network and Data Link layers of the OSI model. These layers are shown in figure 5.2 along with the protocols that operate at each layer.

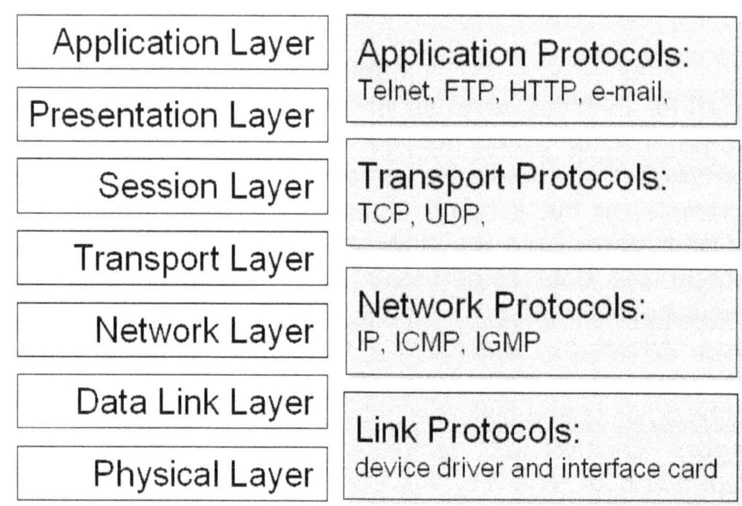

Figure 5.2. TCP/IP Protocols map onto the 7-layer OSI model

As mentioned earlier, each layer has a set of protocols that are used to implement the services at that layer. For example, the application layer handles the details of applications such as e-mail, file transfer protocol (FTP) etc. A message packet created at the application layer will traverse all the lower layers on its way to the destination computer. As it travels down the layers, each transition will add a header to the packet, which corresponds to that layer. This is shown in Figure 5.3 where the original data is created at the application layer. Transition to the presentation layer adds the presentation header (hp). Going down the layers different headers are added as session (hs), transport (ht) network (hn) and data (hd) headers. These headers are used at the destination computer to provide control information at the relevant layer. The physical layer treats all information as raw data and therefore there is no header information added for that layer. When data reaches the destination computer, it will travel up all the layers, using the header at each layer to describe the control actions at that layer.

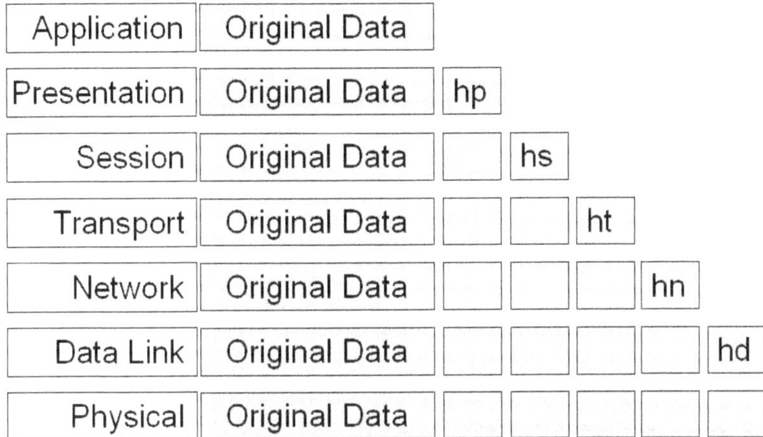

Figure 5.3. Header additions as data travels down the layers

As mentioned earlier, each layer provides a service for the layer above it. Therefore the transport layer provides a flow of data between two hosts, for the application layer. The hierarchy of layers and protocols as data flows through the layers is illustrated in figure 5.4.

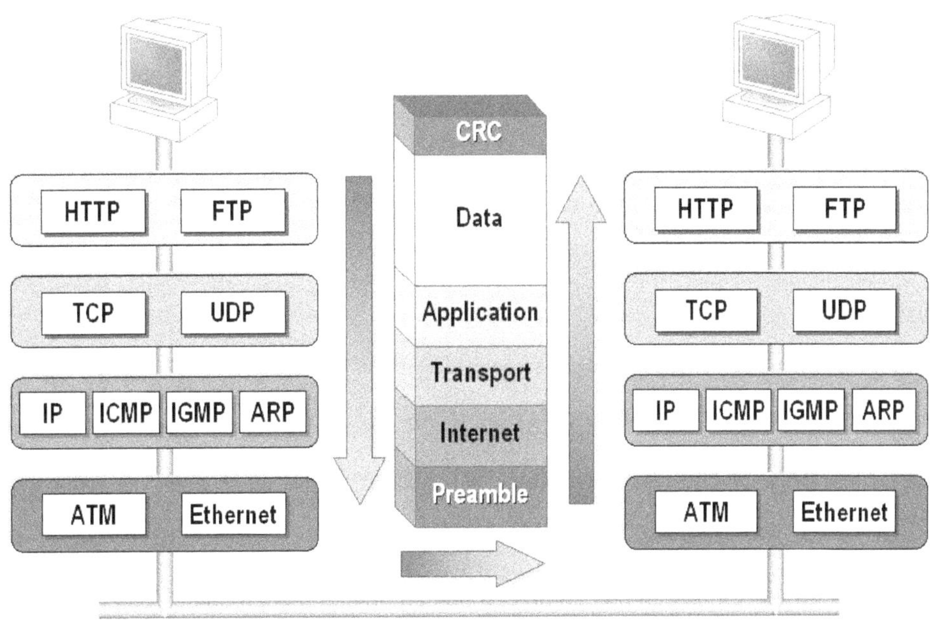

Figure 5.4. Data flow through the network protocols

At the transport layer in the TCP/IP protocol suite there are two vastly different transport protocols. These are the TCP and UDP (User Datagram Protocol) as shown in figure 5.4. The packet in this layer is made up of the header, datagrams, segments and data. TCP is concerned with things such as dividing the data passed to it from the application into the correct size, acknowledging received packets, setting timeouts to ensure packets are being sent from their source, and in general it ensures that data flow is reliable. At the same layer, UDP provides a different service to the application layer. It is responsible for sending packets of data, which are called datagrams from one host to the other. However this service is not reliable and no guarantee is given that the datagrams will reach their destination.

The network layer is sometimes called the Internet layer, and it handles the movement of packets around the network. This movement includes the routing of packets from their source to their destination. The protocols that operate at the network layer include, IP (Internet Protocol), ICMP (Internet Control Message Protocol), and IGMP (Internet Group Management Protocol). More information on these protocols is available from RFCs mentioned earlier. [33] The data-link layer is concerned with providing a flow of data from one device to another. It accepts packets from the network layer and packages these into frames for transmission on the physical layer. It is worth stressing the terminology here, frames travel at data link layer; packets travel at network layer, and these should not be confused. The data link layer adds a header to include control information such as frame type, routing and segmentation information.

The physical layer is responsible for sending bits of digital communications from one computer to the other. It is therefore not concerned with the meaning of bits and no header information is added at the physical layer. Some of the issues that the physical layer is concerned with are as follows,

- Network connection types such as multi-point and point-to-point connections.
- Physical topology of the networks.

- Methods for signalling and data modulation.
- Synchronisation between end-points in communications.
- Multiplexing.
- Devices such as hubs, terminators, couplers, cables, connectors, repeaters etc are associated with the physical layer. Protocols that map onto the physical layer include, Ethernet (IEEE 802.3), token passing bus (IEE 802.4), and token ring (IEEE 802.5).

5.5. Other protocols

There are literally hundreds of protocols that apply to different layers of the OSI model, and are used by various network services. It is not necessary to list them all here and instead few are given for reference purposes. The Microsoft developer Network (MSDN) lists many of the protocols on their website, and can be accessed for more information. [42]

In an inter-networked environment, when a network O/S is installed on a server there will typically be a choice to install a protocol from another vendor. For example, the Windows network O/Ss come with three network protocols, each intended for networks of different sizes and requirements. They are as follows,

- NetBEUI.
- NWLink.
- TCP/IP.

Each of these has different characteristics and therefore applications. NetBEUI is a lightweight protocol generally intended for small, single server networks. NWLink is intended for medium sized networks or networks that require access to a NetWare file server. TCP/IP is designated for large LANs and WANs. Clearly, if a small office network were being installed, without the need for future expansion there would be no point installing TCP/IP when NetBEUI will suffice. In some cases, such as setting up a Windows network by remote installation, TCP/IP stack will not be present before the Windows is installed. In these situations, a boot-up disk with the NetBEUI protocol can come in very handy to get the initial communications up and running.

NetBEUI: This stands for NetBIOS Extended User Interface, and NetBIOS stands for Network Basic Input Output System. This protocol was developed by IBM to support networking using the OS/2 network O/S. It was envisaged as a network supporting small workgroups of less than 200 hosts. The protocol cannot be routed across networks and is therefore constrained to a single network. The advantages that it has over other protocols are mainly due to the fact that it is lightweight.

NWLink: This is the Microsoft implementation of the Novel NetWare IPX/SPX protocol stack. The reason that Windows implement these protocols is so that they can communicate with Novel NetWare servers on the network.

DLC Data Link Control (DLC): The Data Link Control (DLC) protocol is a transport protocol commonly used for communicating with mainframes. IBM maintains the DLC specification.

AppleTalk: AppleTalk includes protocols that interconnect computer workstations, printers, shared modems, and other computers acting as file servers and print servers. Apple Computer, Inc maintains AppleTalk.

Bluetooth: The Bluetooth protocol is a serial bus protocol. The Bluetooth Special Interest Group (SIG) maintains the Bluetooth specification.

More information on the Bluetooth protocol can be found on the Bluetooth website. [43]

Simple Network Management Protocol v2 (SNMP v2): The Simple Network Management Protocol v2 (SNMP v2) conveys management information between agents and management stations. Operations of the protocol are implemented within a framework that defines authentication, authorisation, access control, and privacy policies. The Internet Engineering Task Force (IETF) stores RFCs for SNMP v2.

CIFS Protocol: Client systems use the Common Internet File System (CIFS) protocol to request file and print services from server systems over a network. CIFS is based on the Server Message Block (SMB) protocol. Several variants of the SMB protocol are in use by a variety of servers with differing capabilities. When it first negotiates a session with the server, a CIFS client determines an acceptable variant to use and the capabilities of the server.

ICMP Router Discovery Messages: The ICMP Router Discovery Messages protocol specifies an extension of the Internet Control Message Protocol (ICMP) to enable hosts attached to multi-cast or broadcast networks to discover the IP addresses of their neighbouring routers. The Internet Engineering Task Force (IETF) stores the RFC for ICMP Router Discovery Messages. For information on ICMP Router Discovery Messages, see RFC 1256- ICMP Router Discovery Messages.

Routing Information Protocol (RIP v1, v2): The Routing Information Protocol (RIP v1, v2) exchanges routing information among gateways and other hosts. RFCs for RIP are stored by the Internet Engineering Task Force (IETF). For information on RIP, see RFC 1058- Routing Information Protocol and RFC 2453- RIP Version 2.

Exercises

5.1 What are the main responsibilities of network protocols?

5.2 With reference to the 7-layer OSI model describe the path that data travels as it passes from source to destination.

5.3 What is a protocol stack?

5.4 Describe the 7-layers of the OSI model.

5.5 Explain how the TCP/IP protocol suite maps onto the 7-Layer OSI model.

5.6 What happens with the packet header as it traverses the layers?

5.7 What does the physical layer do and what if any protocols apply to this layer?

5.8 What are the main characteristics of the NetBEUI protocol?

5.9 What are CIFS and how do they relate to SMBs?

5.10 What is SMTP and where is it used?

5.11 Which of the layers of the OSI model does IEEE 802 specify?

6 ROLES OF COMPUTERS ON THE NETWORK

6.1. Introduction

In practical networking there are two basic network types, Peer-to-Peer (PTP) and Client-Server. Hybrid networks include a combination of these two types. Servers are computers that provide shared resources to network users, i.e. shared data, peripherals etc. In client-server networks, client computers access shared network resources provided by the server.

Computers in a network have different roles. In a client-server network, some computers are servers and others are clients. In this case, the server performs a specific service for the clients, and they are classified according to the service they provide. The Internet is a good example of the client-server network. For example, when accessing a URL, web browsers are clients that connect to web servers and retrieve web pages. Another example is e-mail servers such as the Microsoft exchange server. Most people use e-mail clients locally in order to retrieve their e-mail messages from their mail servers. Online chat systems use a variety of clients, which vary depending on the chat protocols being used.

Typically, a PTP networking arrangement is used for a network of approximately ten or fewer computers. There are no dedicated servers in PTP networks and each user has to know how to administer their computer as a server and also how to use it as a client. Thus in PTP networks, the users need more training than in client-server networks. In server based systems the servers are more powerful computers that are designed to meet the demands of all the users on the network.

Network security is much easier to implement in server-based systems. In PTP networks each user can set their own security and if the security settings on a resource are not the same for each user, access to this resource can be compromised. In general therefore, client-server networks provide a much more powerful means and tools for administering the network. Networks of approximately ten computers or more use a server, which never acts as a client and is optimised for servicing user (client) requests. As networks grow, the number of servers can be increased, and specialised servers can be introduced. Some examples of specialised servers include,

File and print servers: Files are stored on the server and when clients use the file, it is loaded into client computer memory. After use, the file is stored on the server. The server also manages all the print resources on the network, and all printing therefore goes through the server.

Application servers: Here only the information that the client needs is passed to the client computer, while the main application remains on the server. For example, SQL server, Oracle server etc.

Mail server: Used to provide message management for users. For example, Unix SquirrelMail and Microsoft Exchange Server, but there are a huge number of alternative mail management systems that are available to run on Windows and also on Linux operating systems. Some of these are- LinksMerak Mail Server 9.0, MDaemon Mail Server, FTGate Mail Server, Winmail.

Communications Server: Handle data flow between the network and other networks, mainframe computers or remote users. These servers include security features for remote access.

Directory Services Servers: These servers are used to administer network components, users, and resources as well as to store and secure information on the network.

It is possible to combine server roles into a single server, such that a server can be an Application Server as well as an e-mail and print server. This very much depends on the size of the network and the loading on the server. Other server roles such as DHCP, Domain naming Service (DNS), and Web etc are discussed later in this text. Server-based network advantages include,

- Data sharing can be centrally administered and therefore easier to locate and support than resources on random computers.
- Security goes through one administrator.
- Back-up is straightforward because data is centralised on servers.
- Redundancy can be built into the network by duplicating server roles to ensure reliability and fault tolerance.

- Large number of users can be supported across diverse geographical locations.
- Client hardware does not need to be expensive because most of the power is in the server.

6.2. Client-server Database

The client-server concept is very common in database applications as shown in figure 6.1. This relies on the server to service the requests of the client. For this to happen both the server and the client must have suitable software installed. The client-server concept can be briefly explained by considering a database application.

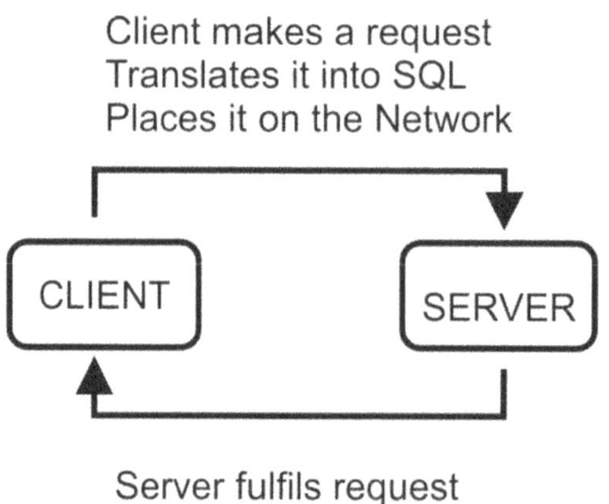

Figure 6.1. Example of a Client-Server database

For example, assume that a database needs to be examined by issuing a Query. In centralised computing there would be a computer containing the central database with connections to all the other computers on the network. If a client requests data from the database the system moves all the data across the network to the client. The client then performs the Query and obtains the desired results. By contrast, in a client-server environment the server only sends the results of a query to the client. This reduces network traffic and speeds up database applications, which is why client-server computing is very popular with database management applications. In the above example of the client-server model the client software would typically use Structured Query Language (SQL) to communicate with the database server.

In the client-server environment there are typically two main components, the front-end application that is the client and the back-end server, i.e. database server. Typically the back-end server would not contain the user-interface since it is the client that is responsible for presenting the data in useful form. This data presentation would include,

- Presenting an interface to the user.
- Formatting requests for data.
- Displaying data it receives back from server.

The client is equipped with front-end tools such as,

- **Query tools:** These use pre-defined queries and built-in reporting to access back-end data.
- **User applications:** Data input and other tools to access back-end database from the client.
- **Program development tools:** High-level programming to design bespoke client tools to access server data.

In database applications, the server is dedicated to storing and managing data. This back-end processing includes sorting data, extracting data, sending information to client. Additionally, database server software performs all the updates, deletions, additions and protection features. Procedures are pre-written and stored on the server and can be used by any client to help service a request.

6.3. Corporate networks

Client-server computing is also very common in corporate networks. These can be very large LANs as well as WANs. In these types of networks such as for example the Microsoft network, the logical organisation of the network is done according to a domain network model. An example of this is shown in figure 6.2. There could be a single domain or a multiple domain network model where domains would further be expanded using trees and forests. Either way each domain would have a number of servers helping to service that domain. For example, a domain naming service (DNS) server would be required on the domain to translate domain names to IP addresses.

Smaller networks of twenty computers or less, such, as for instance, a small business computer network would normally be organised in a logical workgroup network model. (also shown in figure 6.2) In this model the networked computers share files and printers using the network, but there is no centralised server to control network activity.

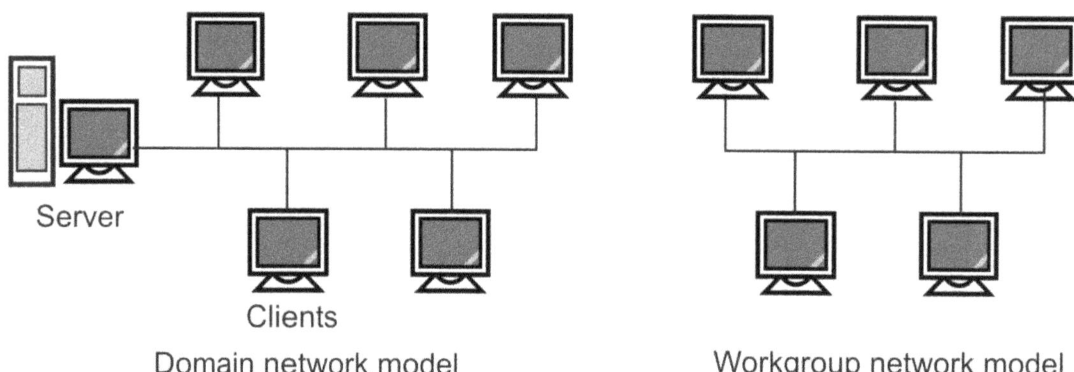

Figure 6.2. Domain and work-group logical networks

Thus it can be said that the physical client-server networks tend to fit in with the logical domain network model. And likewise, the physical peer-to-peer network fits into the workgroup logical network model. The size and scalability of any computer network are determined both by the physical medium of communication and by the software controlling the communication (i.e., the protocols).

6.4. Servers

As mentioned earlier, a server performs services for connected clients within the client-server architecture. For example, a server could be an application program that accepts remote procedure calls (RPCs) in order to service requests from clients. Servers are computers on the network that are designed to run these applications, without user intervention.

For example in a corporate office network a Dynamic Host Configuration Protocol (DHCP) server provides clients with an IP address. A Network Address Translation (NAT) server on the other hand protects a computer from the Internet by hiding the private IP addresses. Other examples of network servers include Directory services, DNS, Proxy services, Remote

Access Services (RAS), web, e-mail, file services and many others. In practical networks these servers are deployed in software and quite often a physical server machine may carry out a number of these server roles. Figure 6.3 identifies some of the common server roles in modern networks.

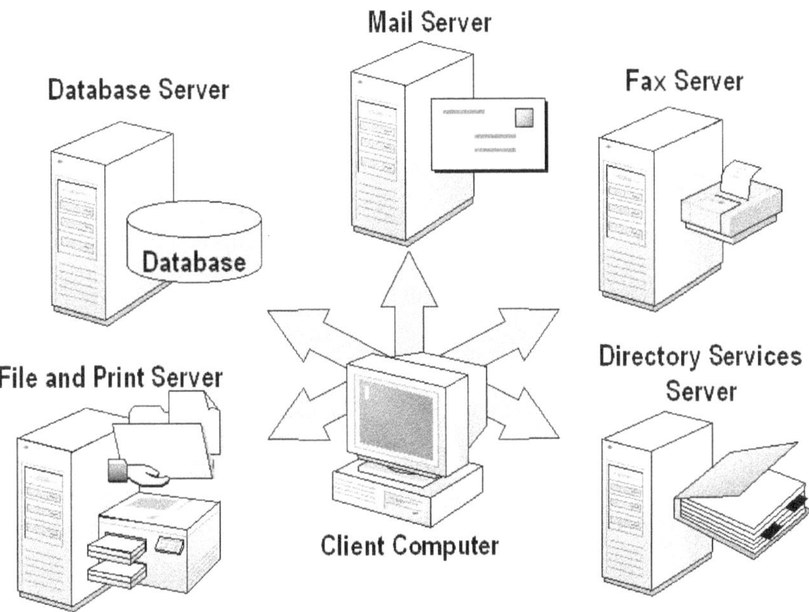

Figure 6.3. Examples of server roles in a network

It is worth mentioning that almost the entire structure of the Internet is based upon a client-server model. The Internet connects millions of servers across the world into a network. These computers run continuously and provide services to client computers. For example, each computer connected to the Internet has to have a unique public IP address; therefore a DHCP server is required to allocate this unique address to the client.

6.5. Server Role Configuration Options

Servers have evolved in parallel with computer networks. Networks allow computers to communicate with each other, and consequently there was a tendency to dedicate some computers to a serving role while other computers assume a client role. For example, Microsoft networking identifies the server roles in their 2003 network operating systems as described next. [44]

Terminal Server

Provides a single point of installation that gives multiple users access to any Windows Server 2003. Users can run programs, save files, and use network resources from a remote location as if these resources were installed on their local computers. Benefits include,

- Rapid, centralised deployment of applications.
- Uniform version of Windows on desktops, reducing maintenance and administrative costs.
- Increased scalability.
- Improved manageability.
- Has an easy-to-use remote desktop connection.

File Server

The file server controls access to files such as data files and network-accessible applications. Benefits include,

- Automatically copies critical data volumes by using the Volume Shadow Copy Restore service, eliminating downtime. Copies are used to restore or archive files, and users can retrieve archived versions of their documents.
- Enables Encrypting File System (EFS), which provides core file encryption technology. EFS is a public key-based system that makes it easy to manage, difficult to attack, and transparent to the user.
- Initiates Distributed File System (DFS), a stable, orderly, location-independent naming scheme for all shared files when using Windows. A single share, or a single drive mapped to such a share, can contain files and directories on any number of file servers.
- Stores, manages, and shares information such as files and network-accessible applications.
- Limits and monitors the amount of disk space available to individual users.
- Securely searches for information, either locally or on the network. It also searches files that are in different formats and languages.

- Helps users manage their disk space by logging and reporting when a user exceeds a specified disk space limit or warning level—that is, the point at which a user is nearing his or her quota limit.

Print Server

Configures and manages access to printers. Benefits include,

- Supports print devices from a variety of hardware vendors.
- Provides printer management via a Web browser. Individuals can pause, resume, or delete a print job and view the printer and print job's status.
- Administrators can manage printers remotely, manage printers by using Windows Management Instrumentation (WMI), or print from a server or client computer to a print server by using a URL.
- Provides increased print driver control and reliability.
- Improves print spooling performance of heavily loaded servers.
- Reduces administrative time by automatically propagating print cluster driver installation to all nodes.
- Users can connect to printers on a network by using Web point-and-print for single-click installations of a shared printer. It also lets users install drivers from a website.

Application Server (IIS, ASP.NET)

Installs Internet Information Services (IIS 6.0) along with other technologies and services, such as COM+ and ASP.NET. The application server role contains all the functionality and other services for development, deployment, and runtime management of XML Web services, Web applications, and distributed applications. Benefits include,

- The Process Recycling tool enhances reliability. This tool recycles processes, thereby minimising resource consumption caused by memory leaks before they compromise performance and reliability. Administrators can schedule periodic IIS processes recycling to release resources any leaking Web application consumes.
- A just-in-time object activation model saves resource infrastructure.

- Resource pooling—database connection pooling and object pooling—uses resources more effectively than in previous Windows operating systems.
- Avoids system resource overloading by using distributed transaction management.
- Automatic XML Web service interfaces access business objects.
- Uniform integrated security across all applications. Authorisation Manager increases reliability and reduces administrative time.

Mail Server (POP3, SMTP)

Installs post office protocol (POP3) and simple mail transport protocol (SMTP) e-mail services components included with the Windows Server 2003 family. The POP3 service implements the standard POP3 protocol for mail retrieval and enables mail transfer when paired with the SMTP service. Benefits include,

- End-users, applications, and devices can use the POP3 and SMTP services to store and send e-mail messages to other end-users, applications, and devices for basic messaging needs.
- Enables users to access the mail server to retrieve e-mail from their local computers by using an e-mail client that supports the POP3 protocol (for example, Microsoft Outlook and Outlook Express).

Remote Access/VPN Server

Remote or mobile users can access corporate networks as if they were directly connected, either through dial-up connection services or over the Internet by using VPN connections. Benefits include,

- Remote access to all the services is available to a locally connected user, including file and print sharing, Web server access, and messaging.
- Administrative control of how and when remote users access the network.
- Provides network address translation (NAT) services for the computers on the network.

- Creates custom networking solutions using application-programming interfaces (APIs).

Streaming Media Server

Provides Windows Media Services to an organisation. Windows Media Services manages, delivers, and archives Windows Media content, including streaming audio and video, over an intranet or the Internet. Benefits include,

- Uses Fast Streaming—a set of features in Windows Media Services—to improve the streaming performance.
- Provides real-time digital video over networks that range from low-bandwidth, dial-up Internet connections to high-bandwidth, and local area networks (LANs).
- Uses server-side play lists and advertisements by enabling Dynamic Content Delivery, which customises content distribution.
- Offers streaming advertisements to potentially generate revenue for a Web site.
- Reliably scales and secures streaming media for even the largest enterprises and content delivery networks.

WINS Server

Configures Windows Internet Name Service (WINS), which maps IP addresses to Net BIOS computer names and vice versa. With WINS servers, individuals can search for resources by computer name instead of by IP address. Benefits include,

- Reduces Net BIOS-based broadcast traffic on subnets by permitting clients to query WINS servers to locate remote systems.
- Supports earlier Windows and Net BIOS-based clients on the network by permitting them to browse lists for remote Windows domains without requiring a local domain controller on each subnet.
- Supports DNS clients by enabling those clients to locate Net BIOS resources when WINS lookup integration is implemented.

Domain Controller (Active Directory) Server

Stores directory data and manages communication between users and domains, including user logon processes, authentication, and directory searches. Active Directory service manages users and computers and is a key feature of the Domain Controller Server role. Benefits include,

- Stores directory data and makes it available to network users and administrators. Active Directory stores information about user accounts, for example, names, passwords, and phone numbers—and enables other authorised users on the same network to access this information.
- Improves availability and reliability of network services by adding extra domain controllers to an existing domain.
- Improves network performance between sites by placing a domain controller in each site, which enables the server to handle the client logon processes within the sites rather than using network bandwidth between sites.

DNS Server

The DNS service enables client computers on a network to register and resolve user-friendly DNS names. The DNS server hosts records of a distributed DNS database and uses these records to answer DNS queries sent by DNS client computers, For example, queries for the names of Web sites or computers on your network or on the Internet. Benefits include,

- User-friendly naming makes naming and locating network resources more efficient.
- Resolves control names for each network segment and replicates changes to the entire network or globally on the Internet.
- Reduces administration time by dynamically updating DNS information.

DHCP Server

Once set up, administrators can manage IP addresses and related information in a central location. Benefits include,

- Prevents IP address conflicts by preventing the use of previously assigned IP addresses.

- Reduces the time spent configuring and reconfiguring computers by selecting the DHCP server to supply a full range of additional configuration values when assigning address leases.
- Prevents clients who frequently change locations, from missing updates by using the lease renewal process.

It is worth pointing out that servers should not be confused with mainframe computers. Mainframes are very large computers that centralise certain information-processing activities in large organisations and may or may not act as servers in addition to their other activities. Many large organisations have both mainframes and servers, although servers usually are smaller and much more numerous and decentralised than mainframes.

6.6. Server hardware

To a large extent the hardware used in server computers is similar to most other general-purpose computers, although their hardware configurations may be optimised to complement their server roles. However, servers run software that is significantly different from that used on desktop computers and workstations.

In terms of performance criteria CPU speeds are far less critical for many servers than they are for many desktops. This is primarily because servers do not need a lot of human operator interaction. Once a server is configured it remains in an isolated area free from constant user intervention. Consequently, the lack of any graphical user interface (GUI) in many servers frees up very large amounts of processing power for other tasks, making the overall processor power requirement lower. If a great deal of processing power is required in a server, there is a tendency to add more CPUs rather than increase the speed of a single CPU, again for reasons of reliability and redundancy.

Because servers must operate continuously and reliably it is necessary to cool them and in some cases, centralised air-conditioning may be used to keep servers cool, in addition to fans. Special uninterruptible power supplies (UPS) should also be used to ensure that the servers continue to run in the event of a power failure. Typical servers feature heavy-duty network connections in order to allow them to handle the large amounts of traffic that they typically generate as they receive and reply to client requests. It is also common for servers to be equipped with SCSI hard drives to enable RAID arrays to be used for fault-tolerance.

More recently advances in server hardware include the introduction of blade servers. [45] The IBM Blade Centre is an example of this technology, while HP and Sun offer their own blade solutions. Avery useful reading on the hardware of HP blade servers can be found in their white paper entitled 'HP BladeSystem p-Class System Overview and Planning'. [46]

Very briefly, the principle characteristic of a blade server is that it is a hardware arrangement, which houses multiples of very thin, modular electronic circuit boards, known as server blades. These blades are literally servers on a card, containing processors, memory, integrated network controllers, an optional fibre channel host bus adaptor (HBA) and other input/output (IO) ports. For example, the HP blade system p–class series hardware solutions typically consist of server blades, blade enclosures, network interconnection hardware (with options), a power subsystem, and management tools that enable adaptive computing and is optimised for rapid deployment. As a result of this reduced hardware overhead blade servers allow more processing power in less rack space, reduced power consumption and less complicated cabling.

The blade server arrangement lends itself to simplified integration of data storage, network components and also server clustering. For data storage integration, blade servers typically connect to a storage pool over a fibre-optic channel providing very fast access to data pools. Integration of network components reduces distances between servers. As a direct result of these two benefits, server-clustering benefits are obtained. Typically a cluster of blade servers would include a number of servers each of which is dedicated to a single task, such as for example a cluster of four blades comprising,

- Blade 1: File sharing.
- Blade 2: Web page serving and caching.

- Blade 3: SSL encrypting of Web communication.
- Blade 4: Streaming audio and video content.

Like most clustering applications, blade servers can also be managed to include load balancing and failover capabilities.

6.7. Server operating systems

Server operating systems provide a means of managing the resources that are available on the server. The requirements of servers include responding to client requests and so the server operating systems are significantly different from those of desktop computers.

It is difficult to design an operating system that handles both environments well; thus, operating systems that are well suited to the desktop may not be ideal for servers and vice versa. The UNIX operating system was originally a minicomputer operating system, and as servers gradually replaced traditional minicomputers, it became the logical choice of operating system for the servers. Server operating systems tend to have certain features that make them more suitable for the server computing. These include,

- GUI is not necessary.
- The ability to be reconfigured without shutting-down the system.
- Movement of data between different volumes or devices, which is transparent to the end-user.
- Advanced backup features to permit online backups of critical data at regular and frequent intervals.
- Advanced networking features (such as daemons in UNIX or services in Windows) make unattended execution of programs more reliable.
- Tight system security, with advanced user, resource, data, and memory protection.
- Operating systems can interact with hardware sensors to detect conditions such as overheating, processor and disk failure and either alert operators, take remedial action, or both, depending on the configuration.

The Microsoft Windows operating system is predominant among desktop computers, and although Windows support servers with the Windows 2003 Server O/S, the most popular operating systems in server applications are derived from the UNIX operating system —such as FreeBSD, Solaris, and Linux. Nevertheless, certain versions of Microsoft Windows operating systems are also used on servers as are recent versions of the popular Mac OS X (also Unix-based) family of desktop operating systems and even some proprietary mainframe operating systems (such as z/OS).

The rise of the microprocessor-based server was facilitated by the development of several versions of Unix to run on the Intel x86 microprocessor architecture. The Microsoft Windows family of operating systems also runs on Intel hardware, and versions beginning with Windows NT have incorporated features making them suitable for use on servers. It is worth mentioning that, in computer networks there is a tendency to arrange the network in native mode. That is all the computers on the network run the same operating system. This makes network administration easier. For this reason most operating systems manufacturers will provide versions of both the server and the client operating systems.

6.8. Clients

A client is an application that cannot function in stand-alone mode because it relies on a service of another network application i.e. a server. Historically, the concept evolved from dumb terminals that could interact with remote computers via a network. These were the clients of the time-sharing mainframe computer on the same network.

In modern day networks clients can have independent processing power and different client services are supported at the network level. For example, distributed database applications have very sophisticated client and server applications. Recent trends on the Internet have seen existing large server applications being switched to websites, making the browser a sort of universal client. An example of this is the increased use of web-mail service providers. These applications use a browser as the client software, which avoids the need to install a separate mail-client application. For example, one of the earliest Webmail services was Hotmail.

As far as client types are concerned they are generally classified as 'Thick clients', 'thin clients', or 'hybrid clients'. The classification is based on the amount of local storage and processing power that they possess.

	Local storage	Local processing
Thick Client	Yes	Yes
Hybrid Client	No	Yes
Thin Client	No	No

Thick client

A thick client (also known as fat or rich) is a client that performs most of the data processing itself. The hardware for this type of client is typically a personal computer, which has significant processing power. The software programming environments of thick clients include Curl, Delphi, Droplets, Java, win32 and X11. Platforms and Languages include web-based frameworks. For example, the Microsoft-based thick client platform includes, [47]

- Net Framework for web applications (C# and VB.Net).
- Net Framework for windows applications (C# and VB.Net).
- ASP/VBScript websites.
- Advanced HTML, DHTML, XHTML and JavaScript.
- Enterprise Services/Serviced Components for n-tier .Net Development.

Examples of thick-client computing applications include corporate databases, web-based business solutions, document management systems (DMS) etc. Typically these applications will have software interfaces to extension applications such as Purchase Ordering, Invoicing, Cashflow Management and Approval Workflow for popular accounting systems like Deltek Advantage and MYOB. [48]

Thin client

A thin client is a minimal sort of client with resources that are sufficient only to connect to the server, and utilise its resources. Generally speaking the main job of a thin client is to graphically display pictures provided by an application server, which performs the bulk of any required data processing.

Thin-client computing can provide a significant cost reduction in some corporations. Additionally, recent trends show that enterprises are now trying to further reduce costs by moving to 'intelligent' Thin Clients. In contrast to the traditional thin clients, which simply acted as terminals allowing access from desktops to server-based applications, the Intelligent Thin Clients come with built-in emulation software; e-mail; a full-function browser--such as Mozilla Firefox or full Internet Explorer--supporting JVM, Flash and XML; and pop-up window support.

These intelligent Thin Clients run Linux or Windows XPe operating systems, and allow access to a file server as well as Web-delivered applications such as Lotus Notes, WebSphere, [49] etc. Programming environments for thin clients include JavaScript/AJAX (client side automation), ASP, JSP, Ruby on Rails, Python's Django, PHP and other (depends on server-side backend and uses HTML pages or rich media like Flash, Flex or Silverlight on client). [50]

Hybrid client

A hybrid client is a mixture of the above two client models. Similar to a fat client, it processes locally, but relies on the server for data storage. This approach provides features from both the fat client (multi-media support, high performance) and the thin client (high manageability, flexibility). For example, the recent emergence of the ASP model was supposed to resolve many of the problems of the client-server model, such as high hardware and software costs, development and implementation costs, as well as the costs of staffing and infrastructure maintenance. Some developers are proposing a hybrid client-server plus ASP (CLASP) approach, while expanding market opportunities for database software and server hardware. [51]

Workstations

A workstation, such as a Unix workstation, RISC workstation or engineering workstation, is a high-end desktop microcomputer designed for high-performance technical applications. [52] Workstations are intended primarily to be used by one person at a time, although they can usually also be accessed remotely by other users when necessary. They have superior performance compared to personal computers, especially with respect to graphics, processing power, memory capacity and multi-tasking ability.

In view of their specialised use, workstations are often optimised for displaying and manipulating complex data such as 3D mechanical design, engineering simulation results, and mathematical plots. This in turn necessitates a high-resolution display, and support for multiple displays and may often utilise a server level processor.

For design and advanced visualisation tasks, specialised input hardware such as graphics tablets or a SpaceBall can be used. Workstations have classically been the first part of the computer market to offer advanced accessories and collaboration tools such as videoconferencing capability. The systems that come out of workstation companies often feature SCSI or Fibre Channel disk storage systems, high-end 3D accelerators, single or multiple 64-bit processors, large amounts of RAM, and well-designed cooling. However, the distinction between workstation and PC is increasingly becoming blurred as the demand for fast computers, networking and graphics have become common in the consumer world, allowing workstation manufacturers to use 'off the shelf' PC components and graphics solutions as opposed to proprietary in-house developed technology. For example, some low-end workstations use CISC based processors like the Intel Pentium 4 or AMD Athlon 64 as their CPUs. Higher-end workstations still use more sophisticated CPUs such as AMD Opteron, IBM POWER, MIPS or Sun's UltraSPARC, and run a variant of Unix, delivering a truly reliable workhorse for computing-intensive tasks.

Exercises

6.1 Discuss the basic features of client-server and peer-to-peer networks.

6.2 Name and discuss the type of servers that you may need in a corporate network.

6.3 What are the main advantages of server based networks?

6.4 Using a database server as an example, explain the client-server concept.

6.5 Explain how the hardware arrangement in a server computer differs from client machine hardware.

6.6 Briefly discuss the features of Blade Servers, and how they can be clustered.

6.7 What are the main features of server operating systems?

6.8 Give examples of server O/Ss.

6.9 Giving examples as appropriate, explain the various client types, i.e. thick, thin and hybrid.

7 NETWORK SERVICES

7.1. Introduction

Corporate networks are becoming more sophisticated and as progress advances are made in networking hardware and software, so the corporate needs are increasing. More and more corporations are resorting to WANs to satisfy their marketing aims. Takeovers and mergers have meant that a degree of integration that a network O/S can provide is a very important factor. In order to facilitate the running of a modern corporate network some mandatory network services need to be provided. These include the following services,

- IP allocation service.
- Domain Name resolution service.
- Network address translation.
- Firewall and proxy service.
- Virtual private networks.

7.2. Dynamic Host Configuration Protocol (DHCP)

DHCP is an extensively used TCP/IP protocol for dynamically assigning IP addresses to devices on a network. It provides a framework for passing configuration information to hosts on a TCP/IP network. In other words, DHCP is a protocol used by networked computers (clients) to obtain IP addresses and other parameters such as the default gateway, subnet mask, and IP addresses of DNS servers from a DHCP server.

DHCP is a successor to the older BOOTP protocol, whose leases were given for infinite time and did not support options. The introduction of DHCP added the capability of automatic allocation of reusable network addresses and additional configuration options. DHCP captures the behaviour of BOOTP relay agents, and DHCP participants can interoperate with BOOTP participants. [53]

Due to the backward-compatibility of DHCP, very few networks continue to use pure BOOTP. As of 2006, RFC 2131 (dated March 1997) provides the latest DHCP definition. As of 2004, the latest non-standard of the protocol is

RFC 3315 (dated July 2003), which describes DHCPv6 (DHCP in an IPv6 environment). DHCP is built on a client-server model, where designated DHCP server hosts allocate network addresses and deliver configuration parameters to dynamically configured hosts. The DHCP server ensures that all IP addresses assigned to clients are unique. This means that no IP address is assigned to a second client while the first client's assignment is valid (its lease has not expired). Thus IP address pool management is done by the server and not by a human network administrator. DHCP supports three mechanisms for IP address allocation namely,

- **Automatic**- In automatic allocation, DHCP assigns a permanent IP address to a client.
- **Dynamic**- In dynamic allocation, DHCP assigns an IP address to a client for a limited period of time (or until the client explicitly relinquishes the address).
- **Manual**. In manual allocation, the network administrator assigns a client's IP address, and DHCP is used simply to convey the assigned address to the client.

A particular network will use one or more of these mechanisms, depending on the policies of the network administrator. Figure 7.1 shows computers on the network having dynamically assigned IP addresses that are subject to lease duration, as well as static IP addresses, where the IP address is assigned permanently. Here the DHCP server assigns IP Addresses 1 and 2 from a pool to the two DHCP client computers. The non-DHCP client has static IP address, which is not assigned by the DHCP server. Nevertheless, the DHCP server will know that the static address has been assigned and this address must not be in the DHCP server pool of available addresses to lease.

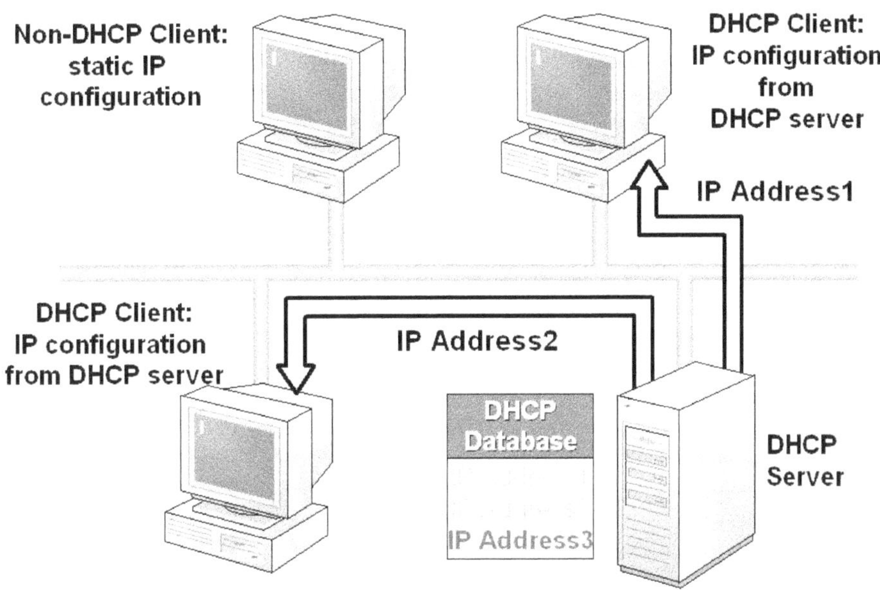

Figure 7.1. Static and dynamic clients can be on the same network

Settings for DHCP options will vary from system to system, but normally the administrator would define pool of addresses that are available for dynamic allocation on a lease basis. The DHCP server would assign these whenever a host logs onto the network. There would also be an option to select IP reservations. These IP addresses cannot be assigned dynamically on a lease basis because that would make it difficult for clients to locate these servers. For example, IP address reservations may be necessary in the following circumstances,

- The computer acts as a server (e.g., a Web server, application server hosting special software or files used staff, proxy server used for internet access etc.)
- Networked printer requires a static IP address in order to receive print jobs.
- The device uses software, which requires the device to have static IP address (e.g., in order for the software license to function or to talk to the device).
- The device is not DHCP-compatible and MUST be configured manually with a specific IP address.

These servers need to be assigned static IP addresses. The DHCP can be configured to assign these automatically, or the administrator can set these manually for the host computer. Either way they are static and are not intended to change during normal network operation.

Dynamic allocation is the only one of the three mechanisms that allows automatic reuse of an address that is no longer needed by the client to which it was assigned. Thus, dynamic allocation is particularly useful for assigning an address to a client that will be connected to the network only temporarily. It can also be used for sharing a limited pool of IP addresses among a group of clients that do not need permanent IP addresses. Dynamic allocation may also be a good choice for assigning an IP address to a new client being permanently connected to a network where IP addresses are sufficiently scarce that it is important to reclaim them when old clients are retired.

Manual allocation allows DHCP to be used to eliminate the error-prone process of manually configuring hosts with IP addresses in environments where (for whatever reasons) it is desirable to manage IP address assignment outside of the DHCP mechanisms. Table 7.1 considers some advantages and disadvantages when comparing static to dynamic IP address allocation methods.

Table 7.1

Manual TCP/IP Configuration	
Disadvantages	Advantages
IP addresses entered manually on each client computer	IP addresses are supplied without user interaction to client computers
Possibility of entering incorrect or invalid IP address	Ensures that clients always use correct configuration information
Incorrect configuration can lead to communication and network problems	Eliminates common source of network problems
Administrative overhead on networks where computers are frequently moved	Client configuration updated automatically to reflect changes in network structure

The main advantage of dynamically assigning IP addresses is that it allows these addresses to be reused, and in this manner the IP address utilisation on the network is improved. Dynamically assigned IP addresses can also enhance security for individual users because their IP address is different every time they log into the network. Another important advantage is that it simplifies network administration because the DHCP server maintains a record of IP addresses and thus relieves the administrator from the task of having to manually assign and maintain a unique IP address to every computer on the network. The principle of operation of the DHCP service can be explained in four basic handshake steps involving the DHCP server and the DHCP client. These are shown in figure 7.2 where the client computer begins in **step 1**, by issuing an IP discovery message to the server. The client does this by broadcasting on the physical subnet to discover the available servers.

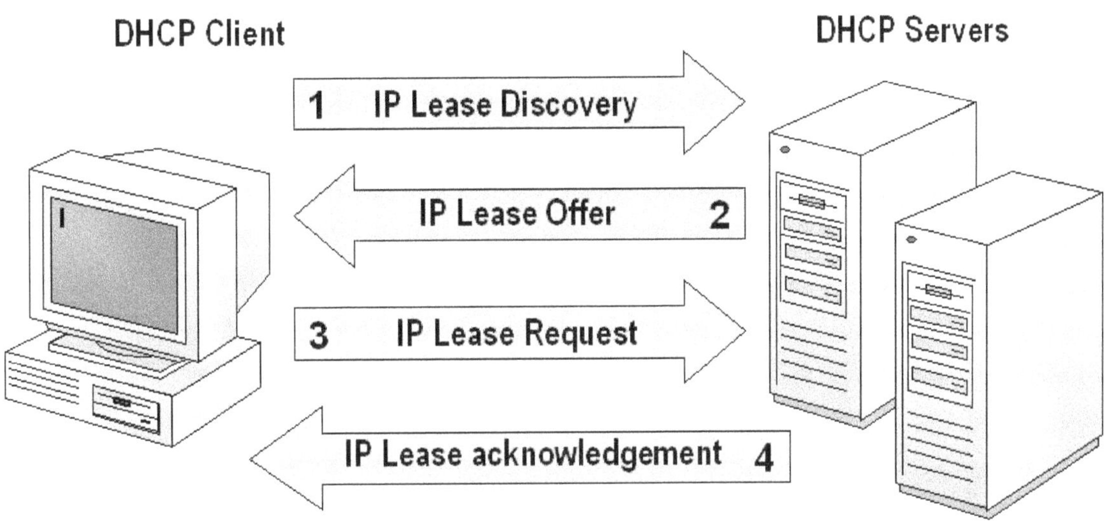

Figure 7.2. DHCP Client – Server handshake

Step 2 of the handshake is for the DHCP server response by sending an IP lease offer message to the client. This message contains the MAC address of the client, offered IP address, lease duration, subnet mask, and the IP address of the DHCP server making the offer.

Step 3 when the client receives the IP lease offer, it must tell all the other DHCP servers that it has accepted an offer. The client first compares the offers with the settings that it requested, and then sends a DHCPREQUEST message containing the IP address of the server that made the offer. This is performed in order to inform all DHCP servers on the network that the lease is being assigned. This message indicating which server it selected is broadcast to the entire network. When the other DHCP servers receive this message, they withdraw IP leases that they offered and return these to the pool of valid addresses. In this handshake a number of DHCP servers can make a lease offer, the client can only accept one.

In **step 4** the DHCP server sends an acknowledgement to the client. This acknowledgement phase involves sending a DHCPACK packet to the client. This packet includes the lease duration and other configuration details that the client might have requested. At this point, the TCP/IP configuration process is complete. Figure 7.3 shows typical information used in the DHCREQUEST and DHCPACK messages that are steps 1 and 4 respectively in the DHCP client-server handshake.

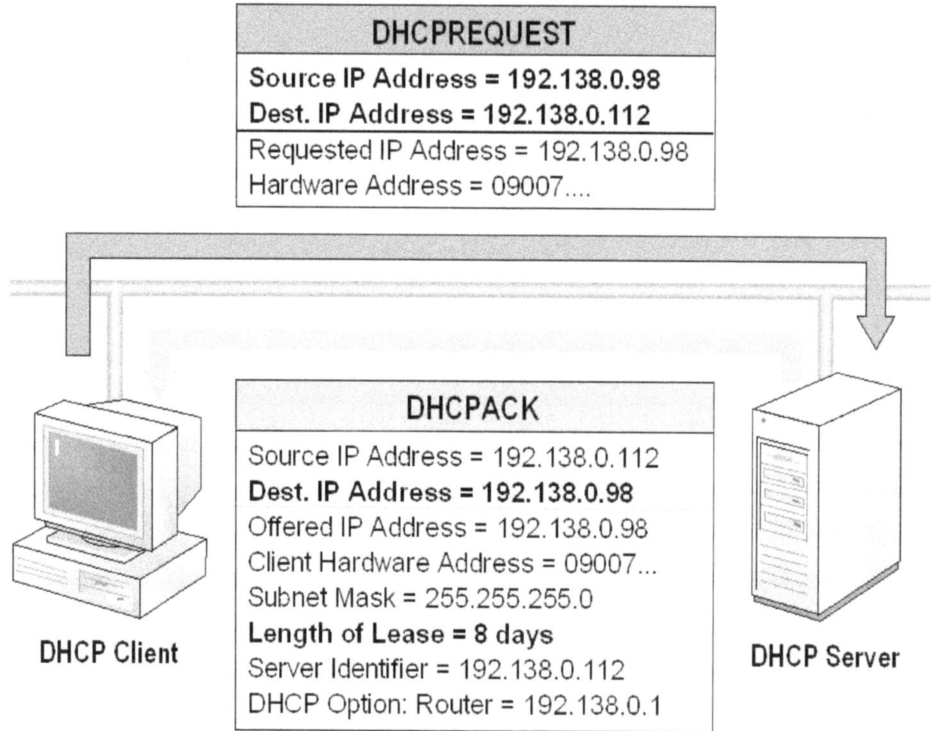

Figure 7.3. Typical messages between DHCP client and server

7.3. DHCP Packet forwarding

One major limitation of DHCP is that it relies on broadcasts for communications. By design and to avoid congestion on a network, broadcasts are normally only propagated on the local network. This means that in order to be able to communicate the client and server always need to be on the same physical network. In the case of large corporate networks this may not be a good solution. Having a different server on every subnet significantly reduces the benefits of centralised configuration management of the corporate network as well as creating major administrative overhead.

In networks where the DHCP server is not on the same LAN as the client the IP address must be allocated by a DHCP server on another subnet. This is possible in some cases where administrators are able to configure a local router to forward DHCP packets to a DHCP server on a different subnet. In other words the router forwards the DHCP packets that the client has broadcast on the local subnet, to the LAN where the DHCP server is located. If the router supports DHCP packet forwarding then configuring this router is all that is required. In this case the client-implementation creates a UDP packet with the broadcast destination of 255.255.255.255 which is effectively a subnet broadcast address.

An RFC 1542–compliant router will forward DHCP requests across subnets. Routers that do not forward packets to a broadcast address are said to be Non-RFC compliant. In this case the client on a subnet that does not have a DHCP server will broadcast its DHCPREQUEST but will receive no reply because the router that it uses as a gateway does not route DHCP packets to a broadcast address. This situation is shown in figure 7.4.

To resolve this issue the subnet without the DHCP server must have a Bootstrap protocol (BOOTP)/DHCP relay agent to forward the DHCP packets to the LAN that has the DHCP server. Thus the BOOTP protocol enables a client and server to be on different networks through the use of BOOTP relay agents. A relay agent is a device that is not a BOOTP server, but which runs a special software module that allows it to act in the place of a server.

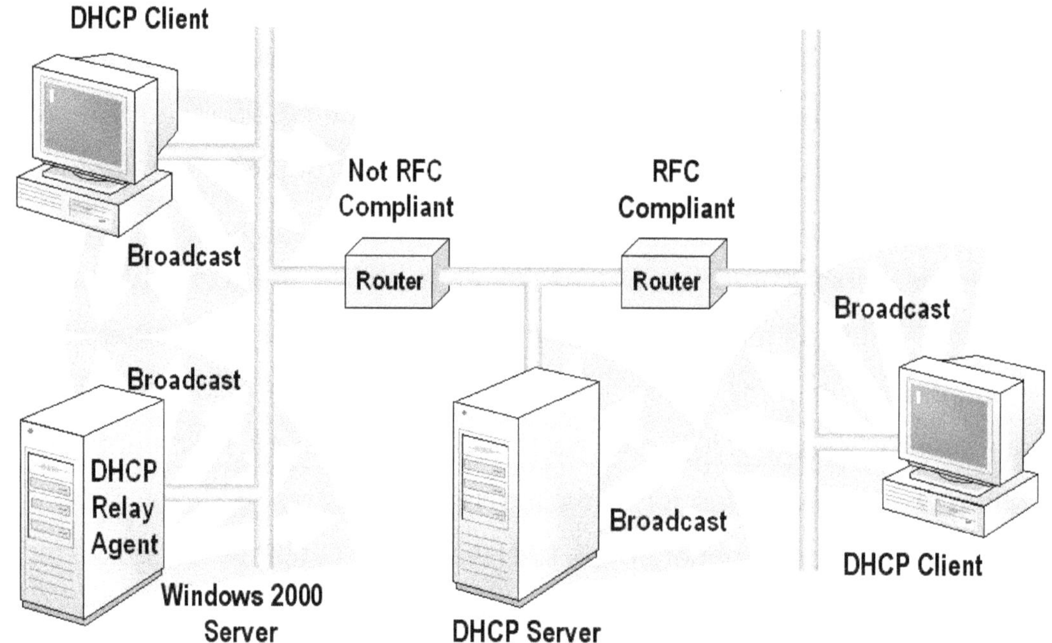

Figure 7.4. Non RFC Compliant router

A relay agent can therefore be placed on networks where there are BOOTP clients but no BOOTP servers. This situation is shown in figure 7.5, which identifies the four steps that are performed to issue the client IP address. The relay agent intercepts requests from clients and relays them to the server. The server then responds back to the agent, which forwards the response to the client. A full rationale and description of operation of BOOTP relay agents can be found in the RFC 1542 and others.

From figure 7.5, using the relay agent on subnet 1 enables the client to obtain an IP address from the server on subnet 2. The four steps are identified as follows,

- **Step 1:** DHCP client broadcasts a DHCP message. This step is the same as from the standard DHCP client-server handshake.
- **Step2:** DHCP relay agent detects the broadcast and responds by sending a message to the DHCP server notwithstanding the fact that there is no DHCP server on the subnet. At this point the relay intercepts the message and forwards it to the server on another subnet.
- **Step 3:** DHCP relay agent receives a reply from the DCHP server and sends a broadcast on the local subnet.

- **Step 4:** DHCP client receives the broadcast.

Thus it is seen that the relay agent takes on the bulk of communications and acts as an intermediary between the client and the server.

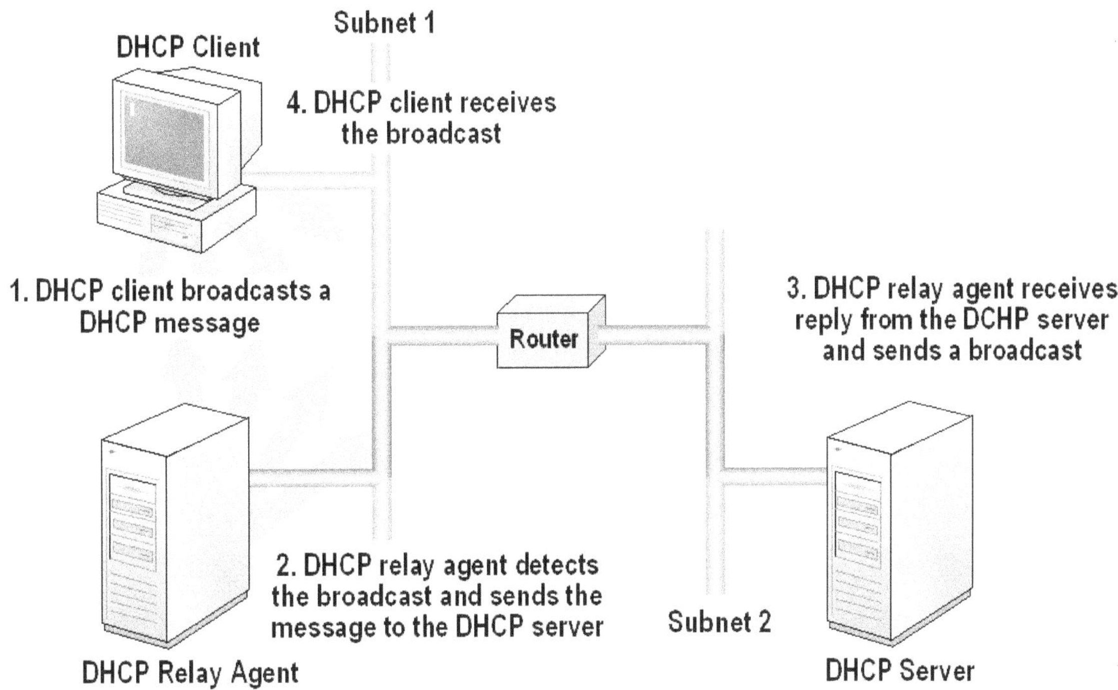

Figure 7.5. Relay agents on a subnet provides communications with server

The designers of DHCP were satisfied with the basic concepts and operation behind BOOTP relay agents, which had already been in use for many years. For this reason, they made the specific decision to continue using BOOTP relay agent functionality in DHCP. In fact, this is one of the reasons why the decision was made to retain the BOOTP message format in DHCP, and also the basic two-message 'request/reply' communication protocol. This allows BOOTP relay agents to handle DHCP messages as if they are BOOTP messages. Further reading on this topic can be found in Cisco, IBM and hp literature. [54-57]

During the network design stages, the tasks of allocating IP addresses and configuring the DHCP server have to be considered jointly. RFC 2131 Dynamic Host Configuration Protocol, March 1997, defines an approach to DHCP design that should be adhered to when designing and documenting DHCP related information. Briefly, the definition of terms includes the following,

- A DHCP client is an Internet host using DHCP to obtain configuration parameters such as a network address.
- A DHCP server is an Internet host that returns configuration parameters to DHCP clients.
- A BOOTP relay agent is an Internet host that passes DHCP messages between DHCP clients and DHCP servers.
- DHCP is designed to use the same relay agent behaviour as specified in the BOOTP protocol specification.
- A binding is a collection of configuration parameters, including at least an IP address, associated with or 'bound to' a DHCP client. DHCP servers manage bindings.

The following list gives general design goals for a DHCP solution,

- DHCP should be a mechanism rather than a policy. DHCP must allow local system administrators control over configuration parameters where desired; e.g., local system administrators should be able to enforce local policies concerning allocation and access to local resources where desired.
- Each client should be able to discover appropriate local configuration parameters without user intervention and incorporate those parameters into its own configuration.
- Networks should require no manual configuration for individual clients. Under normal circumstances, the network administrator should not have to enter any client-specific configuration parameters.
- DHCP should not require a server on each subnet. To allow for scale and economy, DHCP must work across routers or through the intervention of BOOTP relay agents.
- A DHCP client must be prepared to receive multiple responses to a request for configuration parameters. Some installations may include multiple, overlapping DHCP servers to enhance reliability and increase performance.
- DHCP must coexist with statically configured hosts and with existing network protocol implementations.

- DHCP must interoperate with the BOOTP relay agent behaviour as described by RFC 951 and by RFC 1542. [58].
- DHCP must provide service to existing BOOTP clients.

The following list gives design goals specific to the transmission of the network layer parameters. DHCP must,

- Guarantee that any specific network address will not be in use by more than one DHCP client at a time.
- Retain DHCP client configuration across DHCP client reboots. A DHCP client should, whenever possible, be assigned the same configuration parameters (e.g., network address) in response to each request.
- Retain DHCP client configuration across server reboots, and, whenever possible, a DHCP client should be assigned the same configuration parameters despite restarts of the DHCP mechanism.
- Allow automated assignment of configuration parameters to new clients to avoid hand configuration for new clients.
- Support fixed or permanent allocation of configuration parameters to specific clients.

7.4. Domain Names

Computers in a network need to have an address so that other computers can contact them. The Internet protocol (IP) address helps to uniquely identify a computer on a network. Human operators however, do not identify with numbers as easily as with names, and therefore a computer address to name resolution in the form of a Domain Naming Service has been devised. Simply put, the DNS maps IP addresses to domain names and therefore by implication, DNS only applies to those networks that are organised as domains. The DNS system is documented in a number of requests for comments (RFCs), and the most significant of these are as follows,

- 1034 Domain Names—Concepts and Facilities.
- 1035 Domain Names—Implementation and Specification.
- 1123 Requirements for Internet Hosts—Application and Support.

- 1886 DNS Extensions to Support IP Version 6.
- 1995 Incremental Zone Transfer in DNS.
- 1996 A Mechanism for Prompt DNS Notification of Zone Changes.
- 2136 Dynamic Updates in the Domain Name System (DNS UPDATE).
- 2181 Clarifications to the DNS Specification.
- 2308 Negative Caching of DNS Queries (DNS NCACHE).

Domains are logical units of administration of users, computers and resources and domain names are used to identify these. Essentially this means that if an organisation implements a domain naming service across a LAN or a WAN, then anyone with suitable access rights to the network should be able to locate resources by their names. All computer names that are in a domain are published in a DNS database along with their corresponding IP address. Accordingly every domain must have a dedicated DNS server to perform this name to IP address resolution. A local agent, called a resolver, retrieves information associated with a particular domain name. A brief explanation of the process is given with reference to figure 7.6.

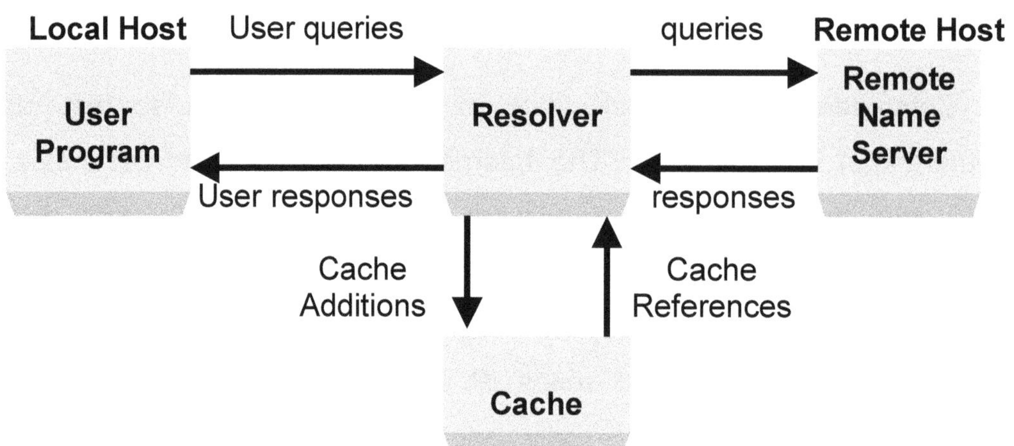

Figure 7.6. DNS service operation

The user sending a DNS query to the resolver receives ether the result of the query or information that it cannot be resolved. In other words, the resolver does all the hard work to retrieve the query and the user is not given the detail of these activities. In order to reduce network traffic and speed up operation, the database, which the resolver must search, is distributed among a number of name servers on the network. Each of these servers stores different sections of the domain space. The resolver begins the search by contacting a named DNS to resolve a query. In return, the resolver either receives the desired information or it receives a referral to another name server. Using these referrals, the resolvers learn the identities and contents of other name servers. To do this, when a name server resolves a request, it caches all of the IP addresses it receives. Therefore for example, once it has made a request to a root server for a .COM domain, it knows the IP address for a name server handling that domain. The next time the server needs to resolve a .COM domain, it only needs to go to the cache. Name servers can do this for every request, but to limit the number of cache entries the information stored in the cache includes a parameter called Time To Live (TTL). Thus, when the DNS server receives an IP address to resolve, it also gets a value for the TTL. The name server will cache the IP address for that period of time that can range from minutes to days and then discard it. This is fundamental to DNS since it allows the changes in name servers to propagate. Those names that are no longer valid will not be available after their TTL has expired.

Typically DNS servers have different query types and look up types as shown in figure 7.7. A DNS query can either be an iterative query, which is relatively quick and returns the best answer, while on the other hand a recursive query takes longer and returns the complete answer. The server can be configured for either of these and the choice will depend on the organisational structure of the network.

Query Types	
Iterative Query	The DNS server returns the best answer that it can provide without help from other servers
Recursive Query	The DNS server returns a complete answer to the query, not a pointer to another DNS server

Lookup Types	
Forward Lookup	Requires name-to-address resolution
Reverse Lookup	Requires address-to-name resolution

Figure 7.7. DNS query and look-up options

DNS servers can also be used for reverse lookup, where an IP address is resolved to a name. If one DNS server cannot resolve a DNS query for a particular domain name then it forwards this query to another DNS server and so on. The larger the network, the more DNS servers need to be contacted in order to resolve a query. Just as IP addresses are unique, so the domain names must be unique on a network. The Internet is a vast network and all the computers that are active on the Internet must have a unique name and an IP address. It is a known fact that domain namespaces have to be registered with domain hosting providers and usually there is registration fee associated with a hosting plan.

The principle here is very simple, however when the sheer number of names that appear on the Internet is considered, the DNS database gains significance. Domains on the Internet are organised in levels of hierarchy. The top-level domain names are usually allocated a significance that identifies the purpose of the domain. For example, .com is a commercial organisation and .gov is a government organisation etc. There are several hundred top-level domain names, including COM, EDU, GOV, MIL, NET, ORG and INT, as well as unique two-letter combinations for every country.

As the hierarchy is traversed down the levels so, the names are appended to the left hand side of the domain name, to indicate subdivisions within a domain. This is shown in figure 7.8. Here the top-level domain is .com. At this level there is a DNS server that holds all the published names in the .com level.

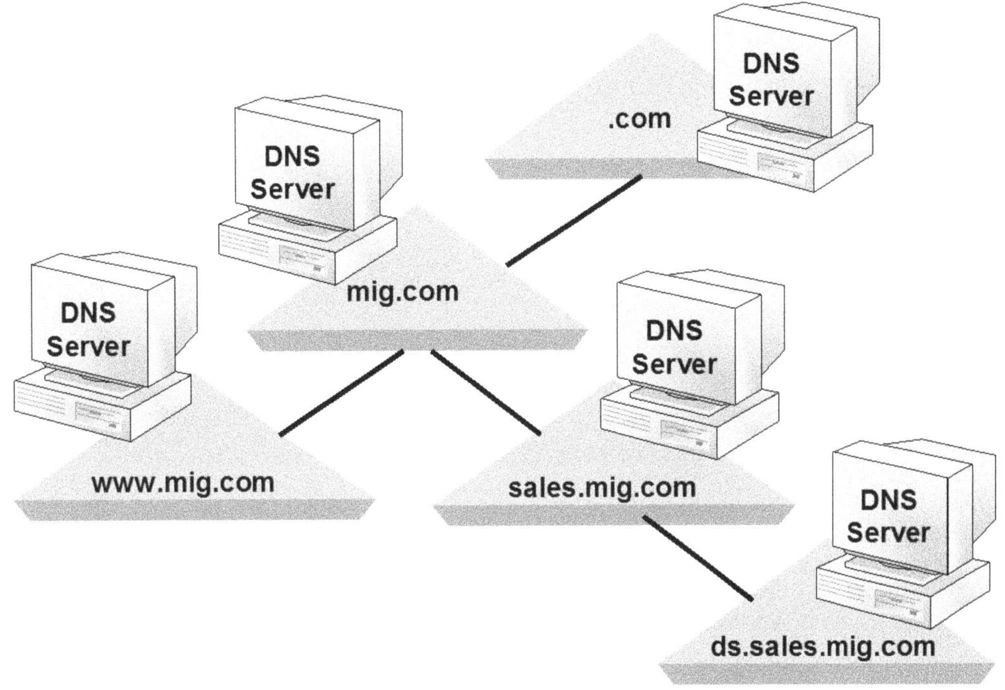

Figure 7.8. Domain hierarchical structure

Similarly as the domain hierarchy is traversed, there is a DNS server at each level that contains a database for all the domain names on that level. In the case of sales.mig.com domain name shown in figure 7.8, it is a third-level domain. The left-most word, such as www or sales, is the actual host name, which identifies a unique computer on the domain (i.e. web server). As mentioned earlier, the DNS server is responsible for resolving the name to an IP address and a single domain can contain any number of host names as long as they are all unique within that domain. Thus, with reference to figure 7.8, the top-level domain DNS server will have a map for all the top-level names and their IP addresses, one of which will be mig.com. The mig domain DNS server will have the entries for all the names in that domain, including www and sales. And the same logic applies to the DNS server in the sales domain, which will contain entries for all the names in that domain, including the ds.sales.mig.com host. The DNS system allows for up to 127 levels, although in practice it is not common to have more than four levels.

A DNS query begins at the top-level domain and the search continues down the hierarch until the name is found. If the name is not found the DNS returns a name not found error message as shown in figure 7.9.

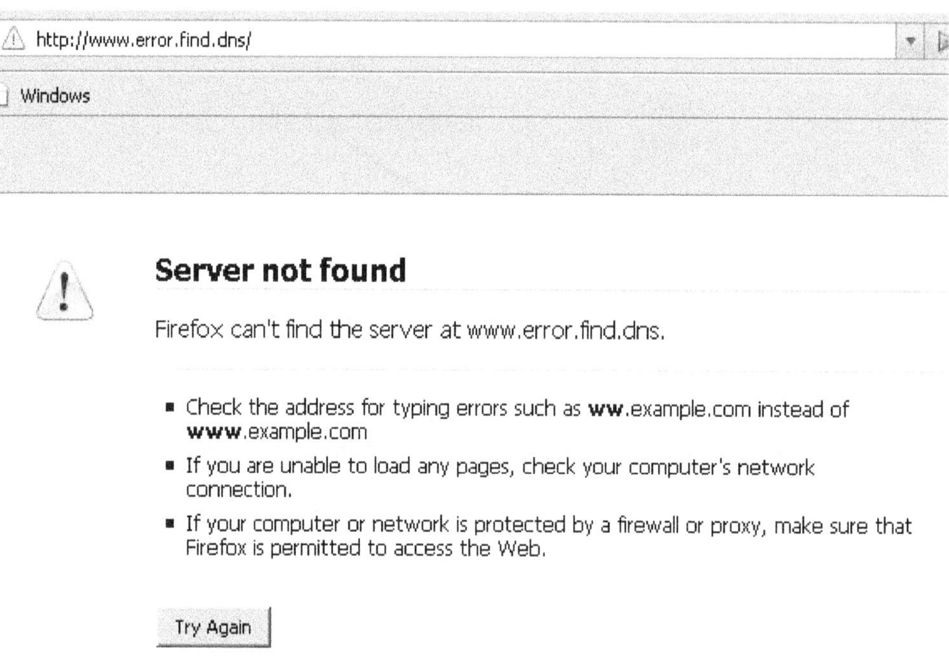

Figure 7.9. Error message from DNS

Resolving a name query on a subnet is quite straightforward, but when the query is on a large network, such as the Internet this task becomes significantly more complex. The reasons for this are briefly discussed next.

Domain names and IP addresses change daily with new domains being registered and old names being withdrawn. This requires that DNS databases be updated regularly. There are billions of IP addresses used on the Internet and as many have DNS names.

Requests to access a host on the Internet happen billions of times a day. Every time a user requests a page on the Internet, a DNS query is invoked. The number of these requests at any one instant in time is enormous. For example, if it is assumed that a single user generates 100 web URL requests every day, and that on average there are 200 million individual users on the Internet every day. The number of DNS requests can be calculated as $DNS_{requests} = 100 \times 200 \times 10^6 = 20 \times 10^9$, which is 20 billion requests per day. The

DNS system is a database, and no other database in the world gets this many requests. Because all of the names in a given domain need to be unique, there has to be a single entity that controls the list of Top Level Domains (TLDs) to prevent name duplication. For the Internet, the Internet Assigned Numbers Authority (IANA) and the Internet Corporation control the name and IP allocation for Assigned Names and Numbers (ICANN).

7.5. DNS Servers

Name servers manage two kinds of data. The first kind of data is held in sets called zones; each zone is the complete database for a particular subtree of the domain space. This data is called authoritative. A name server periodically checks to make sure that its zones are up to date, and if not, obtains a new copy of updated zones from master files stored locally or in another name server. The DNS requires that more than one name server redundantly supports all zones. Designated secondary servers as shown in figure 7.10 can acquire zones and check for updates from the primary server using the zone transfer protocol of the DNS. [59]

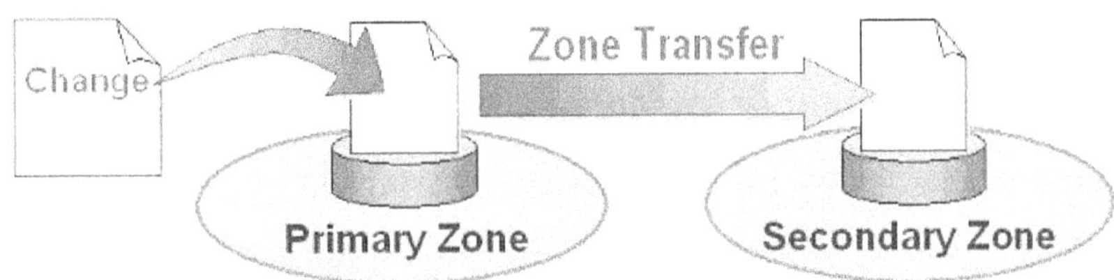

Figure 7.10. DNS zone transfer

The second kind of data is cached data, which was acquired by a local resolver. This data may be incomplete, but improves the performance of the retrieval process when non-local data is repeatedly accessed. As mentioned earlier, cached data is eventually discarded by a timeout mechanism.

DNS Resource Records

The DNS databases store 'resource records' (RRs) under domain names. This data is structured into classes and zones, which can be independently maintained. See (RFC 1034, 1035, 2136, 2181, 2535). All RRs have the same format as shown in figure 7.11. Here the components are explained in the table on the right of the figure. [60]

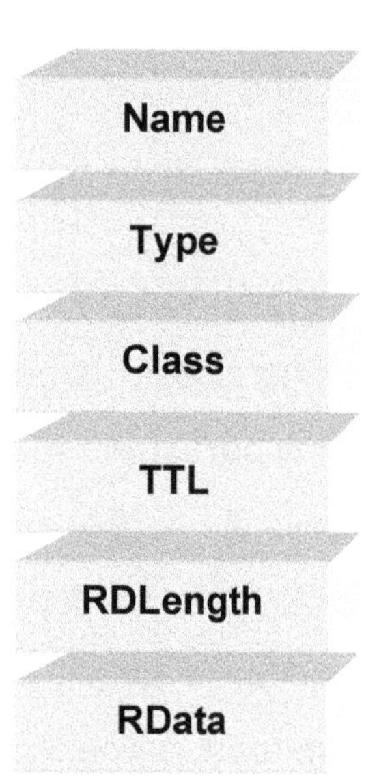

NAME an owner name, i.e., the name of the node to which this resource record pertains.
TYPE two octets containing one of the RR TYPE codes.
CLASS two octets containing one of the RR CLASS codes.
TTL a 32 bit signed integer specifies the interval that the resource record may be cached.
RDLENGTH an unsigned 16 bit integer that specifies the length in octets of the RDATA field.
RDATA a variable length string of octets that describes the resource. The format of this information varies according to the TYPE and CLASS of the resource record.

Figure 7.11. DNS, Resource records structure

Canonical name (CNAME)

DNS allows machines to have a genuine name (i.e. canonical name), as well as an unlimited number of aliases. The CNAME record takes care of aliases. These should only be used when absolutely necessary since they can cause major problems if not used properly. CNAMES are also useful for generic names, for example, having 'www.mig.com CNAME popular.mig.com', so the machine can have its own official name, but users can still find it without knowing its real name. [61]

CNAME resource records incur performance overheads. On low volume DNS servers the additional overheads are not significant but on high volume servers they can become significant. The user must make a choice to balance what many see as the convenience of using CNAME RRs against the possible performances degradation involved. [62]

7.6. DNS Server Network planning issues

All network infrastructure plans must include a DNS strategy. Design considerations begin with planning a capacity strategy. This will help to determine how many DNS servers are needed, and where the primary and secondary zones will be stored. As mentioned earlier DNS servers process large amount of data and the location of these on the network will impact on network loading. [63]

When planning for capacity the number of resource records that need to be stored determines the size of the zone. In typical usage a DNS server will consume 4Mbytes of RAM for minimal services, without storing any zone data. After that every zone that is added will use approximately 300 bytes and another 100 bytes for every resource record that is added to the zone. Thus approximate RAM usage can be calculated as follows,

$$DNS_{RAM} = 4 \times 2^{20} + z(300) + w(100) \qquad (7.1)$$

Where z- number of zones and w-number of RRs.

Thus a DNS server with 256 MB of RAM can potentially hold the following number of records in a single zone,

$$RR = \frac{(256-4)\times 2^{20} - 300\times 2^{10}}{100} = 2{,}639{,}339$$

It is worth noting that since the DNS server service loads all the zones into RAM and works form there, upgrading DNS server RAM can significantly improve performance.

7.7. DNS Server roles

Caching only servers are not authoritative for the zone and therefore they do not store the primary and secondary zones databases. Instead they perform resolution on behalf of the client and then store it in a database. Thus with reference to figure 7.12 a caching-only server at the remote office will look in its cache to resolve the query from a client. If this cannot resolve the query, the server then looks across the WAN to the corporate HQ DNS server, and when it is found, the result is stored in the cache for the next time it is needed. In this manner search traffic is reduced for all the queries stored in the cache. Additionally, caching-only servers do not hold zone information, so there is no zone transfer traffic associated with them.

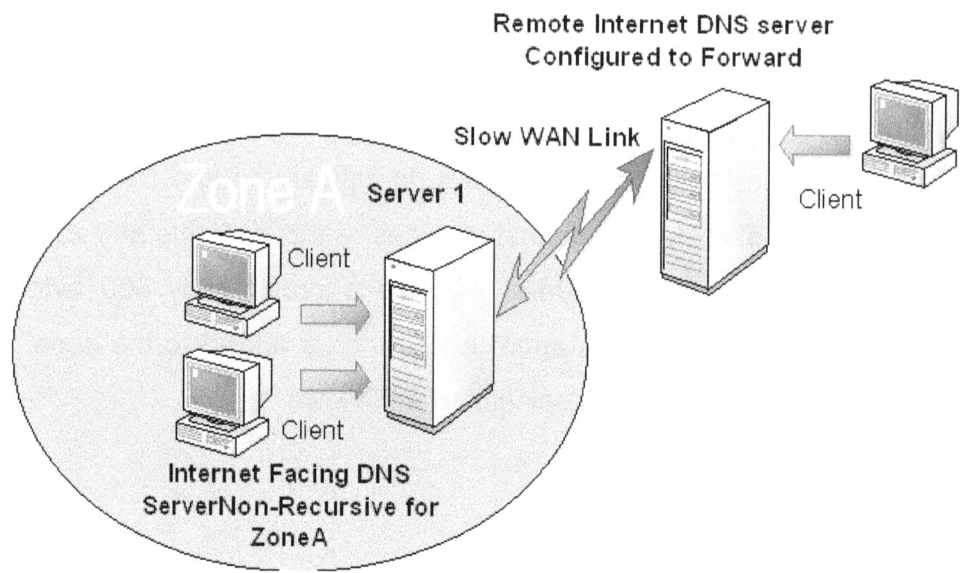

Figure 7.12. Using caching-only server to reduce WAN traffic

Non-recursive servers

These servers are configured to return either a full query result or a negative response. That is to say, they are prevented from forwarding requests to other servers. This is a very useful feature for Internet facing servers because non-recursive servers will only look in their own zones. Figure 7.13 shows server 1 as a non-recursive server for zone A. A query from a client on another network that has been forwarded, will be resolved only if it is within zone A. This will allow the DNS server to respond to queries from other DNS servers for the information in zone A. It will prevent Internet clients to use server 1 to resolve other names on the Internet.

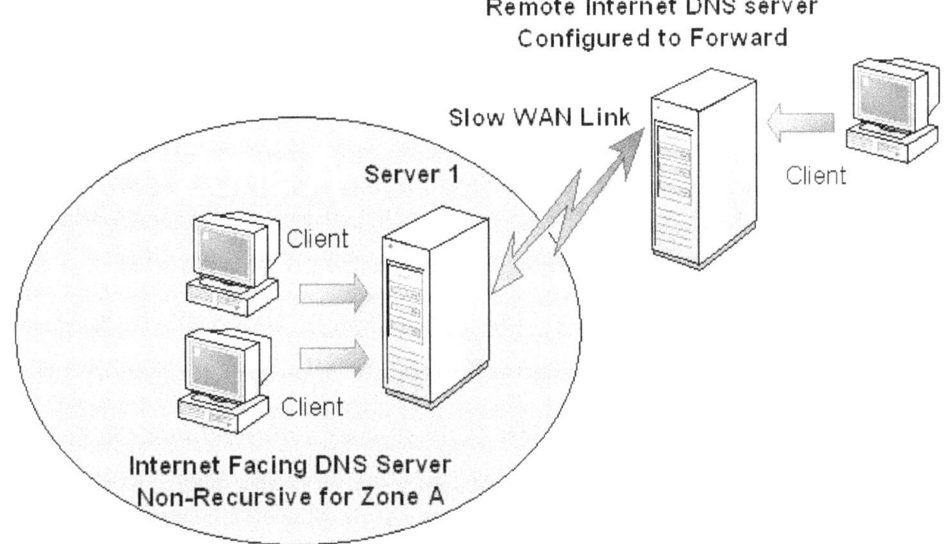

Figure 7.13. Non-recursive server

Forward only servers

In this configuration the DNS server does not resort to standard recursion, when the query cannot be resolved through its forwarders. In a way this is mid-way between non-recursive and fully recursive servers. The server will try its forwarders, and if these fail it will stop, and return a failure, rather than continue with full recursion.

Forwarders are useful for managing the DNS traffic between the local network and the Internet. For example, a single DNS server, configured, as a forwarder can be the single point of access to your network form the Internet. In this case the firewall that is used by the network is configured to allow only the DNS server configured as a forwarder to communicate with the Internet. This server will participate in name resolution and will contact all the forwarders it knows, but if this fails it will not attempt further recursion.

Conditional forwarders

These are selective forwarders that are configured to forward queries for predefined domain names. To do this conditional forwarders are configured to use one or more DNS server IP addresses for each specific domain. In this manner a direct point of contact is created between the DNS servers on the two networks, and consequently recursion traffic is reduced. DNS clients in separate networks can resolve each other's names without having to query the DNS server on the Internet.

7.8. Location of DNS servers

Adding DNS servers to a zone offers redundancy and carefully planned location of these servers can reduce network traffic. For example, if a server is placed in the vicinity of a large client population, this can reduce network traffic. Also, the addition of a secondary server in a suitable location will reduce the load on the primary server for that zone and this can reduce network traffic.

When determining the number of DNS servers the following points need to be considered,

- Estimate the effect of zone transfers and DNS query traffic on slower links in the network. Although DNS is designed to help reduce broadcast traffic between local subnets, it does create some traffic between servers and clients. In LANs and WANs with complex routing arrangements, this traffic can become considerable and the design must take it into account.
- When using a wide area network (WAN) connection, consider setting up DNS servers as caching-only DNS service at these locations to reduce WAN traffic.
- With most installations, there should be at least two DNS server computers for fault tolerance. Note that DNS was designed to have two servers for each zone, one as a primary server and the other as a backup or secondary server. With small LANs, it is possible to configure a single DNS server to function as both primary and secondary DNS for the zone.

Windows Internet Naming Service (WINS)

In heterogeneous networks, where for example Unix hosts are present along with Windows NT machines, the DNS namespace may not contain all the hosts and in this case the Windows Internet Naming Service (WINS) database needs to be integrated. Earlier Windows clients like Win '95 did not use DNS and instead registered their Net BIOS names with the WINS database. As a result these names are not available in a DNS namespace. WINS Lookup is a system that provides a limited gateway between the Domain Name System and the Windows Internet Name System (WINS). Using WINS Lookup, a DNS server can resolve queries for names registered exclusively in WINS. (See RFC2026)

At this point it has to be said that since the introduction of the Windows® 2000 operating system, Microsoft ® have adopted the DNS as the name service for their operating systems. Windows 2000 Server and its successor(s) include an IETF standard-based Domain Name System Server, which is RFC compliant. With Windows 2000 servers and later, DNS clients can resolve host names found in the WINS service by forwarding unresolved DNS queries to the WINS server. During DNS design, if the network needs to resolve WINS clients, it is a good idea to designate a subdomain within the namespace that will house all the WINS clients. In order to forward unresolved DNS queries to a WINS server, needs to be enabled on that zone.

7.9. Network Address Translation (NAT)

Basic NAT is a method (transparent to end-users) by which, IP addresses are mapped from one group of addresses to another group. The need for this IP address translation arises when a network's internal IP addresses cannot be used outside the network either for privacy reasons or because they are invalid for use outside the network. For example, when a local host needs to access the Internet, it requires a unique IP address for the duration of the Internet session. In this case the public IP address must be different from the private address that is assigned to the host while using the local LAN. Typically a NAT operates on a router connecting two networks together as shown in figure 7.14.

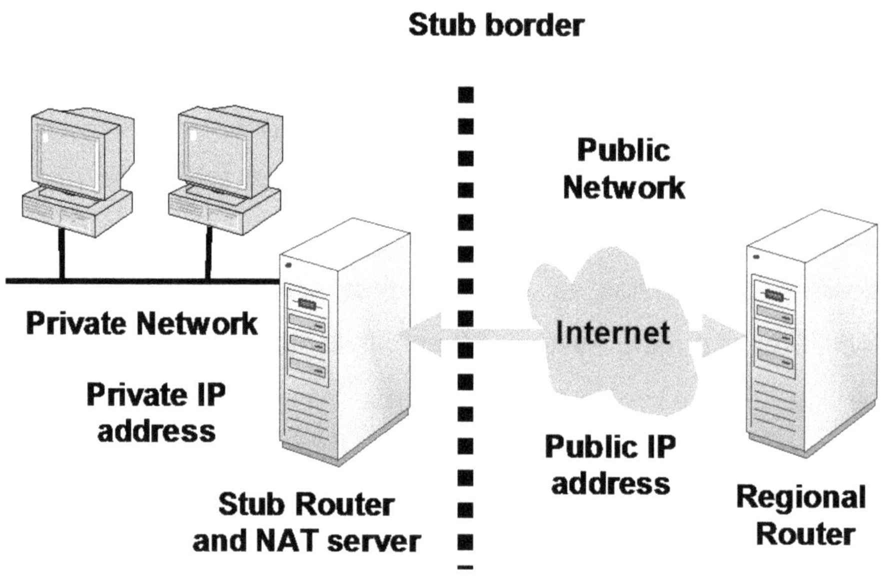

In figure 7.14 one of the networks is designated as private and the other as a public network. Before packets can be forwarded onto the public network, the private IP address of the sending computer needs to be converted into a public address. The NAT server performs this action. In addition to this, another service, namely the Network Address Port Translation (NAPT) is used to translate a number of network addresses and their TCP/UDP ports, into a single network address and its TCP/UDP ports. Together, these two operations are referred to as a traditional NAT. (See RFC 3022)

The need for a NAT service arises from the fact that network topology outside a local domain can change in many ways. Whenever external topology changes, address assignment for nodes within the local domain must also change to reflect these. For example, customers may change providers, company domains may be re-organised or ISPs may merge etc. Therefore the public IP addressing and naming system is a dynamic and constantly changing environment. Changes to the external network can be hidden from users within the domain by processing these changes in a single NAT.

The basic operation of a NAT server is as follows. With reference to figure 7.15, the addresses inside a stub domain are the private addresses and these can be reused by any other stub domain. For example, a Class A address 192.168.1.6 can be used by many stub domains. A NAT is installed at stub boarder to convert this address to a public address. It needs to be emphasised that if there is more than one exit point then it is a requirement that each NAT has the same translation table. For example, consider the NAT configuration shown in figure 7.15.

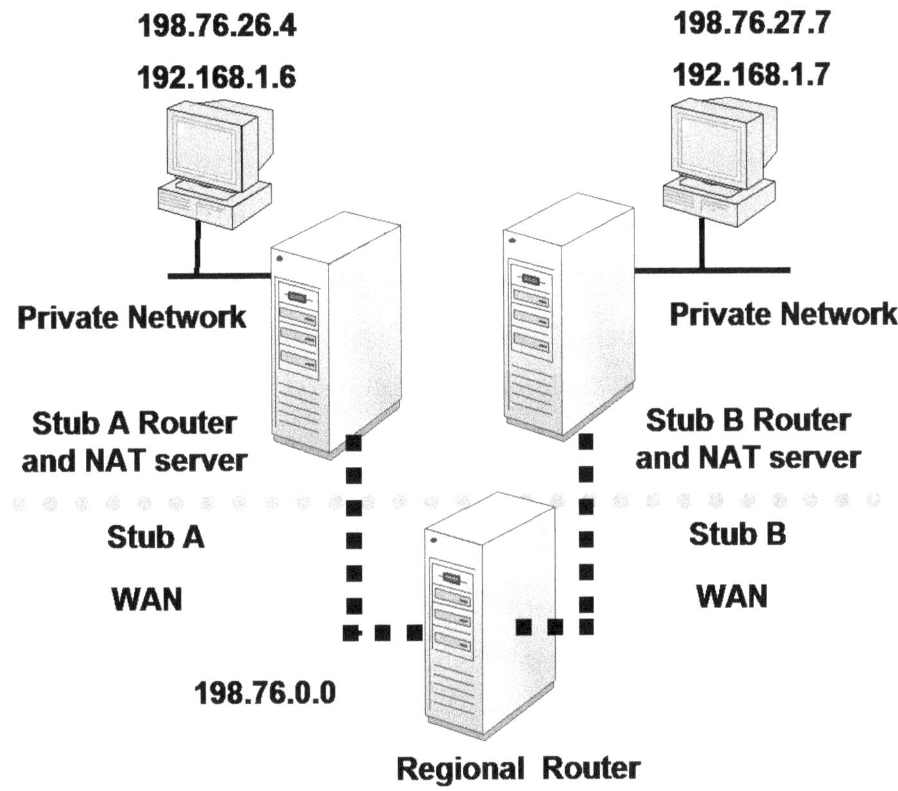

Figure 7.15. Basic NAT Operation

Here, both stubs A and B use the same internal class C network address 192.168.0.0. The two stub domains each connect to the same regional router across a WAN using a dedicated stub router and NAT. Assume that stub A's NAT is assigned the class C address 198.76.26.0, and Stub B's NAT is assigned the class C address 198.76.27.0. These class C addresses are external to the stub domains, and therefore they are globally unique on the WAN. Assume that the translation table maps addresses as given in table 7.2.

Table 7.2

	Private address	Public address
Stub A	192.168.1.6	198.76.26.4
Stub B	192.168.1.7	198.76.27.7

Consider a situation when stub A host 192.168.1.6 wishes to send a packet to stub B host 192.168.1.7. The destination address 192.168.1.7 is a private address and therefore it needs to be translated to a unique public address, assuming that the translated destination address is the globally unique address 198.76.26.4 as given in table 7.2. The packet is therefore sent to the primary router in stub A giving the destination address 198.76.26.4.

The stub A router has a static route for network 198.76.0.0 so the packet is forwarded to the WAN link. However before the package is forwarded, the NAT translates the source address 192.168.1.6 of the IP header with the globally unique 198.76.26.4, which is the address that the NAT has in its translation table. (As shown in Table 7.2). In this manner the translations are transparent and are governed entirely by the mappings that are stored in the translation table. On the return path, the IP packets undergo similar address translations and for this reason, the translation table in stub B router must contain the same entries.

Notice that this requires no changes to hosts or routers. For instance, as far as the stub A host is concerned, 198.76.26.4 is the address used by the host in stub B. The address translations are completely transparent.

7.10. Firewalls

Firewalls are network components that look after the security in an inter-networked environment. In other words, a firewall does not protect the LAN from internal attacks. Firewalls can be implemented in hardware or in software and in a very general sense a firewall will control traffic entering and leaving a network. The level of protection that a firewall provides depends on the size of the network and the type of traffic that it typically carries. Before discussing the firewall, it is worth considering some of the typical threats that a firewall will need to protect against. These are as follows,

Remote login: An unauthorised person is able to log onto the network and have full access to the resources.

Operating system bugs: Some operating systems have backdoors while others provide remote access with insufficient security controls or have bugs that an experienced hacker can take advantage of.

Denial of service: These are very difficult attacks to protect against because they fall into the category of genuine services. The way that this attack works is that the hacker sends a request to the server for a genuine service. When the server responds with the acknowledgement and tries to establish a session, it cannot find the system that made the request. By sending a large number of these, unanswerable requests, to the server, it is slowed down and may even crash.

Macros: Macros are used in many applications, such as for example Microsoft Office, to automate actions by the user. As such they are executable programs within that particular application. Hackers have taken advantage of this to create their own macros that, depending on the application, can destroy data or crash the computer.

Viruses: Arguably the best-known threat to computers and networks are computer viruses. These are malicious programs written by hackers that can copy themselves to computers. In this manner the virus can spread quickly from one system to the next. Once embedded on the machine, viruses can execute and do damage ranging from harmless messages to erasing all data on the computer.

SMTP session hijacking: Simple Mail Transfer Protocol (SMTP) is the most common method of sending e-mail over the Internet. If the network SMTP service is not protected, an unauthorised user can gain access to a list of e-mail addresses belonging to the organisation. An example situation is shown in figure 7.16 where Net A and Net B SMTP servers are not protected.

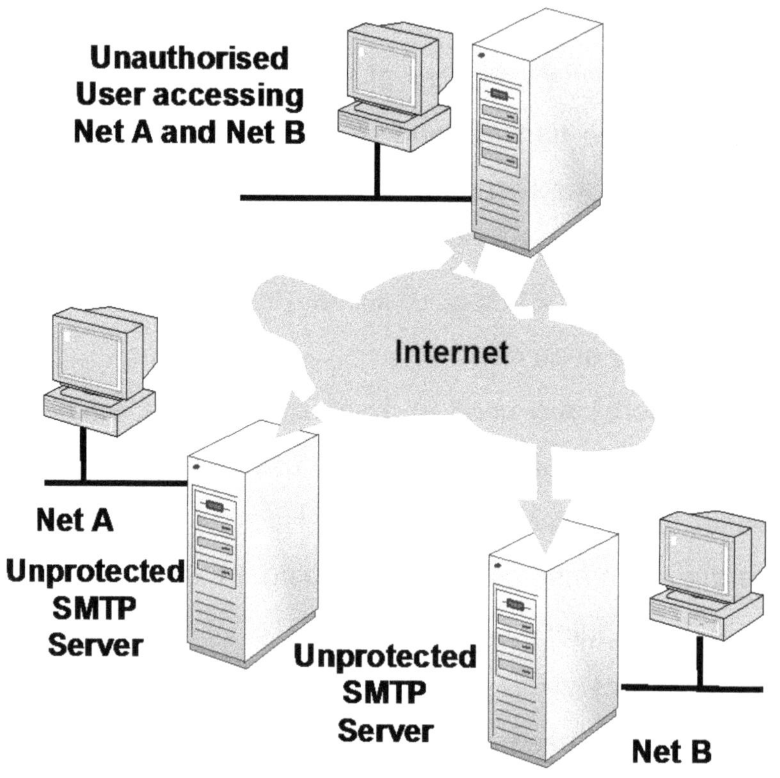

Figure 7.16. SMTP session hijacking

For example, an unauthorised user can obtain all the e-mail addresses in Net A. By redirecting the e-mail through the SMTP server on Net B, a person can send junk e-mail to thousands of users, without revealing the identity of the source. This is done quite often making the actual sender of the Spam difficult to trace. Some web mail servers keep a database of rogue addresses in order to reduce the amount of Spam. Another potential threat on the SMTP service is the so-called e-mail bomb. These happen when someone sends the same e-mail thousands of times to the recipient, until the receiving SMTP server cannot accept any more messages.

Source routing: In general the routers along that path determine the path that a packet travels over the Internet. However, source routing means that the source can specify the path that the packet travels. A hacker can exploit this feature and append the packet with information that makes it look as though it originated from a trusted source. Most firewall products disable source routing by default.

Firewalls are designed to deal with these threats and the level of security that is established determines how many of these threats can be stopped at the firewall. The highest level of security would be to simply block everything. Obviously that defeats the purpose of having an Internet connection. Generally, when configuring a firewall, it is a good idea to stop everything, and then to selectively allow those components that are considered safe. A simple diagram of a firewall is shown in figure 7.17.

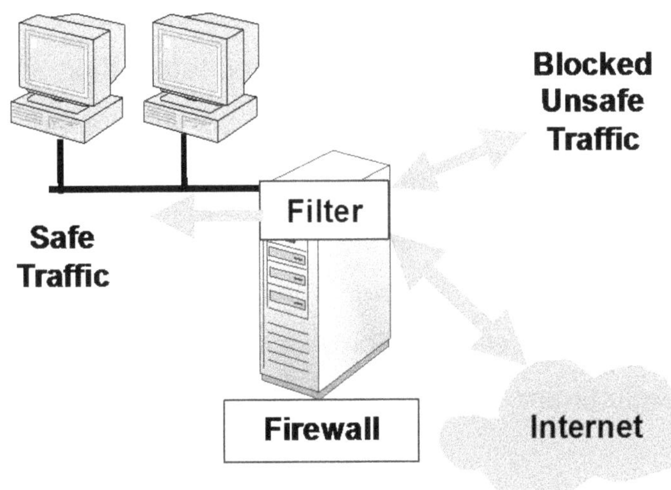

Figure 7.17. Firewall acts as a filter to Internet traffic

Here the Internet facing router is configured as a firewall to control all Internet traffic. Therefore, the firewall can examine this traffic at different levels in order to establish if it is safe. If a rogue packet is detected the entire session will be discarded. Some of the ways that the firewall can inspect the traffic are packet filtering, proxy service and stateful inspection, which are briefly described next.

Packet filtering: Packet filtering is the selective passing or blocking of data packets as they pass through a network interface. The criteria used when inspecting packets are based on the Layer 3 (IPv4 and IPv6) and Layer 4 (TCP, UDP, ICMP, and ICMPv6) headers. The most often used criteria are source and destination address, source and destination ports, and protocol. [64]

The firewall analyses packets and applies a set of filter rules that are evaluated in sequential order, first to last. They specify the criteria that a packet must match and the resulting action. Packets that make it through filters are sent to the requesting system and all others are discarded. This means that a variety of filters can be implemented based on several criteria, some of which are as follows,

IP addresses: Each machine on the Internet is assigned a unique IP address, which can be examined by the firewall. For example, if a certain IP address from outside the network is reading too many files from a server, the firewall can block all traffic to or from that IP address.

Domain names: This works in a similar manner to the IP addresses filtering except that a filter is set to a DNS name rather than an IP address. For example, a company may block all access to certain domain names, or allow access only to specific domain names.

Protocols: A firewall can be configured to allow or block traffic based on the protocol. For example, a firewall may block all ftp protocol traffic, if the network is not designed to allow it. Some common protocols that a firewall filter can be set to exclude are, IP, TCP, HTTP, FTP, UDP, ICMP, SMTP, SNMP, Telnet etc.

Ports: Ports are address locations within a server through which the server provides services to the network. For example, Web services are on port 80, ftp on port 21 etc. An organisation may decide to block all traffic on port 80, thus blocking all HTTP services.

Specific words and phrases: A firewall can be configured to search for words and phrases in a packet. This can be time consuming, but it is an efficient method of filtering by content. For example, offensive words in an email can be filtered.

Proxy service: Information from the Internet is retrieved by the firewall and then directed to a proxy server that is designated to deal with it. Some proxy server functions that would be provided in this case include the following,

- **Web proxy:** Web proxies attempt to block offensive web content. When a computer requests a Web page, it is retrieved by the proxy server and then sent to the requesting computer. Thus the computer hosting the Web page never comes into direct contact with the client on the local

LAN, other than through the proxy server. Caching Proxy servers can also make Internet access more efficient by caching recently accessed web pages.

- **Intercepting (Transparent) proxy server:** This configuration combines a proxy server with a gateway. Connections made by client browsers through the gateway are redirected through the proxy without any client-side configuration. Transparent proxy servers intercept and redirect network connections without user interaction or browser configuration. These proxies ease administrative burden, since no client browser configuration is required.
- **Reverse proxy server:** This is similar to a web proxy except that a reverse proxy server is installed in the vicinity of one or more web servers. All traffic coming from the Internet and with a destination of one of the web servers goes through the proxy server.

Stateful inspection: This method of inspection is similar to packet inspection but it attempts to speed things up. Rather than examining the contents of each packet it only examines certain key parts of the packet. These key parts are identified for packet types according to the protocols that are used, and they are stored in a reference database. Data packets passing through the firewall are monitored for these defining characteristics and compared to the reference database. If this comparison is successful packets are allowed to pass through the firewall, if not, they are discarded. For more information on firewalls and related topics see references [65, 66].

7.11. Virtual Private Networking (VPN)

A VPN is a private network that uses a public highway such as the Internet to establish a connection between remote sites and users. This offers an economical solution to corporations because it avoids the cost of using and maintaining a dedicated connection such as leased line. VPNs allow WAN connections to be established by allowing the user to tunnel through the Internet in a manner that provides the same features and security as in private networks. Therefore, by using a VPN, the network administrator can ensure that only those users on the corporate LAN, who are authorised, can gain access to the protected resources available through the VPN. Additionally, all communication across the VPN can be encrypted for data confidentiality. [67, 68]

Typically a corporate VPN solution must support remote client access to the network and it should also allow remote offices to connect over LAN-to-LAN connections. In addition, the solution must ensure the privacy and integrity of data over the Internet. The following are some of the essential features that a corporate VPN should support,

- **User Authentication**. The solution must authenticate users before allowing them VPN access.
- **Data Encryption.** Data carried on the public network must be encrypted to prevent unauthorised access to the data. This would include key management for client-server communications.
- **Multi-protocol Support.** The solution must handle common protocols used in the public network. These include IP, Internet Packet Exchange (IPX).

Basic operation

Figure 7.18 shows a corporate HQ, which connects to a remote office using the Internet. The Internet is a public network and many millions of users have access to it. In order to secure the communication between the HQ and the remote office, a secure tunnel is established as a VPN connection.

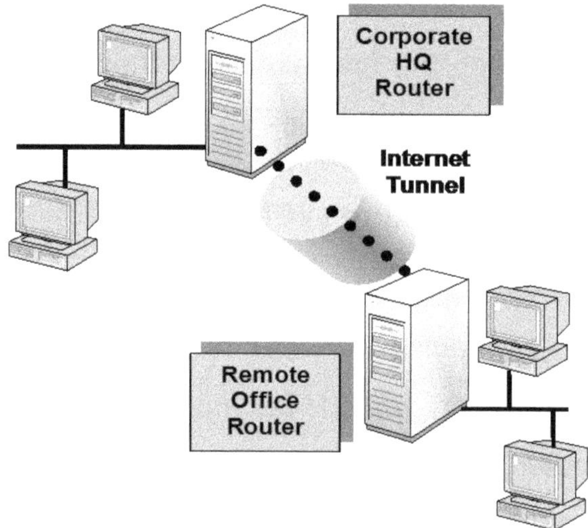

Figure 7.18. VPN uses the public network to connect remote networks

The VPN software at both ends uses the Internet tunnel to create a virtual private network between the branch office router and corporate hub router. Before the data enters the tunnel it is encapsulated by the tunnelling protocol and an additional header is appended to this data so that the destination address and other routing information are known.

Many protocols encapsulate the data; however tunnelling refers to those protocols that carry a protocol from another networking system within an IP packet; such as for example, transmitting NetWare IPX packets within IP. In this manner a tunnelling protocol can be used to transport multiple protocols over a common network. The core of VPN is the tunnelling protocol that is used to support the entire process of encapsulation, transmission, encryption where supported and un-encapsulation of data.

Tunnelling protocols

In a regular protocol, the lower layer protocol encapsulates packets from the higher-level protocol. For example, a network layer 3 packet encapsulates a transport layer 4 packet, and a data link layer 2 packet encapsulates a network layer 3 packet. In contrast, a tunnelling protocol encapsulates a packet of the same or lower layer. For example, generic routing encapsulation (GRE) can contain a layer 3 IPX packet within a layer 3 IP packet. A virtual private LAN service (VPLS) encapsulates a layer 2 Ethernet frame within a layer 3 IP packet.

The principle of tunnelling has been used for some time and the early technologies include the IBM system Network Architecture (SNA) and the Novel Netware Internetwork packet exchange (IPX). When System Network Architecture (SNA) traffic is sent across a corporate IP internetwork, it uses an SNA frame that is encapsulated in a UDP and IP header. User Datagram Protocol (UDP) is one of the core protocols of the Internet protocol suite and is used by computers on the network to exchange short messages.

The IPX protocol works with data packets rather than frames. When an IPX packet needs to be sent, the router wraps it in a UDP and IP header, and then sends it across an IP network. The destination IP-to-IPX router removes the UDP and IP header and forwards the packet to the IPX destination. More recently, newer protocols have emerged which include Point-to-Point Tunnelling Protocol (PPTP), layer 2 tunnelling protocol (L2TP and Internet Protocol Security (IPSec).

For a tunnel to be established, both the source and destination computers must use the same tunnelling protocol. With reference to the 7-layer OSI model, the technology for establishing a tunnel is based on either the layer 2 or the layer 3 tunnelling protocols. Layer 2 protocols correspond to the data-link layer and use frames as their unit of exchange. Layer 2 protocols include, Point to point tunnelling protocol (PPTP), layer 2 tunnelling protocol and Layer 2 Forwarding (L2F). These layer 2 protocols use point-to-point protocol (PPP) frames to encapsulate the data.

Layer 2 Protocols

Point-to-Point Tunnelling Protocol (PPTP). PPTP allows IP, IPX, or NetBEUI traffic to be encrypted, and then encapsulated in an IP header to be sent across the Internet. PPTP provides simple-to-use, lower-cost VPN security. Unlike IPSec technology, PPTP is compatible with Network Address Translators (NAT) and supports both multi-protocol and multi-cast environments. It also combines standard user password authentication with strong encryption without requiring the complexity and expense of public key infrastructure (PKI).

Layer 2 Tunnelling Protocol (L2TP). L2TP allows a point-to-point protocol (PPP) session to travel over multiple links and networks. For example, L2TP allows IP, IPX, or NetBEUI traffic to be sent over any medium that supports point-to-point datagram delivery, such as IP, X.25, Frame Relay, or ATM. L2TP was derived from Microsoft's Point-to-Point Tunnelling Protocol (PPTP) and Cisco's Layer 2 Forwarding (L2F) technology.

Unlike PTPP, L2TP does not include encryption and therefore it is often combined with IPsec to provide secure VPN solutions.

Layer 3 Protocols

Layer 3 tunnelling protocols use packets to send data. Examples of these are, IPSec and Generic Routing Encapsulation, protocols.

IPSec Tunnel Mode. This mode allows IP payloads to be encrypted, and then encapsulated in an IP header to be sent across the network. From a VPN design point of view, IPSec provides advanced security for VPN but it does not support User Authentication and Address Assignment. In addition, it does not support multi-protocol. Therefore it is applicable primarily to IP-only, unicast-only situations, such as remote access by individual users. In practice this covers a large number of VPN applications since there are many organisations that need to support access by employees working with laptop computers at remote locations.

Generic Routing Encapsulation. Is a protocol developed by Cisco systems, which is widely used to tunnel protocols inside IP packets for virtual private networks. It is mainly used to support Cisco routing and for this purpose it is often used with IPSec to transmit routing protocol data from one router to another, which IPSec does not natively support. [69] Layer 2 and Layer 3 protocols support different features and the choice is left to the designer as to which options to select.

Exercises

7.1 Discuss the 3 mechanisms used by DHCP to allocate IP addresses.

7.2 Explain when it would be useful to use static IP addressing.

7.3 Explain the steps involved when a DHCP server and client negotiate an IP address allocation.

7.4 What is Packet forwarding in DHCP service?

7.5 How does a BOOTP/DHCP relay agent work?

7.6 What are general design goals for DHCP service in a computer network?

7.7 Why is a DNS service required in all networks?

7.8 Explain the processes involved between the local and remote hosts during a DNS query.

7.9 Distinguish between forward and reverse lookup queries in DNS.

7.10 Discuss how the domain structure impacts on the DNS service.

7.11 Describe the primary and secondary lookup zones and how they are used in the DNS service.

7.12 What are DNS resource records and how are they structured?

7.13 What is a Canonical Name CNAME?

7.14 Explain the various roles that a DNS server may take.

7.15 What considerations would you keep in mind when locating a DNS server on the network?

7.16 What is WINS, and why is it important in modern networks?

7.17 What is a NAT server?

7.18 Explain the operation of a NAT server with particular emphasis on how the internal IP address is made transparent.

7.19 What are the main functions of a firewall?

7.20 Discuss the threats that a firewall is designed to mitigate.

7.21 Explain how the proxy service is related to a firewall?

7.22 What is a virtual private network? Why is it useful to organisations?

7.23 What are the essential features that a VPN must support?

7.24 Explain the basic operation of a VPN service.

7.25 How is security implemented in a VPN?

7.26 In the context of a VPN distinguish between the protocols at layer 2 and layer 3.

8 ROUTERS

8.1. Introduction

Routers function as a boundary between networks. They are equipped with network interfaces to each of the LANs that they interconnect. A router uses the IP protocol to forward packets from one of these networks to another. By examining the packet header, a router can determine the best path for the packet to travel. Routers operate at the network layer of the OSI model and therefore they can connect networks that use different protocols. Figure 8.1 shows where the router fits into the 7-layer OSI model. Packets received by the router transit the network layer interface where all link layer protocol headers are removed. The router then determines where these packets should go and adds the corresponding data link layer header to the packets before transmitting them. All this activity takes time and therefore routers introduce latency in packet transmission. Reducing the number of hops, i.e. number of routers that are traversed, as the packet travels from source to destination, can reduce latency and improve speed.

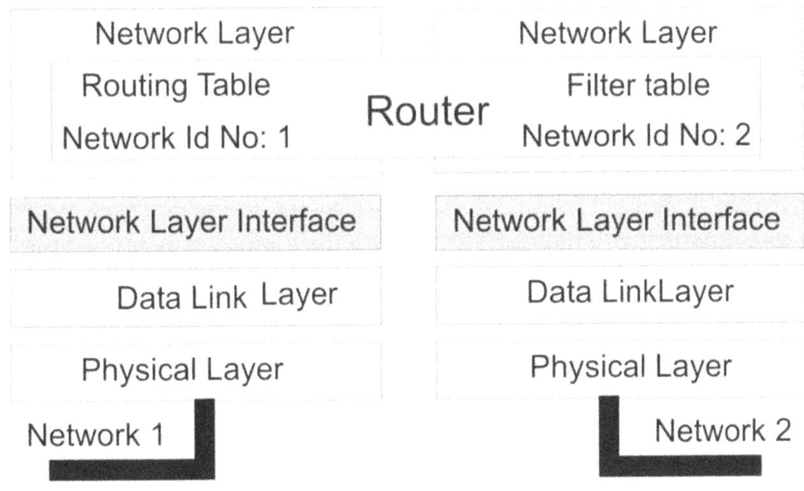

Figure 8.1. Router operates at the network layer

Routers can be used to segment a large network into smaller networks. This may be necessary when subnetting in order to reduce competition for the bandwidth. Additionally, segmenting a network creates separate collision and broadcast domains and this reduces network traffic. Routers are also used to connect two or more LANs via a WAN. Routers can communicate with each other to determine optimum routes. They do this by using the Internet Control Message Protocol (ICMP) protocol, which is also used for error reporting. [70]

8.2. Routing table

A routing table is a set of rules that are used to determine where data packets travelling over an Internet Protocol (IP) network will be directed. All IP-enabled devices, including routers and switches, use routing tables. The routing table contains all the IP destination addresses with the appropriate network interface. A default entry, (i.e. 0.0.0.0); can be used as the route for all addresses that are not in the routing table. A filter table can be used to discard unwanted packets. Access Control Lists (ACLs) that are processed by the router can be configured to do this. Table 8.1 describes entries in the Internet Protocol (IP) routing table.

Table 8.1

Network destination: IP address of the destination host. The network destination is from the default route (0.0.0.0) to broadcast address (255.255.255.255). The default route is used when there is no match with the destination address in an IP datagram.
Subnet mask: This mask is applied to the destination IP address when matching to the ID of the network destination. Within an IP address, a subnet mask distinguishes network identifiers (ID) and host IDs.
Gateway: Indicates the IP address to which datagrams need to be forwarded. This is the IP address of another network adapter of the existing router or the IP address of another router on the network.
Interface: This field indicates the IP address of the network adapter to which datagrams are forwarded. This happens when the gateway is an adapter rather than a router on the network.
Metric: Indicates a measure of the efficiency of a given. When, as is often the case, multiple routes exist to an IP destination, the metric is used to select the best route.

When deciding on which route to take a router will consider the types of routes that are available as well as a metric associated with each route. Internet is an example of a network that has many available routes to any given destination. The types of routes can be broadly classified as follows,

- **Direct routes:** These routes are to subnets that are connected to the router. The Next Hop filed is blank.

- **Remote routes:** These routes are available through remote routers. For these routes, the Next Hop field is the IP address of a local router.
- **Host routes:** These are routes that are specific to particular hosts on the subnet. For, example a DHCP server on another subnet can have a host route configured so that it can be reached from the local subnet. Host routes are configured for a specific IP address. For host routes, the network ID is a specific IP address, and the network mask is (255.255.255.255). If a host route is found the hop count is incremented, but that is the final hop.
- **Default routes:** This is the network route used by a router when no other known route exists for a given destination address. All the packets for unknown destinations are sent to the default route. This route generally leads to another router. The default route destination is 0.0.0.0 with the network mask of 0.0.0.0. The next hop address of the default route is typically the default gateway of the subnet.
- **Metrics:** A router relies on metrics to make routing decisions. A router metric is typically based of information like path length, bandwidth, and load; hop count, path cost, delay, Maximum Transmission Unit (MTU), reliability and communications cost. The routing protocol normally specifies which of these metrics is used to determine the route. When the router does not specify how a metric is defined, the administrator who configures the router has to define the metric. Some examples of metrics are as follows,
    - **Hop count**: The hop count is the number of routers between the starting node and the destination node. An IP packet travelling over the Internet can easily 'hop' through more than a dozen routers and the hop count indicates the number of routers in the path from the source to the destination. Anything on the local subnet is one hop, and each router crossed after that is an additional hop.
    - **Delay:** This indicates the amount of time that the packet takes to reach its destination.

- **Throughput:** Rather than measuring just the time, this metric calculates the amount of data that be sent along the path per second.
- **Reliability:** This metric considers how reliable a particular path is. This will depend on statistical data being available so that a measure of reliability can be given. For example, dedicated T1 lines are generally considered to be more reliable than VPN connections.

8.3. Routing protocols

As mentioned earlier, basic routing performs the task of determining the best path through the network. The router does this by examining the routing table, which holds all routing information received from routing peers. Modern routers are also able to forward packets from one network interface to another. In this case instead of storing a routing table, the router would have a Forwarding Information Base (FIB), which is a database that maps network prefixes to router port identifiers. As a minimum, the FIB contains the interface identifier and next hop information for each reachable destination network prefix. [71]

Forwarding routers examine the destination address and also consult other tables in order to make decisions about the packet, based on characteristics, such as the source address, the IP protocol identifier field, or TCP or UDP port number. Network interface cards in forwarding routers are high specification, fast packet processing card, which include a forwarding engine.

Networks are continually changing and this will have an effect on the contents of routing tables. For consistent operation of a router if a routing path changes then the routing table must be updated. This updating can occur in one of two ways; either by using static routes, or dynamic routes. Static routes are defined and updated manually. Dynamic routes are configured automatically by using routing protocols. Routing protocols are used to exchange information between routers in order to propagate network address and connection information. The two most common IP routing protocols used on intranets are Routing Information Protocol (RIP) and Open Shortest Path First (OSPF).

A manually configured static route specifies the path to another network, which a datagram must take, based on the datagram's destination address. If a route changes, the network administrator must manually update the routing tables. Static routes can work well for small internetworks. However, they do not scale well because they must be administered manually.

With dynamic routing the routing protocol constructs routing tables by exchanging routing information with other routers on the internetwork.

Routing Information Protocol: RIP is a distance vector routing protocol designed for exchanging routing information within a small to medium-size internetwork. [72] Distance vector routing protocols propagate routing information in the form of a network ID and 'distance,' or hop count. Because RIP has a maximum distance of 15 hops, locations that are 16 or more hops distant are considered unreachable. Compared with other protocols, RIP is simple to configure and deploy. However, as networks increase in size, the periodic announcements by each RIP router can cause excessive traffic on the network. RIP is typically used in networks with up to 50 servers. RIP is also the name of a similar but separate routing protocol for Internetwork Packet Exchange (IPX) networks.

Open Shortest Path First (OSPF): This protocol is based on the Shortest Path First (SPF) algorithm, which computes the shortest path between nodes in a network. It is a link-state protocol, which is to say that it propagates routing information in the form of link-state advertisements (LSAs). Link state implies that the state information of the link is included with the protocol. This information includes the cost, delay and bandwidth information, and can be used to decide on which route to take.

The link-state database is a 'map' of the network that is updated after any change in the network topology. The advantage of OSPF, compared with other routing protocols, is that it operates efficiently in large networks because it computes the best route to use and requires fewer status messages. Unlike RIP, OSPF does not advertise all known routes to other routers, but only the changes to its routes. The disadvantage of OSPF is its complexity; it is harder to configure and requires more management time than RIP. [73, 74]

8.4. Access Control Lists (ACL) s

Access Control Lists are implemented on routers in order to specifically permit or deny access to networks that the particular router connects. Control of access is an increasingly important security measure and network designers need to take these into considerations when specifying network infrastructure. Infrastructure ACLs are used to minimise the risk and effectiveness of direct infrastructure attacks by explicitly permitting or denying access to equipment.

CISCO systems are renowned router manufacturers and they provide some guidelines and recommended deployment techniques for infrastructure protection access control lists.[75] ACLs can be configured to protect the network in the following ways,

- **Receive ACLs (rACLs):** These are used to increase security on routers by protecting the router's gigabit route processor (GRP) from unnecessary and potentially harmful traffic. For example, Cisco 12000 and 7500 platforms support rACLs that filter all traffic destined to the RP and do not affect transit traffic. Authorised traffic must be explicitly permitted and the rACL must be deployed on every router. [76]
- **Hop-by-hop router ACLs:** These ACLs permit only authorised traffic on router interfaces and all other traffic is denied. Transit traffic is allowed only if it has been explicitly permitted. This ACL is logically similar to a rACL except that it does affect transit traffic, and therefore can have a negative performance impact on the forwarding rate of a router.
- **Edge filters:** This ACLs can be applied to the edge of the network. For, example, in the case of a service provider (SP), this filter would be placed at the edge of the address space. An ACL can be configured to explicitly filter all traffic destined for the infrastructure address space.

A scripting type language that is supported by the router can be used to specify an ACL. As a general format, an infrastructure ACL is composed of four sections, as follows,

- Special-use address and anti-spoofing (AS) entries. These are configured to deny illegitimate sources and packets with source addresses that belong within your AS list.
- Explicitly permitted externally sourced traffic destined to infrastructure addresses.
- Deny statements for all other externally sourced traffic to infrastructure addresses.
- Permit statements for all other traffic for normal backbone traffic en route to destinations outside the network infrastructure.

IP Access Control Lists (ACLs), filter IP packets based on the following information about the packet,

- Source address.
- Destination address.
- Type of packet.

In order to filter network traffic, ACLs control whether routed packets are forwarded or blocked at the router interface. The router examines each packet to determine whether or not to forward it based on the permit or deny rules within the ACL. Therefore, the ACL can be described as a sequential collection of permit and deny conditions that apply to an IP packet. The router tests the packets against the conditions in the ACL one at a time. ACL rules can include the following information,

- Source address of the traffic.
- Destination address of the traffic.
- Upper-layer protocol.

CISCO provides the command syntax formats of extended ACLs are given in table 8.2 [77]

Table 8.2

IP
access-list access-list-number [dynamic dynamic-name [timeout minutes]] {deny | permit} protocol source source-wildcard destination destination-wildcard [precedence precedence] [tos tos] [log | log-input] [time-range time-range-name][fragments]
Internet Control Message Protocol (ICMP)
access-list access-list-number [dynamic dynamic-name [timeout minutes]] {deny | permit} icmp source source-wildcard destination destination-wildcard [icmp-type [icmp-code] | [icmp-message]] [precedenceprecedence] [tos tos] [log | log-input] [time-range time-range-name][fragments]
Transport Control Protocol (TCP)
access-list access-list-number [dynamic dynamic-name [timeout minutes]] {deny | permit} tcp source source-wildcard [operator [port]] destination destination-wildcard [operator [port]] [established] [precedence precedence] [tos tos] [log | log-input] [time-range time-range-name][fragments]
User Datagram Protocol (UDP)
access-list access-list-number [dynamic dynamic-name [timeout minutes]] {deny | permit} udp source source-wildcard [operator [port]] destination destination-wildcard [operator [port]] [precedence precedence] [tos tos] [log | log-input] [time-range time-range-name][fragments]

Example ACLs

The following are example configuration scripts according to the syntax described in table 8.2. [40]

1. Allow a Select Host to Access the Network

An ACL is created to PERMIT a selected host (192.168.1.1) traffic from NetB to reach NetA, and to DENY all traffic from NetB to reach Net A.

In order to permit access through the router, for a host on NetB with the IP address 192.168.1.1, the ACL is as configured as shown in table 8.3.

Table 8.3

Router1 ACL permit
hostname Router1 ! interface EthernetB ip access-group 1 in ! access-list 1 permit host 192.168.1.1

This configuration allows only the host with the IP address 192.168.1.1 through the Ethernet B interface on Router1. This host has access to the IP services of NetA. No other host in NetB has access to NetA, because, by default, there is an implicit **deny all** clause at the end of every ACL. Anything that is not explicitly permitted is denied. As a result no **deny** statement needs to be configured in the ACL.

2. Deny a Select Host to Access the Network

An ACL is created to DENY a select host (192.168.1.1) traffic from NetB to reach NetA, and to PERMIT all traffic from NetB to reach Net A.

In order to permit access trough the router, for a host on NetB with the IP address 192.168.1.1, the ACL is as configured as shown in table 8.4.

Table 8.4

Router1 ACL deny
hostname Router1 ! interface EthernetB ip access-group 1 in ! access-list 1 deny host 192.168.1.1 access-list 1 permit any

This configuration denies all packets from host 192.168.1.1 through EthernetB on Router1 and permits everything else. Because of the implicit deny all at the end of the ACL, in order to explicitly permit everything else, it is necessary to include the following command,

access list 1 permit any

It must be noted that the order of statements is critical to the operation of an ACL. For example, if the order of the entries in table 8.4 is reversed as shown in table 8.5. then, the first line matches every packet source address. Therefore, the ACL fails to block host 192.168.1.1 from accessing NetA.

Table 8.5

```
hostname Router1
!
interface EthernetB
ip access-group 1 in
!
access-list 1 permit any
access-list 1 deny host 192.168.1.1
```

These are just two examples of ACLs and it should be clear that other variations could be configured. ACLs provide routers with the ability to control access to networks and therefore offer a layer of security that is increasingly important in modern networks.

Cisco systems [40] and IBM [78] are useful sites to refer to regarding ACLs. Additional white papers and other on-line reference material can be found on the references [79,80].

Exercises

8.1. What is the main purpose of using routers?

8.2. Explain where the router fits in the 7-layer OSI model.

8.3. What is a routing table?

8.4. Discuss the factors that influence the choice of a route through networks.

8.5. What are routing protocols used for?

8.6. What are ACLs used for?

8.7. Explain the main features of RIP and OSPF routing protocols.

8.8. Write an ACL to perform each of the following,

a. Allow a Select Host to Access the Network.
b. Deny a Select Host to Access the Network.
c. Allow Access to a Range of Contiguous IP Addresses.
d. Deny Telnet Traffic (TCP, Port 23).
e. Allow Only Internal Networks to Initiate a TCP Session.
f. Deny FTP Traffic (TCP, Port 21).
g. Allow FTP Traffic (Active FTP).
h. Allow FTP Traffic (Passive FTP).
i. Allow Pings (ICMP).
j. Allow HTTP, Telnet, Mail, POP3, FTP.
k. Allow DNS: a) Permit Routing Updates b) Debug Traffic Based on ACL.

9 NETWORK PERFORMANCE ISSUES

9.1. Introduction

In modern computer networks there is much emphasis on the speed of data transfer between endpoint nodes. More devices, faster and less expensive computers, more applications as well as the increased use of the Internet all impact on network utilisation and consequently on performance. Some of the major factors that affect network performance include bandwidth, latency, throughput, capacity, wire-speed, and utilisation. Additionally network performance is compromised by network bottlenecks, efficiency, frame rate and collisions. During the planning stage it is necessary to consider utilisation trends, as well as the current traffic sources and also future growth.

The RFC 2544 document discusses and defines a number of tests that may be used to describe the performance characteristics of a network-interconnecting device. In addition to defining these tests it also describes specific formats for reporting the results of the tests. [81] Network performance measurement tools are available to technical teams to monitor issues that impact on network performance. These include traffic monitoring tools and protocol analysers, network management software as well as hand-held diagnostic tools.

9.2. Planning for network performance

When planning a network infrastructure it is necessary to keep in mind the factors that influence network performance. Some of the major factors that need to be considered are as follows,

- **Bandwidth:** Bandwidth is measured in bits per second (bps), usually kbps and Mbps. It represents the maximum amount of data that can travel on the network.
- **Latency:** Data travels at a given speed and latency is described as the amount of time it takes for a packet to travel from its source to its destination. As defined in RFC 1242 it is the time interval starting when the last bit of the input frame reaches the input port and ending when

the first bit of the output frame is seen on the output port. Variability of latency can be a problem as future applications are likely to be sensitive to network latency. [82] Furthermore, increased device delay can reduce the useful diameter of net.

- **Throughput:** This is the actual data measured in Mbps, passing through the network. It is defined as the maximum rate at which none of the offered frames are dropped by the device. [82] Since even the loss of one frame in a data stream can cause significant delays while waiting for the higher level protocols to time out, it is useful to know the actual maximum data rate that the device can support. On an Ethernet network the number of collisions increases with the number of users, which significantly affects throughput. Maximum throughput is reached when there are only two nodes and this happens in a switched network. The minimum throughput occurs when the maximum number of users is 1024.
- **Capacity:** Capacity in this context relates to the actual data-carrying capability of the network. It is determined by technology and transmission medium. Usually given in Mbps.
- **Wire-speed:** This is the actual speed that the data travels on the medium. It is measured in Mbps.
- **Utilisation:** This is defined as the percentage of time that the wire is occupied and includes both collisions and successful data transfer. In theory utilisation + idle time=100% Utilisation is affected by a number of factors, including frame size, bandwidth as well as latency. Figure 9.1 shows how latency and utilisation are related for busy, quiet and overloaded network activity. Here low utilisation and low latency is experienced in quiet networks. As the network becomes busier latency rises exponentially with increase in utilisation.

For comparison only, examples of recommended Ethernet utilisation limits for shared and for switched Ethernet are given in table 9.1. Here it is seen that compared with shared Ethernet; the switched Ethernet provides much higher data throughput rates with superior utilisation.

Table 9.1

Ethernet Type	Wire speed	Average Utilisation	Raw Data throughput	Peak Utilisation	Peak Data Throughput
Shared	10Mbps	30%	3 Mbps	80%	8 Mbps
Switched	10Mbps	85%	8.5 Mbps	90%	9 Mbps

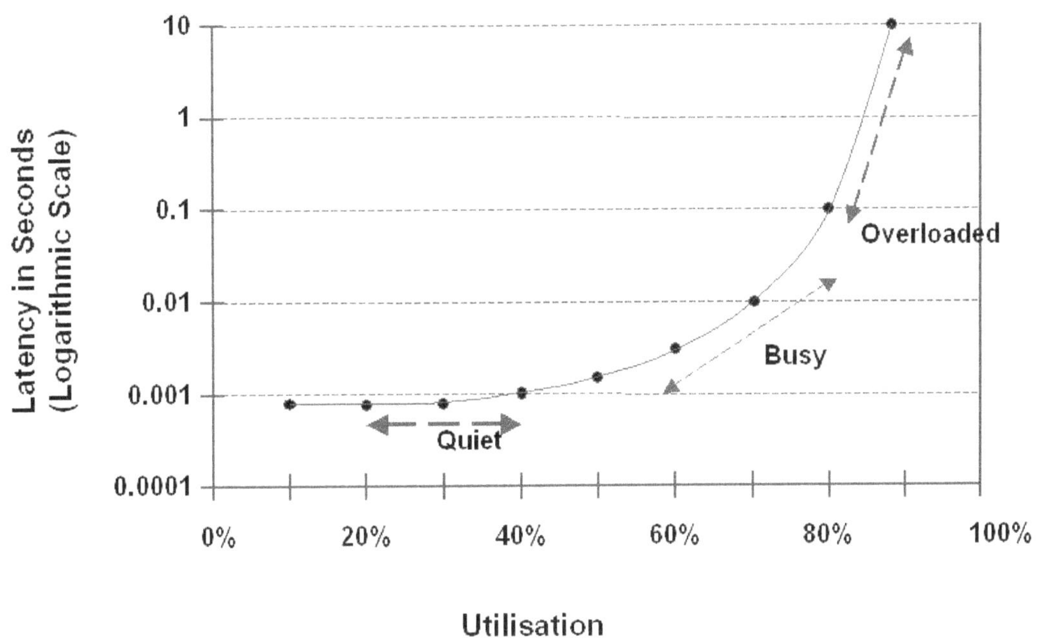

Figure 9.1. Utilisation and Latency for different network loads

- **Jitter:** The variation in the time between the arrival of packets caused by network congestion, timing drift, or route changes. It can be caused by distortion in a digital signal caused by a shift in timing pulses, which in turn can cause data interpretation errors.
- **Jabber:** An error in which a faulty network interface card continuously transmits corrupted or meaningless data onto a network.
- **Bottleneck:** The delay in transmission of data that occurs when one part of the network is slower than others. Typically, the delay typically occurs when a system's bandwidth cannot support the amount of information being relayed at the speed it is being processed.

- **Collisions:** In network segments that use CSMA as the access method, collisions occur when two or more computers attempt to broadcast frames at the same time. This is detected and the computers retry after a variable period of time. Since frames have not been transmitted, this causes a slowdown in performance.
- **Efficiency:** In this context efficiency is defined as the percentage of actual data contained in the frame compared to the total frame size. Ethernet packets contain data as well as a header and trailer overheads. Frames can vary in size which primarily depends on how much data they contain. (See figure 9.2) If the frames are made large the header and trailer overheads are a smaller percentage of the frame than if the frame was small. In this sense therefore, large frames are more efficient than small frames.

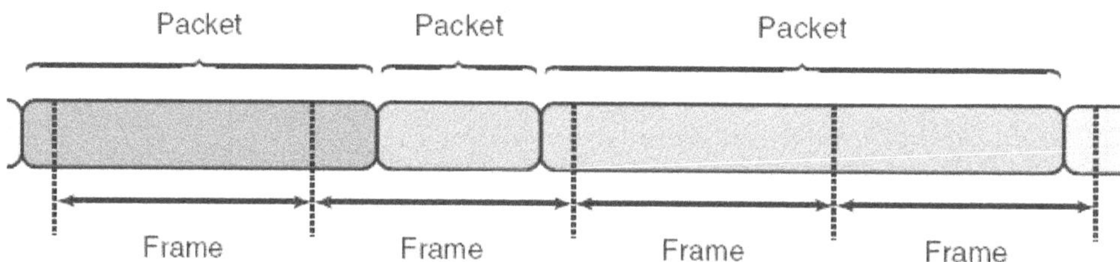

Figure 9.2. Difference between packets and frames

- **Frame rate:** This represents the number of frames per second and depends on the frame size. On an Ethernet segment the maximum frame rate is 14,880 frames per second. However, this assumes that only a single transmitting station has exclusive access to the Ethernet. In the event that multiple stations are transmitting, the throughput drops to between 2 and 4 megabits per second and the network analyser will typically show the interactions at (approximately) 5,000 frames a second. [83]

9.3. Ethernet performance calculations

The simplest form of Ethernet network uses a passive bus operated at 10Mbps. A single LAN may have up to 1024 attached systems, although in practice most LANs have far fewer. The IEEE 802.3 standard covers all the characteristics of Ethernet.

Ethernet frames of data are created according to the Medium Access Control (MAC) protocol, and encoded using Manchester line encoding. Ethernet is a broadcast type Baseband network where any connected computer is allowed to broadcast on the network. The access method used is the Carrier-Sense Multiple Access protocol with Collision Detection (CSMA/CD). The network topology can be a bus or a star topology as well as a hybrid of these two. In a star type topology active or passive hubs are used as the central point of connection between nodes. The majority of Ethernet networks use a passive hub in a star or hybrid topology and run at 10Mbps. If a switch is used instead of a hub then the two nodes that wish to communicate are simultaneously connected through the switch. This avoids broadcasting through the hub, and reduces the rate of collisions. Consequently, Ethernet switch networks are much faster because they do not have many collisions. Using a fast Ethernet switch, networks can run at speeds of 100Mbps. 1Gbps networks usually operate between a pair of Ethernet switches.

To get an idea of speed it is worth mentioning that Ethernet sends information across a network in variable size frames. These frames contain bytes that make up the payload and also those in the header and trailer.

The minimum size of an Ethernet frame is 64 bytes. This consist of the following fields,

Destination Address	**Source Address**	**Frame Type**	**CRC Checksum**	**Data**	**Total Bytes**
6 bytes	6 bytes	2 bytes	4 bytes	46 bytes	64 bytes

The minimum number of bytes passed as data in a frame must be 46 bytes. If the size of the data to be passed is less than this, then padding bytes are added. The frame size is made up of 46 data bytes and the 18-byte overhead.

The maximum size of an Ethernet frame is 1518 bytes. This is made up of 1500 data bytes and the 18-byte overhead.

Destination Address	**Source Address**	**Frame Type**	**CRC Checksum**	**Data**	**Total Bytes**
6 bytes	6 bytes	2 bytes	4 bytes.	1500 bytes	1518 bytes

The maximum frame rate (FR) can be calculated by assuming that no collisions occur and dividing the maximum bit-rate (bps) by the minimum frame size (FS) (in bits). This is given by equation 9.1.

$$FR_{max} = \frac{bps_{max}}{FS_{min}} \qquad (9.1)$$

As mentioned earlier the minimum Ethernet frame size is 64 bytes. Before the frame is transmitted a short delay period is introduced. The purpose of this is to allow a small time interval for the receiver electronics in each of the nodes to settle after completion of the previous frame. A node starts transmission by sending an 8-byte preamble to create this delay period.

Therefore the minimum actual frame size is 64+8=72 bytes. Ethernet frame transmission requires an inter-frame gap or 9.6 microseconds. This delay can be converted to an additional byte overhead of 12 bytes at the speed of 10Mbps.

$$i.e.\ bits = (9.6 \times 10^{-6}) \times (10 \times 10^{6}) = 96 => 96/8 = 12 bytes$$

Therefore the overall minimum frame size at 10Mbps is 72+12=84 bytes, which is 672 bits. The maximum number of frames per second is given by (9.1)

$$FR_{max} = \frac{bps_{max}}{FS_{min}} = \frac{10 \times 10^{6}}{672} = 14880\ frames\ per\ second\ (fps)$$

This is the theoretical maximum for a 10Mbps Ethernet segment. The theoretical minimum frames per second are obtained if it is assumed that the maximum size frames are transmitted. The IEEE 802.3 standard gives 1500 bytes as the maximum frame size on an Ethernet segment. Adding the overhead of 26+12 bytes gives the total frame size of 1538 bytes. Using (9.1) the frame rate obtained is,

$$FR_{min} = \frac{bps_{max}}{FS_{max}} = \frac{10 \times 10^{6}}{1538 \times 8} = 812\ fps$$

The size of the frame depends on the Ethernet network interface used. When the interface sends a frame to the network device driver, it supplies the length of the received frame. During the Ethernet connection process, the system selects the smallest common value of the maximum frame values. The actual maximum frame size used can become even smaller if the bridge cannot support the value selected by the system.

RFC 2544 recommends that the maximum frame rate to be used for LAN-WAN-LAN configurations should be at least 110% of the slowest link speed. Table 9.2 offers a guide on the maximum frame rates to be used with specific frame sizes for different technologies. [84]

Table 9.2 maximum frame rates to be used with specific frame sizes [86]

Size (bytes)	**Ethernet (fps)**	**16Mb Token Ring (fps)**	**FDDI (fps)**
64	14880	24691	152439
128	8445	13793	85616
256	4528	7326	45620
512	2349	3780	23585
768	1586	2547	15903
1024	1197	1921	11996
1280	961	1542	9630
1518	812	1302	8138

To calculate the actual data throughput (ADT) Microsoft provide a formula [86]

$$ADT = (utilisation - collisions) \times efficiency \times wirespeed \quad (9.2)$$

Utilisation can be calculated by considering the percentage of time that the physical link is transmitting data. If it is assumed that there are no collisions, for each node that is transmitting on the Ethernet segment, then the total number of bits that are on the cable can be obtained by multiplying the frame size (bits) by the frame rate (fps). That is, $number\_of\_bits = \sum FR \times FS$

Dividing this by the available wire speed gives a measure of utilisation. Utilisation is obtained as a percentage in equation (9.3)

$$utilisation = \frac{\sum FR \times FS}{wirespeed} \times 100\% \quad (9.3)$$

It is intuitive from (9.3) that utilisation increases as more nodes transmit on the network. For utilisation calculated using equation (9.3) the effects of collisions are not taken into account. Equation (9.2) takes into account collisions to calculate the average data throughput. Efficiency can be calculated by working out the actual payload bits being transferred in frames. This is to say remove the overhead and only take into account the payload.

$$efficiency = \frac{FR_{\min} \times payload}{wirespeed} \times 100\% \quad (9.4)$$

Example

Average (20% utilisation)

Actual data throughput = *(0.2–0.03) x (1-0.038) x 100Mbps = 16.49*

Max: (50%) ADT= (0.5-0.03) x (1-0.038) x 100= 45.21

All information is given in the question and we just need to work out where efficiency comes from.

9.4. Improving performance

Network performance can be improved by analysing the network traffic and implementing measures that deal with any problems. A variety of tools exist for network performance monitoring in order to determine if the system is experiencing a performance bottleneck. Typically in order to measure performance it is necessary to gather network performance data to determine the maximum throughput the system is capable of. Effectively this serves as a baseline for comparison purposes. Request for Comments document RFC1242, entitled 'Benchmarking Terminology for Network Interconnection Devices' defines the terminology and the RFC 2544 document discusses and defines a number of tests that may be used to describe the performance characteristics of a network-interconnecting device. In addition to defining these tests it also describes specific formats for reporting the results of the tests. [87] Performance measurements tools normally send packets from one machine to another and measure the throughput. Interactive monitoring tools track the number of network packets arriving and departing from the system at the current instance of time. This serves as a measure of the workload. For example Intellipool [88] provide monitoring tools for a broad range of operating systems. For reference purposes only, in order to identify the features that manufacturers of monitoring software consider important, the advertising brief for their monitoring tool is given in table 9.3.

Table 9.3

One server monitoring system for all your servers

A unique feature of Intellipool Network Monitor is the wide selection of operating system it can monitor, without needing to install anything on the monitored host.

Supported operating systems:

AIX (4.2 and above)	OpenBSD
	OpenSUSE 10.2
CentOS	Red Hat Enterprise Server
Debian	Solaris
Fedora	Ubuntu
FreeBSD	Windows NT, 2000, XP, 2003 and Vista
HP-UX	
Generic Linux	

Summary: Monitor virtually any type of network resource with the 37 different types of tests. Managed by an easy to use web interface that can be secured by SSL. No need for installation of software on monitored resources.

Logging options include XML logfile, ODBC database, Syslog and Windows

9.5. Sniffers

A sniffer is a computer program that captures all of the traffic flowing into and out of a computer attached to a network. Sniffers range in complexity and speed and simple packages are relatively easy to implement in C or Perl. Typically these use a command line interface and dump captured data to the screen. More complex projects use a GUI; they produce a graph of traffic statistics, track multiple sessions and offer several configuration options. Sniffers are also used to support other programs. For example Intrusion Detection Systems (IDS) use sniffers to match packets against a rule-set designed to flag anything malicious or strange. Network monitoring programs often use sniffers to gather data necessary for metrics and analysis. Government bodies and law enforcement agencies use sniffer programs to collect intelligence.

Sniffer programs work by programming the Network Interface Card (NIC) in a computer, to work in a state known as promiscuous mode. In this mode the NIC listens to all the traffic that is broadcast on the network. Once a NIC is promiscuous, a status that requires administrative or root privileges, a machine can see all the data transmitted on its segment. The program then begins a constant read of all information entering the PC via the network card. Having captured packets of data a sniffer can perform additional processing to reveal the information contained in the packet.

For example, packet headers contain protocol information and a sniffer can peel away the layers of encapsulation and decode the relevant information stored within such as source computer, destination computer, targeted port number, payload, in short - every piece of information exchanged between two computers.

In order to show the type of data that a sniffer works with the following information can be obtained by using a program called tcpdump. This is a UNIX version of a program that is available for many platforms. WinDump is the Windows version of tcpdump, which is fully compatible with tcpdump and can be used to watch, diagnose and save to disk network traffic according to various complex rules. It can run under Windows 95, 98, ME, NT, 2000, XP, 2003 and Vista. WinDump captures data by using the WinPcap library and drivers, which are freely downloadable from the WinPcap.org website. WinDump supports 802.11b/g wireless capture and troubleshooting through the CACE Technologies AirPcap adapter. WinDump is free and is released under a BSD-style licence. [89]

Figure 9.3 shows a network data capture snippet, which is part of an exchange between a machine and the SecurityFocus Web server. [90] Figure 9.3 shows two packets; on the top is the HTTP request by the client and below that is the server's response. Note that the first few lines of each sniffed packet provide a summary of the transaction, which includes timestamps, source and destination MAC addresses, source and destination IP addresses and several other bits of information. The numbered lines (0x00##) show the data transmitted by each packet in hexadecimal format. Additionally, an ASCII decode of the payload is located to the right. It is clear from this that data is vulnerable to hackers who are using sniffers on a network. The best way to protect data from malicious attacks is to use encryption. In this manner even if data is accessible, the fact that it is encrypted means that it is relatively safe from abuse.

```
21:06:30.786814 0:1:3:e5:46:6b 0:4:5a:d1:46:ad 0800 650: 192.168.1.3.32946 >
66.38.151.10.80: P [tcp sum ok] 1:585(584) ack 336 win 64080 <nop,nop,timestamp 608776
899338> (DF) (ttl 64, id 7468, len 636)
0x0000   4500 027c 1d2c 4000 4006 8074 c0a8 0103        E..|.,@.@..t....
0x0010   4226 970a 80b2 0050 54ac b070 78ef d6c3        B&.....PT..px...
0x0020   8018 fa50 c663 0000 0101 080a 0009 4a08        ...P.c........J.
0x0030   000d b90a 4745 5420 2f63 6f72 706f 7261        ....GET./corpora
0x0040   7465 2f69 6d61 6765 732f 6275 696c 642f        te/images/build/
0x0050   626c 6c74 5f72 645f 312e 6769 6620 4854        bllt_rd_1.gif.HT
0x0060   5450 2f31 2e31 0d0a 486f 7374 3a20 7777        TP/1.1..Host:.ww
0x0070   772e 7365 6375 7269 7479 666f 6375 732e        w.securityfocus.
0x0080   636f 6d0d 0a55 7365 722d 4167 656e 743a        com..User-Agent:
0x0090   204d 6f7a 696c 6c61 2f35 2e30 2028 5831        .Mozilla/5.0.(X1
0x00a0   313b 2055 3b20 4c69 6e75 7820 6936 3836        1;.U;.Linux.i686

21:06:30.886814 0:4:5a:d1:46:ad 0:1:3:e5:46:6b 0800 402: 66.38.151.10.80 >
192.168.1.3.32949: P [tcp sum ok] 2363393025:2363393361(336) ack 1437810754 win 8616
<nop,nop, timestamp 899338 608766> (ttl 61, id 10825, len 388)
0x0000   4500 0184 2a49 0000 3d06 b74f 4226 970a        E...*I..=..OB&..
0x0010   c0a8 0103 0050 80b5 8cde 8401 55b3 4042        .....P......U.@B
0x0020   8018 21a8 0543 0000 0101 080a 000d b90a        ..!..C..........
0x0030   0009 49fe 4854 5450 2f31 2e31 2032 3030        ..I.HTTP/1.1.200
0x0040   204f 4b0d 0a41 6765 3a20 320d 0a41 6363        .OK..Age:.2..Acc
0x0050   6570 742d 5261 6e67 6573 3a20 6279 7465        ept-Ranges:.byte
0x0060   730d 0a44 6174 653a 2054 7565 2c20 3132        s..Date:.Tue,.12
0x0070   2046 6562 2032 3030 3220 3033 3a30 343a        .Feb.2002.03:04:
0x0080   3538 2047 4d54 0d0a 436f 6e74 656e 742d        58.GMT..Content-
0x0090   4c65 6e67 7468 3a20 3433 0d0a 436f 6e74        Length:.43..Cont
0x00a0   656e 742d 5479 7065 3a20 696d 6167 652f        ent-Type:.image/
0x00b0   6769 660d 0a53 6572 7665 723a 2041 7061        gif..Server:.Apa
0x00c0   6368 652f 312e 332e 3232 2028 556e 6978        che/1.3.22.(Unix
0x00d0   2920 6d6f 645f 7065 726c 2f31 2e32 360d        ).mod_perl/1.26.
```

Figure 9.3. Network data captures using tcpdump [90]

9.6. Load balancing

Network Load Balancing is used to balance network sessions like web, email, etc over multiple connections in order to spread out the amount of bandwidth used by each LAN user, thus increasing the total amount of bandwidth available. For example, consider a user with a single WAN connection to the Internet operating at 1.5Mbps. Assume that this user adds a second WAN connection operating at 2.5Mbps. If they implemented load balancing across the two connections this would provide a total of 4Mbps of bandwidth during balancing sessions.

Load balancing therefore balances sessions across each WAN link. This is particularly useful with web browsers because when browsers connect to the Internet, they open multiple sessions, one for the text, another for an image etc. These can be balanced to improve performance. It is worth mentioning at this point that an FTP application does not use multiple sessions and therefore it cannot be balanced across two separate WAN connections. However if a secondary FTP connection is made on the secondary WAN link, then it is possible to provide load balancing by distributing traffic across the two connections and so provide an overall increase in throughput.

Furthermore, network load balancing can be used to provide network redundancy so that in the event of a WAN link outage, access to network resources is still available via the secondary link.

Exercises

9.1 Discuss the factors that need to be considered when planning for network performance.

9.2 Networks have performance limitations on the amount of data that they can transfer in a given period of time. Explain how load balancing can improve the performance of a LAN.

9.3 For an Ethernet frame, calculate the maximum and the minimum frame rates.

9.4 You are the administrator of an Ethernet network running at 10Mbps with a passive hub. The network uses a streaming media server to enable users to review the company's video advertisements. Your routine tests have identified that the network is too slow to meet the requirements. For this network perform the following steps,

i) Explain how network performance would be affected if you replaced the passive hub with a switch.

ii) For the network, calculate the maximum and the minimum possible frame rates.

iii) Explain how the frame size is determined for this network.

9.5 Explain what network sniffers do.

9.6 What is load balancing and how is it achieved?

10 IP ADDRESSING

10.1. Introduction

TCP/IP protocol requires that each and every computer on a network segment must be identified with a particular Internet Protocol (IP) address and name. DHCP server normally does the allocation of IP addresses, while the computer name is given by the administrator of the network and registered with the DNS server on the network. DHCP services are defined in request for comments documents, i.e. RFC 2131 and DNS are defined in RFC 1034 and 1035. The Internet Assigned Numbers Authority (IANA) is the entity that oversees global IP address allocation; DNS root zone management, and other Internet protocol assignments. IANA is broadly responsible for the allocation of globally unique names and numbers that are used in Internet protocols that are published as RFC documents. It maintains a close liaison with the IETF and RFC Editor in fulfilling this function. [91]

IP addresses can be private or public. For example a computer on the Internet is identified by its public IP address. In order to avoid address conflicts, IP addresses are publicly registered with the Network Information Centre (NIC) and ultimately with IANA. On the other hand, computers on private network do not need public addresses, since they only need to be unique on the local network.

On a privately assigned IP network the network administrator is responsible for arranging the allocation of IP addresses to hosts. The allocation of IP addresses can be static or dynamic. The administrator allocates static IP addresses, and these are fixed addresses that are not going to change. It is common to allocate static IP addresses to network servers whose address must always be known. The DHCP server allocates dynamic IP addresses to host computers on the network. On a network that uses a DHCP server, the administrator can allocate a pool of IP addresses to be issued by a DHCP server to hosts as and when these are needed.

Although IPv6, the new version of the IP protocol offers a virtually unlimited number of unique addresses (see RFC 2460), the traditional IP address (IPv4) uses a 32-bit number that defines both the network and the host computer.

IP addresses are numeric and uniquely identify one network interface on a computer network, which means that an IP address has to be unique on the network. This is true whether it is a LAN or a WAN. For example, all computers connected to the Internet at any one time have a unique public IP address. Each address is written as four fields (octets as in 8 bits), separated by dots, and each field can be a number ranging from 0 to 255. This notation is described as dotted decimal ('#.#.#.#') form by the RFC 1123, and an example address could be,

192.138.1.1

In total this takes up 32 bits, so that in binary it looks like,

11000000.10101000.00000001.00000001

Figure 10.1 is a quick reminder of how binary numbers are represented. Here an 8-bit binary number is shown with 1s in selected powers of 2. To convert to decimal, the decimal equivalent of each of the powers 2 that have a 1 against them are added together. Thus, in this example $2^7+2^3+2^0=128+8+1=138$

2^7	2^6	2^5	2^4	2^3	2^2	2^1	2^0
128	**64**	**32**	**16**	**8**	**4**	**2**	**1**
1	0	0	0	1	0	1	0
1*128	0*64	0*32	0*16	1*8	0*4	1*2	0*1

128 + 0 + 0 + 0 + 8 + 0 + 1 + 0

138

Figure 10.1. Binary number representation

The 32-bit IP address is used to represent two separate network identifiers. These are the network identifier and the host (computer) identifier. The network identifier will be the same for all computers on the same network, and the host identifier will be different for each computer on the same network segment. Figure 10.2 shows three network segments. The network identifiers for these are 192.168.1.0, 192.168.2.0, and 192.168.3.0. Notice that the last octet in the 32-bit number is zero for each network identifier. These octets are used to provide unique host identifiers for each computer in the corresponding network segment.

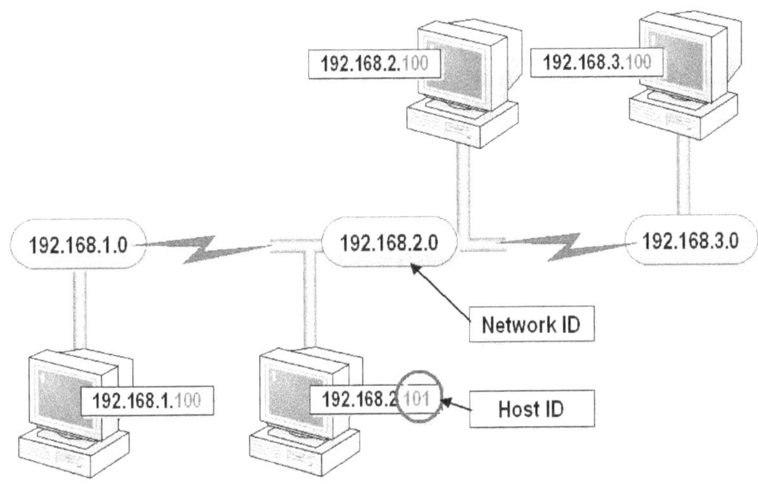

Figure 10.2. Network and Host identifiers

A subnet mask, which is also 32 bits long, is used to identify the network address and the host address from a single IP address. For example, a network mask 255.255.255.0 will have a binary value,

1111111.11111111.11111111.00000000

The way that the IP address for the network and for the host is identified is to perform a logical AND function between the IP address and the subnet mask. This is shown in table 10.1

Table 10.1

	Binary	Decimal
IP address	11000000.10101000.00000001.00000001	192.168.1.1
Subnet Mask	11111111.11111111.11111111.00000000	255.255.255.0
Result after ANDing	11000000.10101000.00000001.00000000	192.168.1.0

10.2. Classful IP Addressing

The network class determines how many of the 32 bits in the IP address are used for the network address, leaving the remaining bits for use as the host address. The four octets can be arranged to represent either a sequence of host identifiers or network identifiers, which leads to the concept of network class. Figure 10.3 shows that two octets are allocated to the network ids and two octets to the host ids.

The octets used in the subnet mask of a classful IP addressing system all have the same value. Thus, a subnet mask octet can have a value of either 0 or 255. Typically the subnet masks will have a 255 in the octet representing the network ID and a 0 in the octet representing the host ID.

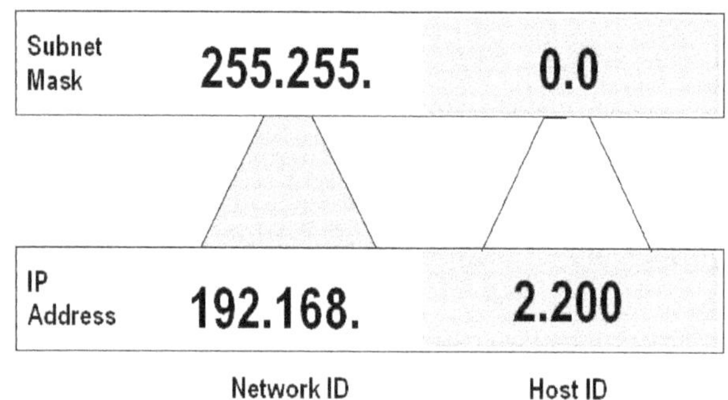

Figure 10.3. Network ID and host ID relationship to the subnet mask

Initially IP addressing was divided into classes according to the number of octets in the subnet mask that had all binary 1s.Thus, as shown in figure 10.4 a Class A network used one octet for the subnet mask, class B used two and class C used three octets. Since the IP address was made up of four octets those octets that are not used in the subnet mask are retained for hosts. For example, if the first octet represents the network ID and the remaining three represent the host id, then this is considered to be a class A address.

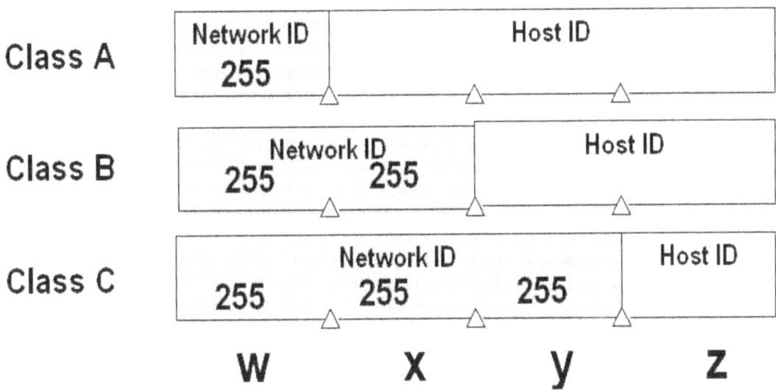

Figure 10.4. Classful IP addresses

It should be relatively clear that class A networks have the most host identifiers (approximately 2^{24}) and that Class C networks have the least number (approximately 2^8). It is worth noting at this point that a host ID must not have all 1's and must not have all 0's in the octet. Thus the range of available host addresses is always (2^n-2), where n is the number of bits available for allocating host IDs.

There are a number of rules that apply when designing the IP addresses in a network. These are as follows,

- The first number in the Network ID cannot be 127 because this is a reserved address for loopback test.
- The Host ID cannot be all 1s because this will interfere with the mask octet, which is in fact used as the broadcast address.
- The Host ID cannot be all zeros since this will interfere with network identifiers.
- The Host ID must be unique on the local network ID, which means that all hosts have a unique address on the network segment.

The available network address ranges for the different classes are shown in table 10.2.

Table 10.2

	Number range	**Number of possible networks**	**Number of hosts on each network**
Class A	1-126 (127 reserved)	127	(2^{24}-2)=16,777,214
Class B	128-191	16,383	(2^{16}-2)=65,534
Class C	192-223	2,097,151	(2^8-2)=254
Class D	224-239	N/A	N/A
Class E	240-254	N/A	N/A

It is worth noting that Class D addresses are reserved for multi-casting; Class E addresses are reserved for future use. They should not be used for host addresses. Another important note is that there are three IP network address ranges that are reserved for private networks. The IANA has reserved these addresses so that they will never be registered publicly. These are known as private IP addresses, and are found in the ranges shown in table 10.3.

Table 10.3 private address range

From	To
10.0.0.0	10.255.255.255
172.16.0.0	172.31.255.255
192.168.0.0	192.168.255.255

These private addresses can be used by anyone setting up internal IP networks, such as a lab or home LAN behind a NAT or proxy server or a router. It is always safe to use these because routers on the Internet by default will never forward packets coming from these addresses. These addresses are defined in RFC 1918.

As mentioned earlier, the four octets are logically ANDed with the subnet mask in order to determine the network ID. All hosts on the same network must have the same network ID. For example, three networks connected by a router are shown in figure 10.5. They are identified by their unique network addresses as shown in the figure and in table 10.4.

Table 10.4

Arbitrary Name	IP Address	Subnet Mask	Network ID
Net A	105.10.5.10	255.0.0.0	105.0.0.0
Net B	172.16.20.11	255.255.0.0	172.16.0.0
Net C	192.168.2.1	255.255.255.0	192.168.2.0

For any computer on a network if the IP address and the subnet mask are known, it is possible to work out the network ID of the segment that the host is connected to. This is done as shown in table 10.1, by logically ANDing the IP address and the subnet; the result of this operation gives the network identifier.

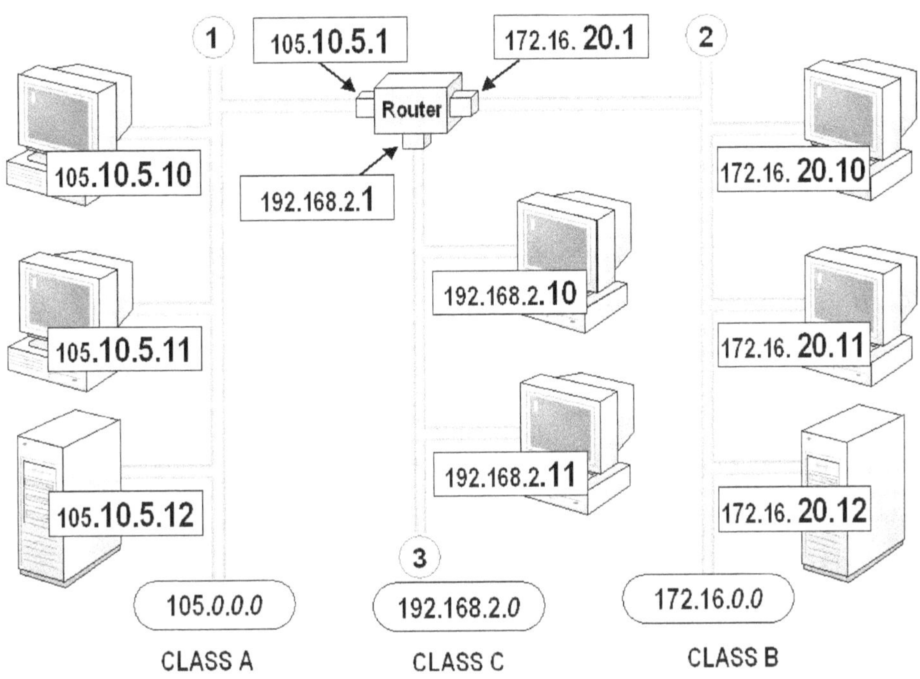

Figure 10.5. Three networks separated by a router

Exercise 10.1

Given the IP addresses and subnet masks in table 10.5, determine which (if any) of the hosts belong to the networks shown in figure 10.5.

Table 10.5

IP Address	Subnet Mask	Network ID	Network (A,B,C or none)
105.10.5.71	255.0.0.0		
172.16.20.11	255.255.0.0		
105.101.21.21	255.0.0.0		
192.168.1.101	255.255.255.0		
105.10.5.71	255.255.0.0		
192.168.2.101	255.255.255.0		

10.3. Subnetting

Conventional classful IP addressing has a tendency to waste IP addresses. This is because the actual number of addresses that are available in each class of network is fixed. For example, if a network consisted of 1000 hosts the allocated class to this network would need to be Class B. This is because Class C only has 254 available addresses for hosts.

However, allocating class B means that 65, 534 addresses are available out of which only 1000 are actually needed. Therefore, 64,534 addresses are wasted. Given the rapid expansion of the Internet this level of waste of IP address space cannot be tolerated. Consequently network designers have resorted to the principle of subnetting. Subnetting is covered in a number of RFC documents. The growth of networking since the time of STD 5 (1981), RFC 950 (1985) and RFC 1123 (1989), has resulted in larger and more complex network subnetting.

As discussed earlier, a classful IP address is a two-layer hierarchy, comprising of a network identifier and a host identifier fields. This subnet scheme creates the possibility of an optional 'subnet' layer and field. This is to say that stealing some bits from the host field of the address can create a new subnet field. [92] The details of the subnet field are site specific and all three classes of networks (A, B, and C) may be subnetted. The use of subnets is an optional local decision. The fact that a network has subnets is invisible outside that network and the change is local which means that is implemented at a given site without any global Internet effects.

Therefore, returning to the example of a client that needs to accommodate 1000 hosts. In a class B framework, additional bits can be added to the default subnet mask by stealing a few from the host's bits. The number of hosts that need to be accommodated will give the indications of how many bits can be sacrificed to the new subnet mask. The class B subnet has 16 bits allocated to the hosts. (i.e. 2^{16}=64K). For 1000 hosts 10 bits should be sufficient (i.e. 2^{10}=1K=1024). Thus, at a glance we can identify that six of the higher bits in the host ID range can be used as the additional bits for the subnet mask. Therefore as a general rule, in order to calculate the number of subnets or nodes, use the formula (2^n-2) where n is the number of bits in the defaults subnet mask that will be used for further subnetting.

Consider the following example of subnetting where 1000 hosts need to be accommodated by subnetting a class B address range. The various numbers are shown in binary and dotted decimal notation in table 10.6. In this example a 6-bit subnet mask was used as mentioned earlier, in order to accommodate 1000 hosts. Consequently, it is possible to provide (2^6-2) =62 subnets with this size mask. Each subnet has (2^{10}-2) =1022 nodes. So it is seen that we can accommodate the required 1000 hosts with this subnet mask. When allocating IP addresses it is important to note that each subnet can have nodes assigned to any address between the subnet address and the broadcast address. The broadcast address is obtained by assigning all of the 6 bits the value 1, and the subnet address is obtained when these 6 bits are all given values 0. These are shown in table 10.6, in binary and in dotted decimal notation.

Table 10.6

Binary	Dotted decimal	Comment
11111111.11111111.00000000.00000000	255.255.000.000	Class B default Subnet Mask
11111111.11111111.11111100.00000000	255.255.252.000	Sub-netted Subnet Mask
10100000.10001100.10111101.11001100	160.140.189.200	IP Address of host
10100000.10001100.10111100.00000000	160.140.188.000	Subnet Address (unused mask bits all 0s)
10100000.10001100.10111111.11111111	160.140.191.255	Broadcast Address (unused mask bits all 1s)

The maximum available hosts for the network subnetted in this way are obtained by a simple multiplication of the number of subnets times the number of nodes available per subnet. For the example, this gives a total of 62x1022=63,364 nodes for the entire class B address subnetted this way. Notice that this is less than the 65,534 nodes that a class B would have if it were not subnetted.

10.4. Classless Inter-Domain Routing (CIDR)

Classless Inter-Domain Routing (CIDR) refers to an Address Assignment and Aggregation Strategy as defined in the RFC 1519 paper. It was designed to provide a more economical means of allocating the available IP addresses. The main motivation for the introduction of CIDR is cited in RFC 1519 as the evolution of the Internet. As the Internet has evolved and grown in recent years, it has become evident that several serious scaling problems were on the horizon. These include,

- Exhaustion of the class B network address space. One fundamental cause of this problem is the lack of a network class of a size which is appropriate for mid-sized organization; class C, with a maximum of 254 host addresses, is too small, while class B, which allows up to 65534 addresses, is too large for most organisations.
- Growth of routing tables in Internet routers is beyond the ability of current software, hardware, and people to effectively manage.
- Eventual exhaustion of the 32-bit IP address space.

Although subnetting can relieve to some extent the burden on classful IP addressing for inter-network communications each subnet has to be connected to other subnets through a router. Consequently each router has to maintain a routing table for all the subnets that it connects.

The routing table stores the routes (and in some cases, metrics associated with those routes) to particular network destinations. This information contains the topology of the network immediately around it. The construction of routing table is the primary goal of routing protocols and static routes. Thus, while it is always possible to subnet, the consequence is that routing tables become massive. The need to record routes in large numbers of routers using limited storage space represents a major challenge in routing table construction. Figure 10.6 shows that a router maintains a routing table for each subnetted network. Since in a network each node presumably possesses a valid routing table, routing tables must be consistent among the various nodes otherwise routing loops can develop. This is particularly problematic in the hop-by-hop routing model in which the net effect of inconsistent tables in several different routers could be to forward packets in an endless loop. Routing loops have historically plagued routing, and avoiding these is a major design goal of routing protocols. In the Internet, the currently dominant address aggregation technology is a bitwise prefix-matching scheme called Classless Inter-Domain Routing (CIDR). [93] Whereas classful IP allocation uses prefixes (network identifiers) that are either 8, 16 or 24 bits, CIDR uses prefixes freely from 13 to 27 bits. Figure 10.7 shows how the 32-bits can be individually selected to be a part of the host or the network identifier.

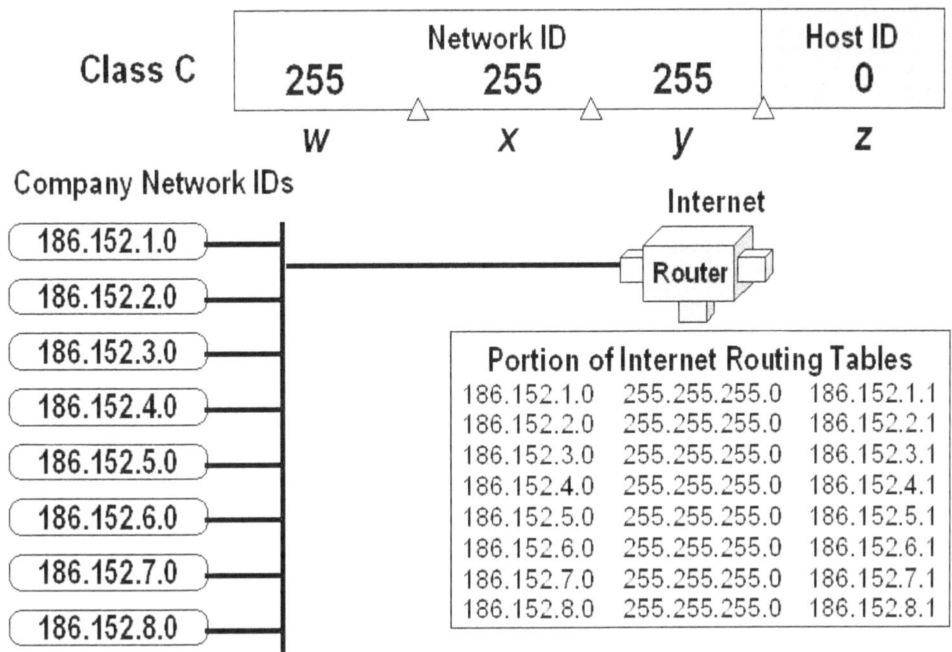

Figure 10.6. Binary IP Addresses

By moving the slide left or right one bit at a time, the number of hosts and networks changes. In this manner blocks of addresses can be assigned to networks as small as 32 hosts (32-5=27 bits in CIDR mask and 2^5=32) or to those with over 500,000 (32-19=13 bits in CIDR mask and 2^{19}=512K) hosts. This allows for address assignments that much more closely match the needs of an organisation. A CIDR address includes the standard 32-bit IP address and also information on how many bits are used for the network prefix. For example, in the CIDR address 138.89.107.15/20, the '/20' indicates that the first 20 bits are used to identify the unique network leaving the remaining bits to identify the specific host.

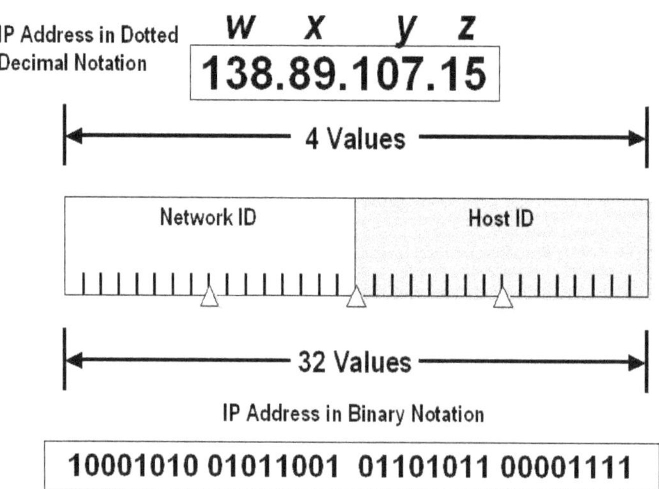

Figure 10.7. Binary Subnet Masks

CIDR notation for a network using the /20 prefix is shown in figure 10.8. Here the first 20 bits are used in the network identifier, which provide for 2^{20}=1M networks. Each network could accommodate approximately 2^{12}=4K hosts

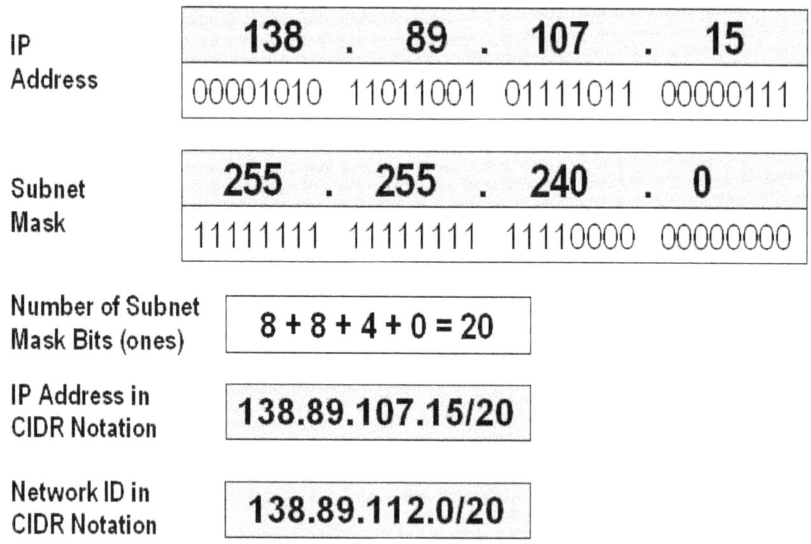

Figure 10.8. IP Address Allocation Using CIDR

This ability to allocate bits to host or network identifiers gives CIDR a major advantage over the classful notation, since IP addresses can be allocated to networks much more precisely. Table 10.7 shows a breakdown of the theoretical number of networks and the number of possible nodes for different CIDR prefixes. For comparison the number or the fraction of the classful networks that these correspond to is also shown.

In general, CIDR helps to reduce the routing table entries in such a manner as to allow aggregation of routing information along topological lines. For simple, single-homed clients, the allocation of their address space out of a transit routing domain's space will accomplish this automatically. Rather than advertise a separate route for each client, the transit domain may advertise a single aggregate route which describes all of the destinations connected to it. [93] CIDR is currently practiced in the Internet community and Internet Service Providers (ISPs) are assigned big blocks of public IP addresses, which they then allocate to their customers.

Table 10.7

CIDR Block Prefix	# Equivalent Class C	# of Host Addresses
/27	1/8th of a Class C	32 hosts
/26	1/4th of a Class C	64 hosts
/25	1/2 of a Class C	128 hosts
/24	1 Class C	256 hosts
/23	2 Class C	512 hosts
/22	4 Class C	1,024 hosts
/21	8 Class C	2,048 hosts
/20	16 Class C	4,096 hosts
/19	32 Class C	8,192 hosts
/18	64 Class C	16,384 hosts
/17	128 Class C	32,768 hosts
/16	256 Class C	65,536 hosts
/15	512 Class C	131,072 hosts
/14	1,024 Class C	262,144 hosts
/13	2,048 Class C	524,288 hosts

For example, assume that a large ISP called XYZ is assigned a CIDR address block with a prefix of /15. According to table 10.7 this is equivalent to 512 Class C addresses or 131,072 host addresses. Typically this ISP will assign its customers CIDR addresses with prefixes ranging from /27 to /19. The prefix allocated will very much depend on the demand from the customers some of whom may be small ISPs. The principle of allocation can proceed down this hierarchy where each customer can sell their CIDR allocation in smaller chunks.

However, aggregation means that in the global routing tables all these different networks and hosts can be represented by the single ISP XYZ Internet route entry. In this way, the growth in the number of routing table entries at each level in the network hierarchy has been significantly reduced. As a guideline, present day global routing tables can have in the region of 100K entries. [94] The Internet is currently a mixture of both CIDR addresses and Class A, B and C addresses. New routers support CIDR and the Internet authorities encourage all users to implement the CIDR for IP allocation. Once again it is worth noting that this applies to public address space. On a private network the choice of the notation is up to the administrator. Further reading on routers and routing protocols can be found on the Cisco website. [96]

Exercises

10.1 Explain the problems with classful IP addressing.

10.2 What is a subnet mask and how is it used to determine the network id, and the host id from an IP address?

10.3 What is subnetting and what are the main problems with subnetted networks on the Internetwork?

10.4 What are the number ranges for the Classful IP addresses A, B, C?

10.5 What are classes D and E used for?

10.6 What are the private address ranges used for?

10.7 What is address aggregation in CIDR?

10.8 Why do you need CIDR if you can subnet?

10.9 You are a network engineer for a market research company that has a pool of 5,000 data-inputting employees. Design an IP addressing scheme using a subnetted class B system.

10.10 Repeat the above with a CIDR system and compare the results.

11 Network infrastructure design

11.1. Introduction

Network infrastructure design process is evolutionary and the team takes the design from concept through to various stages including logical design as well as physical design. Each stage adds new layers to the design and each of these is built on top of the preceding stage. The concept is typically a model of the system architecture. This includes the proposed method of addressing the issues identified as being in the scope. During this stage preliminary requirement specifications are used to set the scope and then they are further refined to more clearly identify the design goals. Design goals need to take into account the business goals, which is to say that the business needs will be addressed within the scope of the design.

Network infrastructure design typically begin by obtaining a scenario from the client with the initial set of requirements. An example of this is given next.

11.2. Example scenario

MIG Consulting Ltd is expanding its services into the Asia-Pacific region and has recently acquired a building in Sydney, Australia, where they intend to house the subsidiary for the Asia-Pacific region. The corporate headquarters for the company are in Oxford. The Sydney subsidiary has the following areas,

- Sales.
- Human resources.
- Network Infrastructure.

Client requirements

Initial discussions with key stakeholders have identified the initial client requirements for each of these areas. A summary of these is outlined in table 11.1.

Table 11.1

<table>
<tr><td>Sales: There will be 5 users initially and this will increase to 10.
Initially there will be 3 desktop computers and 2 laptops. The laptops will use wireless access 803.11b. All NICs will support 10/100Mbps Ethernet.
All hosts will be members of the sydney.mig.com domain.
One domain controller, one print server and two printers will be located in the sales area.</td></tr>
<tr><td>Human resources: There will be 4 employees who will work closely with the corporate HQ in Oxford.
There will be 4 desktop computers (one for each employee).
All NICs will support 10/100Mbps Ethernet.
All hosts will be members of the hr.oxford.mig.com domain. Domain controllers for this domain are located in Oxford.
One printer will be in secured location in Oxford headquarters to service hr needs.
One remote client will need a VPN connection to Oxford HQ.
All data on the WAN must be encrypted.</td></tr>
<tr><td>Network Infrastructure: Computer room will be divided into two areas. One of these will be secure print services area. The other is the computer area.
The computer room will have 1-Gbps fibre optic link to a 24-port 10/100Mbps switch.
A single Cat 6e cable will be taken to all offices and work areas and will terminate in a 100-Mbps 16-port switch.
Internet is provided via a dedicated T1 line to the local ISP that provides DNS and Firewall.
256-kbps leased line to the local telephone company will be used to connect to Oxford HQ</td></tr>
</table>

Bandwidth requirements

Based on experience of the organisation the estimated bandwidth requirements are given in Table 11.2.

Table 11.2

Bandwidth requirements	**Average (kbps)**	**Peak (Kbps)**
Sales desktop	60	1200
Sales notebook	30	1000
Human resources desktop	20	800
Human resources printer	80	10000
Human resources WAN link	100	500

Global requirements

In Table 11.3 the key stakeholders have identified the global requirements that need to be considered during the design and planning stages.

Table 11.3

LAN is private and only accessible by corporate users.
All managers must use Smart Card authentication.
Consider using a 1Gbps layer 2 switch instead of a 10/100Mbps switch in area subnets.
Consider the use of port authentication on these layer 2 switches.
Isolate departmental traffic as much as possible.
Use subnetting to optimise bandwidth usage.
Ensure that adequate bandwidth is available to all areas.
Services needed include NAT, Firewall, DHCP, WINS.
Provide fault tolerance and backup.

Given this initial specification you need to analyse these in order to design the network infrastructure. The design of a network infrastructure involves careful consideration of both the physical and the logical network components. Accurate planning of all the stages allows the designers to correct any design defects early on so that these can be corrected in a timely manner. Consequently the planning stage involves significant documentation effort.

Network infrastructure diagrams are the blueprints used to build the network infrastructure. There are three components to these; the physical and logical network diagrams and the network configuration document.

11.3. Physical network diagram

This diagram shows how the network components connect to each other. The information includes the cable types and all the details of physical connections that are available to the designer. Table 11.4 shows some of the components that may be included in these diagrams.

Table 11.4

Cable Type	ThinNet	Technologies	ATM
	ThickNet		Frame Relay
Segments	UTP		ISDN
Lengths	STP		
Bandwidths	Fibre Optic		
	Wireless		
Topology	Bus	Devices	PDC/BDC
	Star		DHCP
	Token-Ring	Servers	DNS
	Hybrid	Type	Routers
		Location	NATs
		Firmware Versions	Proxy
		Static IP address	Printers
			Hubs
			Switches

Returning to the previous example the simplified physical network diagram as per the specification is given in figure 11.1. Here I have not included details of cable types in order to not clutter the diagram, but this information would normally be included.

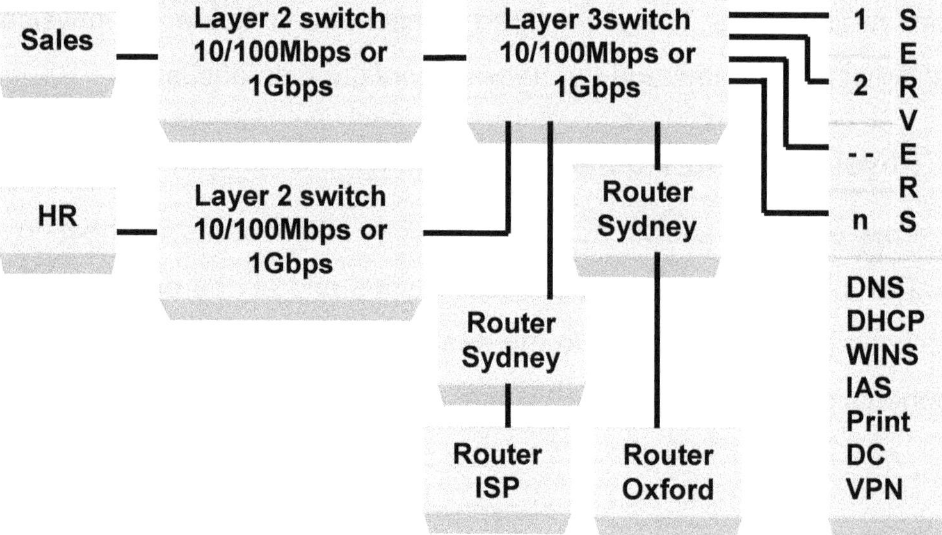

Figure 11.1 Physical network diagram

11.4. Logical network diagram

This shows the domain architecture and how the network is organised in relation to the domain. The information will include details that will help to administer the network. Some of these details are shown in table 11.5.

Table 11.5

Domain Architecture	Hierarchy
	Names
	Addressing
	Naming Conventions
Server roles	DHCP
IP addressing schemes and details	WINS
	DNS
	Proxy
	NAT
	Router
Trust relationships	Transitive
	One-way
	Two-Way

Once again, returning to the previous example the simplified logical network diagram as per the specification is given in figure 11.2. Once again I have not included details of cable types which would normally be included.

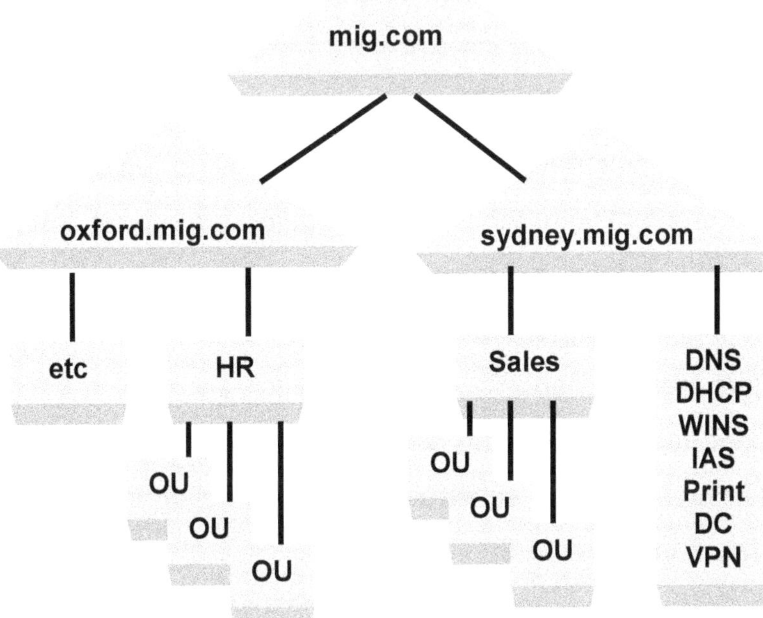

Figure 11.2. Logical network diagram

Network configuration document

This contains the information that is required for network administration purposes. Some of the information that needs to be included is given in table 11.6. It has to be said that all design work relies to an extent on expert judgement as well as experience. Therefore these documents serve as a starting point towards the final design, and they are refined as more time is spent on the project.

Table 11.6

Name resolution service	DNS, WINS
	DHCP
IP addressing methods	Classful/ CIDR
IP configuration	Pools
	Reservations
	Static Ips
Remote dial-up networking	VPN
Bandwidth	ISDN
	FDDI
	Satellite/RF
Administration	Directory services
	Security
	Business rules

11.5. Network planning issues

The aim of any network design project is to provide a satisfactory solution to the problem within the time schedule and budget limits. The risk of poor design or budget overruns is high, which is why the effective management of risks is generally perceived as one of the most important areas of project management. [96]

In project management the designer must consider trade-offs between resources, features and the schedule. This can be done using the trade-off triangle as shown in figure 11.3.

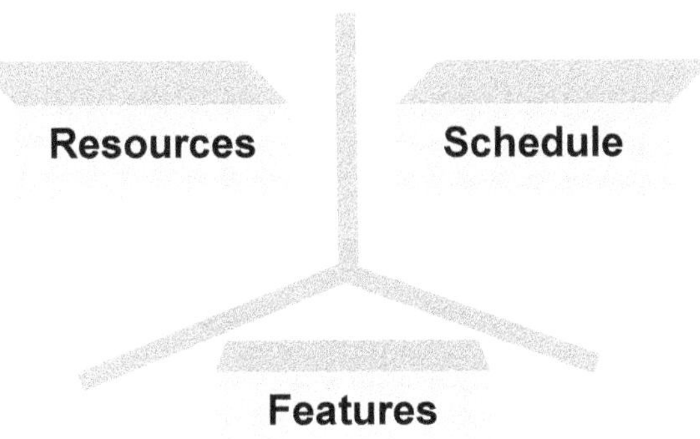

Figure 11.3. Trade-off triangle

The trade-off triangle maintains a balance between resources, schedule and features, all of which have an impact on the overall budget. A change in one of these will require an adjustment to the other two. In using this approach it is often a good idea to use risk-driven scheduling. The essence of this approach is to prioritise the highest risk tasks; therefore the support for identification of the most risky process areas and their potential improvement is especially worthwhile.

Current risk identification practices adopt primarily two techniques; checklists and group effort (e.g. brainstorming). Checklists help to control the identification scope and protect from overlooking significant risks. Group effort benefits from synergetic use of human intuition and experience. Both are valid techniques for identifying risk areas.

Another useful technique in planning is to use time-boxing. Simply put, time boxing sets a fixed time that is available to work on a given task. The plan is to do the best we can within that time frame. Therefore, by applying this technique, a project can be split into distinct time periods. Groups of tasks can then be performed within these time frames. Additionally, it is useful to schedule a buffer time as the last task prior to each major milestone, so that a contingency measure is built into the plan.

As with all complex engineering tasks network infrastructure design requires careful planning. With network infrastructure design there are a large number of issues and it is difficult to prescribe a single approach to every network design challenge. Nevertheless, in general the approach involves three stages, which are, the Requirements, Planning and Implementation stages. The outputs from the requirements stage normally provide the requirements specification. The documents that support this include the following,

- **Scope document**. This describes the project goals and constraints. It outlines the details of the project, the needs it will meet, its features, and an initial schedule.
- **Structure document**. This outlines the structure of project organisation and describes the management process. It identifies the team leaders for each role and outlines their responsibilities.
- **Risk assessment document**. This gives the preliminarily assessment of risk. Additionally, it provides details of contingency plans to manage risk.

The starting point of all network infrastructure projects is the master project schedule. This includes details of the teams involved in various tasks, as well as the time-frames associated with each task.

Table 11.7

Master Plan	Budget Plan	Purchasing Plan
	Capacity Plan	Security Plan
	Deployment Plan	Pilot Plan
		Test Plan
Key Stakeholders	Support Plan	
Experts	Internal structure of organisation	
	External links	
	Project leader	
	day-to-day operations leader	
	End-user requirements	
Scope	Describes relationships between resources, features and project schedule. This is usually in the form of a trade-off matrix	

The master project schedule includes planning schedules for components such as for example plans for; the budget, capacity, deployment, pilot, purchasing, security, support and test etc. Each of these plans has to be documented as the design progresses through the various iterations. Typically the master plan will also include a description of the key stakeholders. These are individuals that are key to the success of the project and include experts in various areas as identified in table 11.7. The master plan also includes a definition of the scope, which describes relationships between resources, features and project schedule.

11.6. Practical considerations

Before the master plan can be put together it is necessary to obtain a client requirement specification so that the scope can be defined. This would normally be done in collaboration with a client and after a number of meetings and discussions a document outlining a requirement specification should be drafted. Typically this document would cover information needed for the physical network design and also the logical network design.

Returning to the previous example, the scenario and the initial documents provide sufficient information to begin with the design. As this progresses, additional information may be required and the specifications may have to be amended. In all cases, the design will have an iterative nature such that it is refined and improved after every iteration. In a general network infrastructure design problem there are some basic questions that need to be answered and decisions to be made during the early stages of design. For example, for the physical network design we need to know,

- How many hosts are required on the networks.
- Where are the hosts located.
- What is the budget.
- What locations are available to house the hosts.
- What cable types are required and where.
- Wireless access requirements.
- Bandwidth requirements.

For the logical network design we need to know,

- How many distinct organisational units (areas) need to be supported? (i.e. sales, marketing, engineering .etc).

- How many users will log-on locally?
- What are the functions of these users?
- Any remote access users.
- Security of data and network.
- What software will be deployed?
- Any business rules that apply, policies and internal politics of the organisation.

11.7. Number of hosts

The number of hosts on the network will be the guiding factor in the design of the network. This will determine the network size and therefore influence the topology and technologies employed in the network. When making design decision the following need to be taken into account.

Peer to peer network: 2-10 users

As a guideline peer-to-peer networks are recommended as a cost-effective solution for networks of fewer than 10 computers where security is not a major issue. In this type of network there are no servers and each computer is managed both as a client and the server by the administrator of that computer. This is an efficient option that has good functionality and offers the following features,

- File sharing.
- Printer sharing and other hardware resources.
- E-mail.
- Low bandwidth Internet connection sharing.
- No centralised administration overhead.

PTP networks are not as good for networks that require centralised administration. These are typically server-based networks that provide the following,

- Centralised security and back up.
- High bandwidth Internet/Wan access.
- Database applications.
- Central administration.

Single server networks: 11-50 users

Client-server networking can be very economical and efficient in small networks of between 11 and 50 users. The single server can be used to provide network services such as DHCP, DNS, file service, print service etc. as well acting as the directory services server to administer users, computers and other resources.

Single server networks incur the cost of a network server operating system as an extra in comparison with PTP networks. Other than that they are not necessarily much more expensive in the hardware. They are much better than PTP for networks that have the following requirements,

- Secure login.
- Archiving and backup.
- Simple administration.
- Internet/WAN access.
- Group and policy management.
- Access control to data and services.

Single server models are not so good for networks that are very demanding where a multi-server network would be a better choice.

Multi- server networks: 51-250 users

As the network grows the single server model can become overwhelmed and additional servers are needed to share some of the burden. Adding more servers to the network makes them multi-server networks. Figure 11.4 shows a simple arrangement of three servers connecting through a router or bridge. Each server is dedicated to a particular task and all clients on the network are able to access each of the servers.

In multi-server networks the network architecture needs to be considered at an early stage of design. Performance issues such as bottlenecks, latency and traffic jam need to be anticipated and design measures put into place to mitigate them.

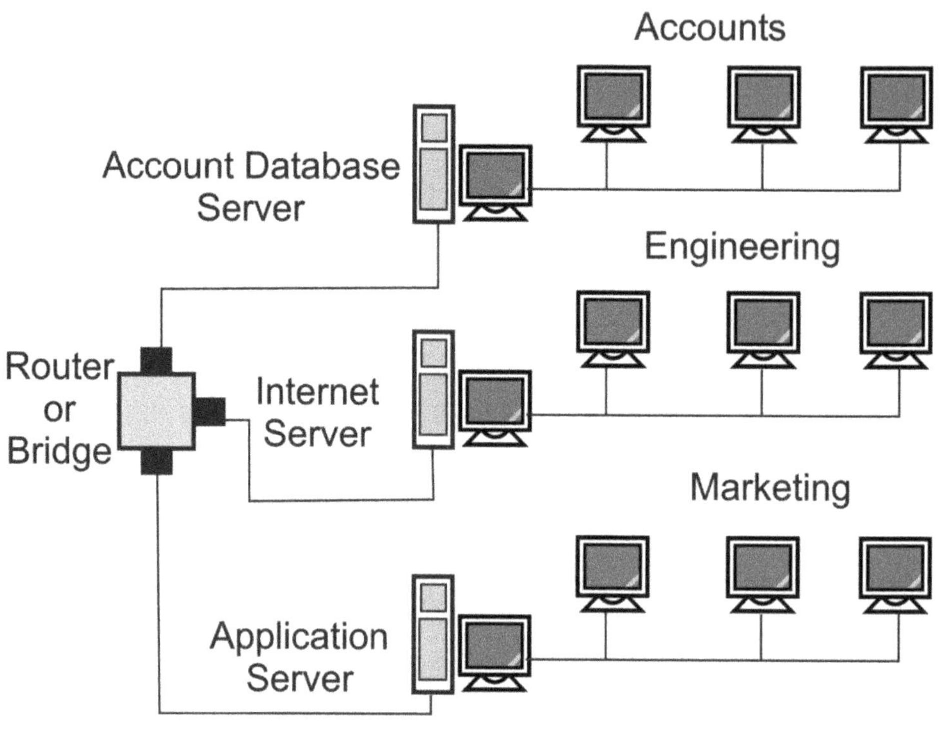

Figure 11. 4. Multiple server configuration

Additionally, these networks number in the region of up to 250 users and they can be spread across different locations. The practical aspects of connectivity, transmission and other technology issues need to be taken into account. In general the following guidelines apply to multi-server networks. Like single-server solutions they are good for,

- Secure login.
- Organised data.
- Archiving and backup.
- Simple administration.
- Internet/WAN access.
- Group and policy management.
- Access control to data and services.

Additionally they are good for,

- Application serving.
- Distributed organisations.
- Large organisation with WAN networks.
- Organisations with complicated internal organisational structure.

A large percentage of corporate networks fall into this category and considerable cost saving and efficiency improvements can be achieved with careful network design.

Multi- server High-speed backbone network 251-1000 users

This is a variant of the multi-server model except that it is deployed across fast media such as fibre optic cables. This is shown in figure 11.5. Furthermore, the larger number of supported users means that typically there will be a larger geographical area of coverage. This type of network is very costly because it requires a high-speed backbone. Typically this would be a FDDI ring topology linking all the servers in a backbone arrangement. An FDDI to Ethernet router must be located at the boundary of the ring and the Ethernet segment that is logically assigned as an organisational unit.

These networks are very expensive because of the cost of the high-speed backbone and the choices have to be based on a compromise of cost against performance.

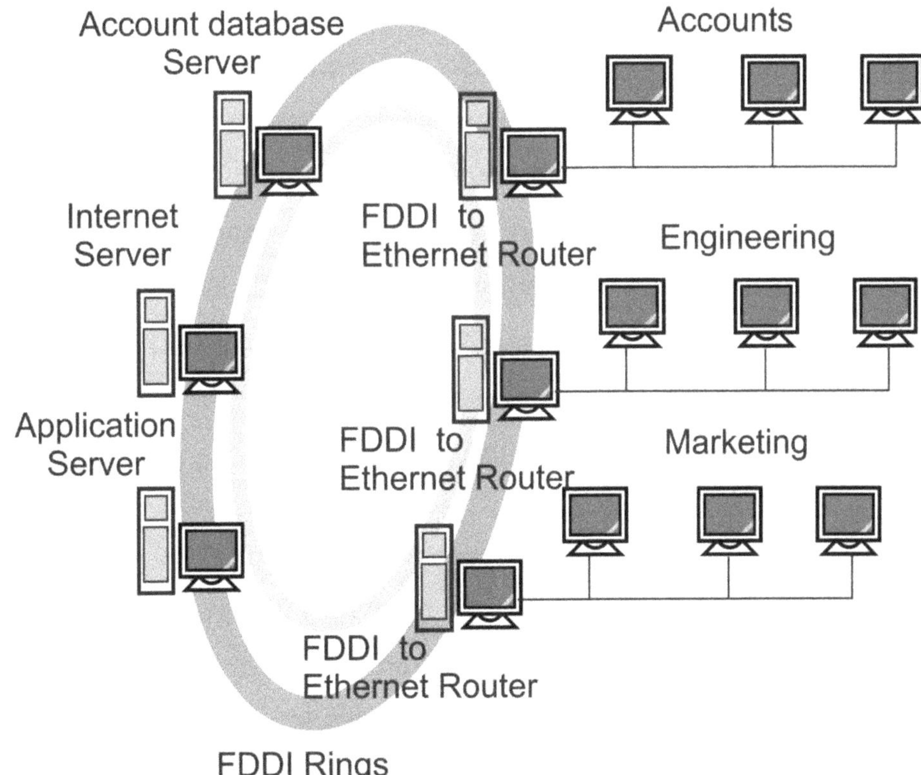

Figure 11.5 Multi- server High-speed backbone network

Enterprise networks (>1000 users)

These networks are very large and as a result it is very likely that they include local and wide area networks within their infrastructure. In order to better administer networks of this size it is a good idea to split them into smaller networks. These smaller networks would for all intents and purposes be functional networks and they would be integrated to form a larger enterprise model. With such enterprise networks the choice of operating system becomes a major factor. This is because the administration of integrated networks of this size is a very challenging task. In some cases very large servers called mainframes or minicomputers are connected to the network to provide an additional layer of services to users.

Some operating systems, such as UNIX and the Mac OS, have networking functions built in. The term network operating system, however, is generally reserved for software that enhances a basic operating system by adding networking features. Examples include, Novell Netware, Sun Solaris and IBM z/OS, Artisoft's LANtastic, Microsoft Windows 2003 Server. The Cisco IOS (Internet Operating System) is also a network operating system with a focus on optimising Internetworking capabilities of network devices.

It must be said that present day enterprise network design has to take into account a broader range of concerns. Network management challenges today go well beyond simple network availability. Issues like Quality of Service (QoS), Service Level Agreements (SLA), network growth/deployment, and most importantly, network security are all critical areas that require advanced troubleshooting, diagnosis, and management tools.

11.8. Network technologies

An equally important decision on network infrastructure design is the choice of technologies for the networks. Ethernet is a very common technology that can be used on wired or wireless networks. Token ring is another technology, which tends to prevail in fibre optics media. ATM and Frame Relay are more common in wide area networks.

Ethernet networks

As mentioned earlier Ethernet can use wired or wireless transmission media. In wired transmission the most commonly used cabling systems include, coaxial cable, twisted pair and fibre optic. Table 11.8 shows the basic characteristics of the various cable types.

Table 11.8

Type	Description
1000Base-LX/FX	Gigabit Ethernet over fibre optic cable.
1000Base-T	1000Mbps, 1 Billion bits per second over copper cabling. All four pairs of Cat6 cable utilised at 250Mbps per pair.
100Base-FX	100Mbps Ethernet data transmissions over Fibre optic cable
100Base-LX	1300nm - Long wavelength fibre optic transmissions at 100Mbps.
100Base-SX	850nm - Short wavelength fibre optic trans. at 100Mbps.
100Base-T2	100Mbps Ethernet running baseband signalling over two twisted pairs
100Base-T4	Four pairs of Cat3 or better cable. Transmits at 25 Meg on all four pairs.
100Base-TX	100Mbps Ethernet running baseband signalling over twisted pair copper. Full duplex
10Base-2	Thin Ethernet, sometimes-called thin net or coax, capable of data transmissions up to 185 meters. (Rarely used now)
10Base-5	Thick Ethernet cable capable of data transmissions up to 500 meters. (Rarely used now)
10BaseT	10Mbps Ethernet running baseband signalling over twisted pair copper cable

Coaxial cables

The 5-4-3 Rule for Ethernet topologies with Co-axial cables: 5-segments, 4-repeaters and 3 segments populated with nodes.

10 base5 or ThickNet uses thick coaxial cable

Table 11.9 gives the basic characteristics. ThickNet uses a BNC type connector and at both ends of the cable it is necessary to install a terminator (50 Ohms) to eliminate signal bounce. The cable is covered in PVC coating and marked every 2.5 meters for connection points. This is done because devices must not be connected too close together due to signal distortion. To make a new connection to a ThickNet cable a Tap is used, which is also called a transceiver. The transceiver is connected using the AUI cable (sometimes known as transceiver cable or drop cable). Table 11.9 gives the basic characteristics.

Table 11.9

Description	Constraint
Maximum segment length	500 m
Maximum segments	5
Maximum segments with nodes	3
Maximum repeaters	4
Maximum overall length with repeaters	2.5 km
Maximum Taps	100
Minimum distance between Taps	2.5 m
Maximum AUI cable drop	50 m

10 base2 ThinNet uses thin coaxial cable

The maximum cable length for a ThinNet segment is 185m. It uses BNC connectors and requires a 50 Ohm terminator at each end. It is significantly cheaper than ThickNet however it is still more expensive than UTP cable. ThinNet specification is significantly different from ThickNet primarily because the transceiver for ThinNet is built into the network interface card (NIC). (See table 11.10)

Table 11.10

Description	Constraint
Maximum segment length	185 m
Maximum segments	5
Maximum segments with nodes	3
Maximum devices per segment	30
Maximum repeaters	4
Maximum overall length with repeaters	925 m

Twisted pair cables

10 baseT uses unshielded twisted pair cable

Unshielded twisted pair (UTP) cable costs less than ThinNet and it is easier to install and wire around buildings and offices. 10baseT Ethernet networks use wired star and connections are RJ-45 type. Although physically it appears as a star, logically the network operates as though it were on a bus.

UTP cable is classified according to categories defined by the Electrical Industries Association into categories 1 to 6. Cat 1 and 2 are voice-grade cable. Categories 3,4,5 and 6 are data grade. Cat 5 has been widely used and its enhanced version cat 5e is installed in most modern LANs. More recently

TIA/EIA-568-B.2-1 Category 6 has been ratified. Cat 7 cable specifications are also on the way.

Brief history of categorisation is that the previous TIA/EIA-568-A 'Commercial Building Telecommunications Standard' was published in 1995. This document was written for Category 5, 100-Ohm copper cabling systems. This transmission system was developed to replace the previous version of Ethernet, which was 10 Base-T. The 10 Base-T transmission standard provided signal transmission of up to 10MHz of bandwidth over Category 3; usually Unshielded Twisted Pair (UTP) copper cabling.

Category 3 cable was also available in Shielded Twisted Pair (STP) and Screened Twisted Pair (ScTP) cables as well, but UTP was the preference throughout the network communications cabling industry. At around the same time the IEEE 802.3 committee was developing the standard for the 100 Base-T Ethernet transmission systems, which required up to 100MHz of bandwidth.

Category 3 cabling systems could not support this bandwidth. And therefore category 5 cabling was developed and introduced to support 100MHz bandwidth Ethernet transmission systems. To further improve on transmission speeds category 6 cabling was intended to yield 200MHz of bandwidth. The IEEE requested that all testing be done to 250MHz to ensure that Cat 6 systems will operate with sufficient margin. Cat 6 standard provides the best performance specification for UTP and ScTP cabling systems. The requirements for Cat 6 cabling are much more stringent than they were for Cat 5 and Cat 5e. It is very important that installers maintain ½' or less of untwist at the termination, proper bend radius, and avoid short links, less than 15 meters.

When properly installed, Cat 6 cabling systems will provide far better performance than Cat 5e. The frequency range is more than double than for 5e, at 250MHz, where 5e is at 100MHz. Cat 6 performance requirements are also significantly better than Cat 5e when compared at the same frequency. [97]

For more details about Cat 6 cabling see chapter 4 of this text.

Fibre optic

10baseFL uses single or multi-mode optical fibre. This is a 10Mbps baseband signalling system over a fibre-optic cable. It is a star wired network because it requires a network hub, which is also called a concentrator. A segment can only have two nodes; one is the hub and the other the station. The hub can be either active or passive. An active hub has electronics to detect and retransmit the signal. A passive hub has optics that split the light and reflect it to other network stations. Since the signal is split between ports in this way, the number of ports cannot be large otherwise the signal will be too weak. Additionally, since there are no electronics in the passive hub, it does not have any error correction circuits. Table 11.11 gives the basic characteristics.

Table 11.11

Description	Constraint
Maximum segment length	2km
Maximum segments	1024
Maximum segments with nodes	1024
Maximum nodes per segment	2
Maximum nodes per network	1024
Maximum hubs in chain	4
Maximum number of repeaters (repeaters come in pairs, a pair counts as 1 repeater)	2

Token ring

Token ring is an access method developed by IBM conforming to the IEEE 802.5 standard. All hosts connect to a central wiring hub called the 'Multi-station Access Unit' (MAU). Using copper, it can connect up to 255 nodes in a star topology at 4, 16 or 100Mbps.

Although the MAU is configured as a central hub, the operation of a token ring is significantly different from the Ethernet star topology. With an Ethernet central hub, all users broadcast a request and therefore they all compete against each other to access the network. On the other hand the token ring MAU ensures that all users get regular turns at transmitting their data.

In copper media two types of token ring networks are supported, Type 1 and Type 3. Type 1 networks support up to 255 hosts per network and use shielded twisted pair wires with IBM style Type 1 connectors. Type 3 allows up to 72 devices per network and use unshielded twisted pair with RJ-45 connectors. Cabling for token ring can be copper of fibre optic depending on the bandwidth requirements.

Fibre distributed data interface (FDDI)

Although somewhat different from the token ring, FDDI also uses token passing as the access method. It includes its own network management system and can optionally run at the same speed over copper wire (CDDI) with distance limitations. FDDI-II defines additional optional protocol mechanisms that allow an FDDI data link to be used to provide circuit-switched services in addition to packet-switched services. The mode of transmission that is used to provide circuit-switched services is called isochronous transmission. Therefore, FDDI-II can handle voice and video as well as data by adding an isochronous data transmission. FDDI-II can support basic mode, in which the ring supports standard FDDI packet switching, and hybrid mode, in which the ring supports both packet-switched and isochronous data. [98, 99]

FDDI provides an optional dual counter-rotating ring topology that contains primary and secondary rings with data flowing in opposite directions. If a line breaks, the ends of the primary and secondary rings can be bridged at the closest node to create a single ring.

FDDI nodes can be configured as Single Attached Stations (SAS) connected to concentrators or as Dual Attached Stations (DAS) connected to both rings. Groups of stations are typically wired to concentrators connected in a hierarchical tree to the main ring. Large networks can be configured as a 'dual ring of trees,' in which the dual ring provides the backbone to which multiple hierarchies of concentrators are attached. [100] An unbroken FDDI network can run up to 100km with nodes being up to 2km apart on multi-mode fibre (62.5/125μm), and 10km apart on single-mode fibre. There can be up to 500 nodes on any one ring.

If the primary ring fails and the FDDI wraps, then the network design must be such that the total ring length must not exceed 200km and the number of nodes must not exceed 1000. Because the secondary ring is there purely for redundancy, the design of FDDI should be such that 500 dual-attached nodes and 100km maximums are not exceeded. It is worth noting that no data travels on the secondary ring unless there is a failure in the primary ring.

The maximum packet size is 4.5Kb (compared with Ethernet's maximum size of 1.5 Kb), which means that FDDI packets must be broken up so that they can go onto Ethernet. Data normally travels on the primary ring (anti-clockwise) unless a fault occurs at which point the working stations wrap onto the secondary ring (clockwise) to maintain the network. The upstream neighbour of a particular station is the one that is sending data to this station on the primary ring. The downstream neighbour is the one receiving data from this station on the primary ring.

Copper-stranded Distributed Data Interface (CDDI) is the UTP equivalent that requires stations to be no more than 100m apart. There is also a shielded copper equivalent called Shielded Distributed Data Interface (SDDI). [101]

Exercise

Your client has two separate locations for their business, one in London, which is the Headquarters and the other in Liverpool, which is concerned with sales and marketing. Both the Liverpool and London office networks are shown in figure 11.6. The client wants you to improve the networks both at London and Liverpool. You have had discussions with the managing director and the technical director for the company and you have obtained the following initial requirement specifications.

- Security in communicating between London and Liverpool is very important and so is the cost of providing this secure communication.
- The volume of communications between Liverpool and London is governed by corporate needs and these are,
    - i. E-mails between Sales and Headquarters. This can be pretty heavy at peak times and needs to be secure and reliable.
    - ii. Liverpool has a lot of Video clips that they need to look at for marketing purposes. Occasionally these are streamed to the London Headquarters.

iii. Headquarters is keen to allow senior staff in Liverpool direct access to some corporate information on their servers. However they want this to be strictly controlled so that only the senior management group can access this information. The managing director wants him and the technical director to have access to everything in both locations.

iv. The technical director is adamant that he wants complete access to all Back-Up information.

After this first meeting you return to your office and plan a strategy. For your assignment you are required to produce documentation to show how you will provide this client with the solution to their networking needs. Your design should proceed along the following guidelines. The contents of the design report that you produce should reflect this. The contents should include the sections as recommended next.

- Introduction and definition of the problem with a statement on the aims and objectives for your study.
- Initial design to include, initial specification as given above and a plan of action. This will necessarily include arranging further meetings with directors to establish detailed requirements. Please include in your report any questions that you would ask in order to establish requirements.
- Final specification for the solution to network needs of the corporation.
- Design for the implementation of the solution. Include Physical and Logical network diagrams.
- Post-implementation and maintenance needs.
- Costs of implementing the solution and maintenance.
- Project management and planning.
- Discussions.
- Conclusions.

The diagrams are given over the page.

SALES AND MARKETING - LIVERPOOL office Network

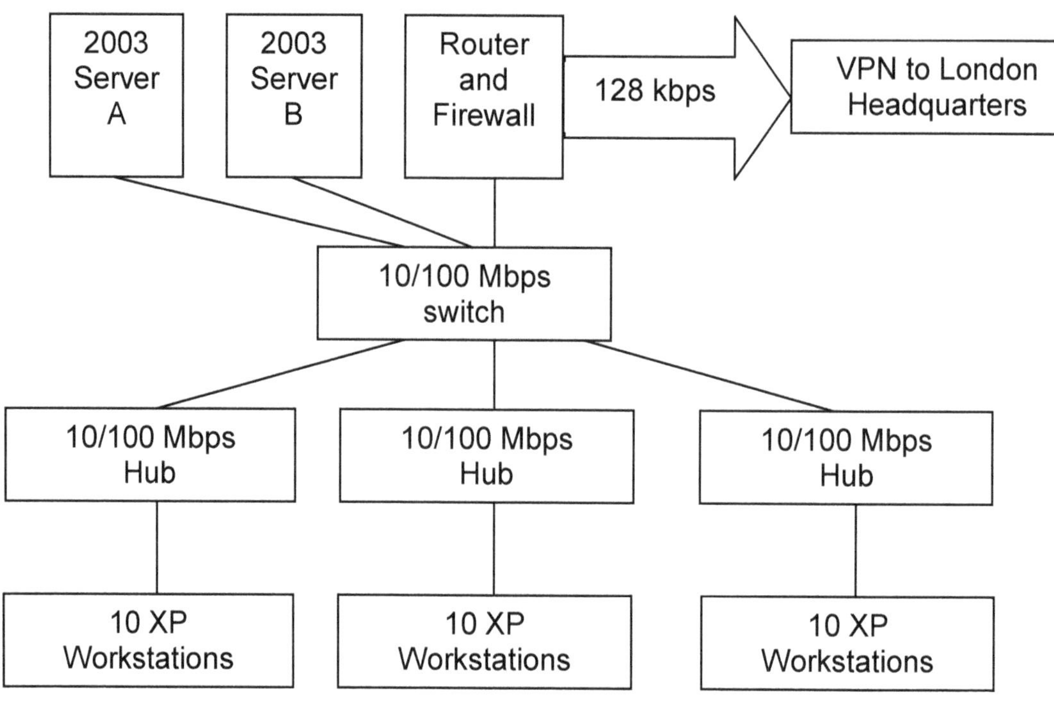

LONDON HEADQUARTERS office Network

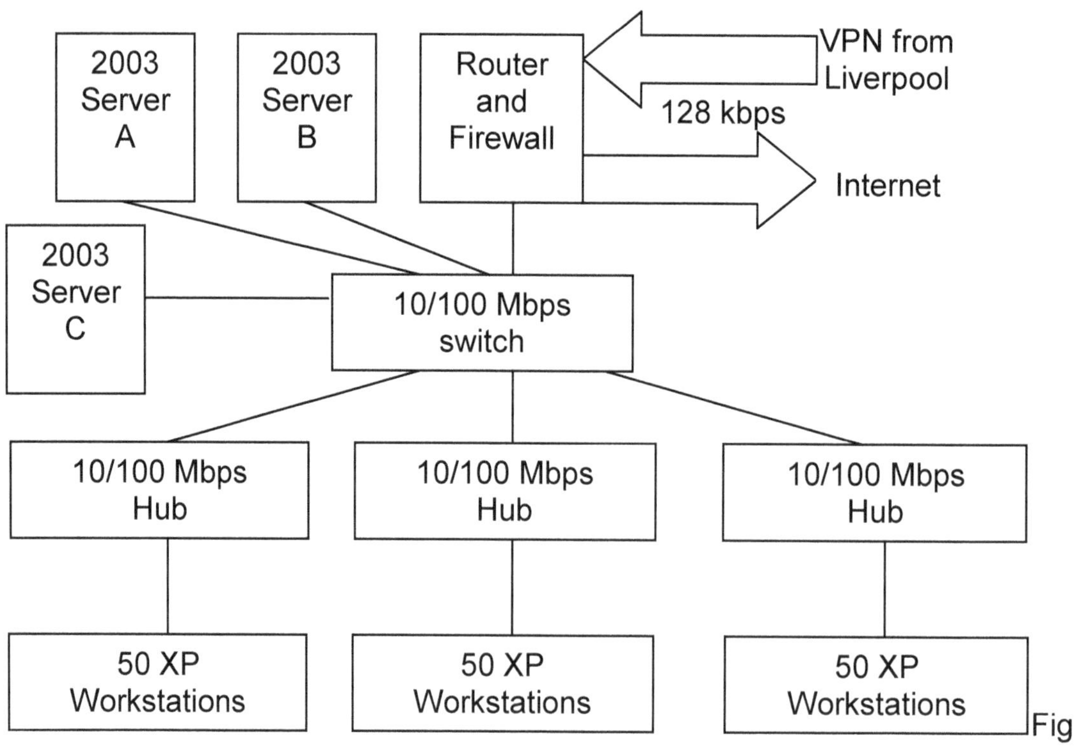

Figure 11.6 Network for the exercise in this chapter

12 NETWORK SECURITY

12.1. Introduction

The increased use of the Internet for e-commerce and other security sensitive data communications has prompted network engineers to develop and implement security measures to secure data integrity and protect the network from external attacks. Network security is made up of a large number of components and therefore any security system is really a combination of measures, each of which is not fully effective in isolation but which work effectively together. As with any system that is made up of individual components, a network security system is only as strong as its weakest link.

The level of security that is implemented can be adjusted to suit the needs of the network. At the same time, the level of security has a direct impact on the usability of the system. In general it is true to say that security always adversely affects how easy the system is for legitimate users. For example, if the network were set-up to deny users access to most of the network resources then network security would be excellent. But in this case the functionality of the network would be severely limited. Thus, to avoid unnecessarily obstructing legitimate users a security system should counter the most credible threats and take into account the seriousness of any consequences. For example, dealing with sensitive information like bank account details deserves more stringent and hence more invasive security measures than, communicating marketing information for a company.

The main components of a security system are a combination of people and technology. In computer security, these include the users, as well as professional staff administering the computers and networks. These users need to be trained to use the technology appropriately. An important source of security lapses is the failure to use technologies properly. Human error is a frequent cause of lapses and the most effective means to minimise these error is to employ technologies that are automated. These technologies are installed, configured, and maintained by professional system administrators. But even with this professional administration, users still have an important role, including vigilance and avoiding common errors. To make users more effective in this role, policies that outline procedures and measures for users to follow need to be in place. Thus the following are identified as some of the essential elements of a security system,

Software. As the Internet provides global access to any computer, security software preventing and detecting malicious access is essential. There are a large number of software solutions to cover a variety of security threats and these have to be kept up to date with upgrades and service packs.

Training. Users need to be trained on how to use the available technologies and on the consequences of any errors and mistakes that they make.

Services. Administrators must be able to manage any computer, install, configure, and maintain specialised security tools, and monitor for intrusions.

Policies. Users must adhere to security policies. These apply to practical rules such as physical access to the network and also user policies on the network.

12.2. Information Security

Services, Mechanisms, Algorithms

The immediate requirements that a network security system must provide include the following,

- **Confidentiality.** Protection from disclosure to unauthorised persons.
- **Access control.** Unauthorised users are kept out.
- **Authentication.** Assurance of identity of person or originator of data.
- **Non-repudiation.** Protects against the originator of communications later denying it.
- **Availability.** Legitimate users have access when they need it.
- **Integrity.** Maintaining data consistency. Protects from unauthorised data alteration.

Software tools support most of these requirements and this happens at different layers of the 7-Layer OSI model. At given layers, different protocols support the appropriate security actions. A typical security protocol provides one or more services.

- Services are built from mechanisms.
- Mechanisms are implemented using algorithms.

SSL - Services in security protocols
Mechanisms - Hashing, Signatures, Encryption
Algorithms

Figure 12.1. Services are delivered via protocols

With reference to figure 12.1, SSL is a secure socket layer protocol that allows information to be encrypted before it is transmitted on the Internet. It supports mechanisms such as hashing, digital signatures and data as well as key encryption. Encryption algorithms are used to perform actual data and key encryption in a secure and known manner, so that the verified recipient can decrypt the data.

12.3. Conventional Encryption

To communicate data securely it is encrypted using a software key, which is shared between the sender and the recipient of data. Therefore the task of communicating a large message in secret is reduced to communicating a small key in secret. Besides other issues this reduces the encrypting effort and also impacts on actual data being transmitted on the network. The major significance here is that by providing a shared key, it is possible to securely send data across an insecure channel, such as the Internet. This is show in figure 12.2.

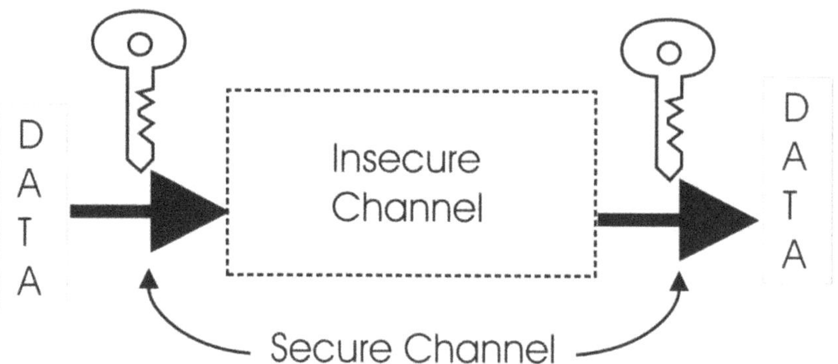

Figure 12.2. Key is used to send securely across an insecure channel

Public-Key Encryption

PKE combines a public and a private key pair to encrypt the data. Anyone can encrypt with the public key while only one person can decrypt with the private key. Both the private and public keys of the pair belong to the recipient and the sender needs the recipient's public key in order to send the encrypted data. This is illustrated in figure 12.3.

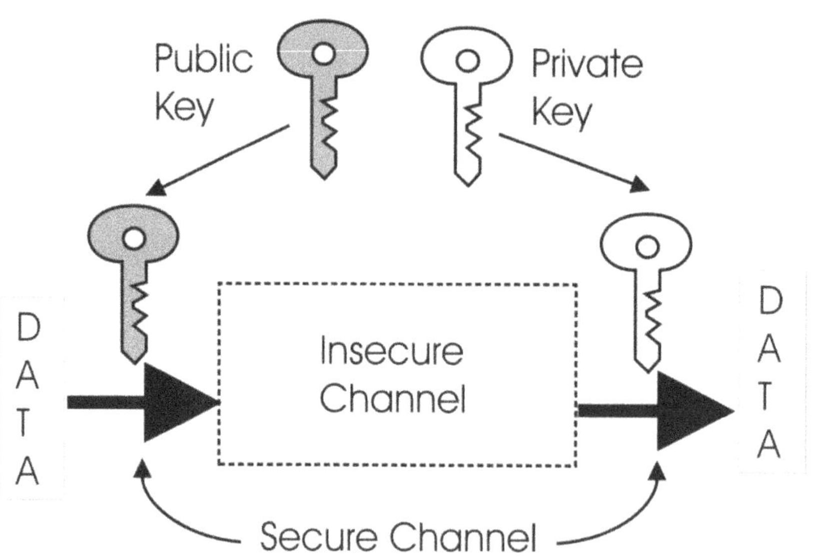

Figure 12.3. Private and public keys used to secure the data

It is also possible to have a so-called 'key agreement', which allows two parties to agree on a shared key. This is also called a session key and it provides part of the required secure channel for exchanging a conventional encryption key. This is described briefly later on in this chapter.

Hash Functions

Hashing is used to encrypt and decrypt digital signatures in order to authenticate message senders and recipients. A hash function algorithm is used to transform a string of characters into a shorter fixed-length value or key that represents the original string. The digital signature is transformed with the hash function and then both the hashed value (known as a message-digest) and the signature are sent in separate transmissions to the recipients. Using the same hash function as the sender, the recipient is able to retrieve the message-digest and the signature.

As shown in figure 12.4 the hash function is used to index the original value and it is used every time the data associated with that value needs to be retrieved. Thus, hashing is always a one-way operation. A good hash function also should not produce the same hash value from two different inputs. If it does, this is known as a collision. A hash function that offers an extremely low risk of collision may be considered acceptable.

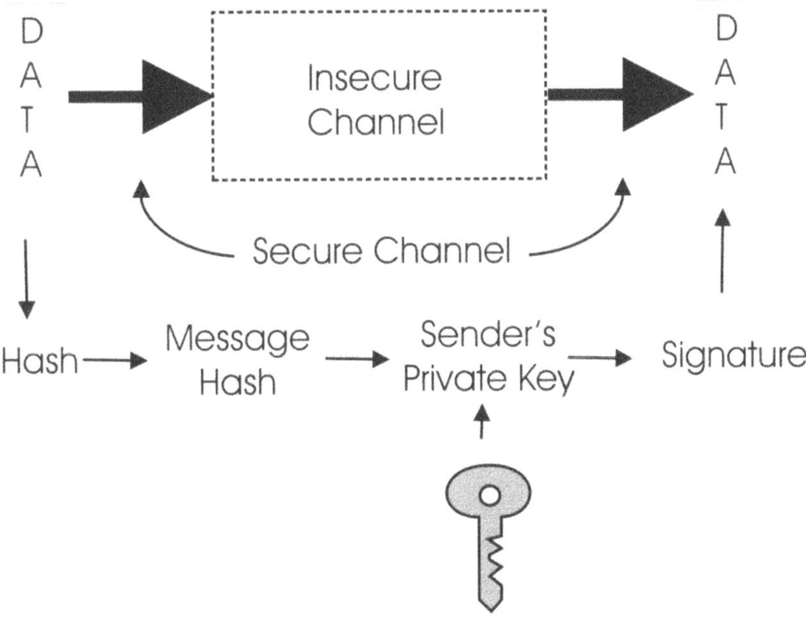

Figure 12.4. Hashing is used to protect the message

Digital Signatures combine a hash with a digital signature algorithm to provide additional security. Digital signature is a mechanism by which a message is authenticated i.e. proving that a message is coming from the authorised sender. [102]

12.4. Message and Data Encryption

In some situations it is necessary to encrypt the data as well as the key used to authenticate the recipient of this data. This process combines conventional and public-key encryption. Public-key encryption provides a secure channel to exchange conventional encryption keys. It is a cryptographic system that uses two keys. One is a public key known to everyone and the other is a private or secret key known only to the recipient of the message. For example, when the sender X wants to send a secure message to the recipient Y, X uses Y's public key to encrypt the message. Y then uses their private key to decrypt it. A session key is used to encrypt both the public key and the data. This is shown in figure 12.5.

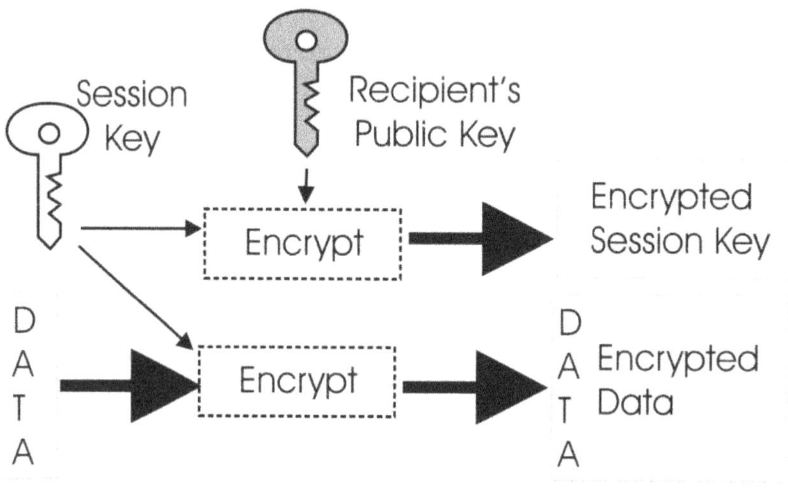

Figure 12.5. Encryption phase of the Data/Key encryption

An important element to the public key system is that the public and private keys are related in such a way that only the public key can be used to encrypt messages and only the corresponding private key can be used to decrypt them. Moreover, it is virtually impossible to deduce the private key even if the public key is known. In order to receive the data the recipient must have the session key and the appropriate private key. The session key is used to decrypt the private key of the recipient, which is matched to the public key as a pair. Session key is also used to decrypt the data. If either the session or the private keys fail in the decryption process the data cannot be received. This is illustrated in the diagram of figure 12.6.

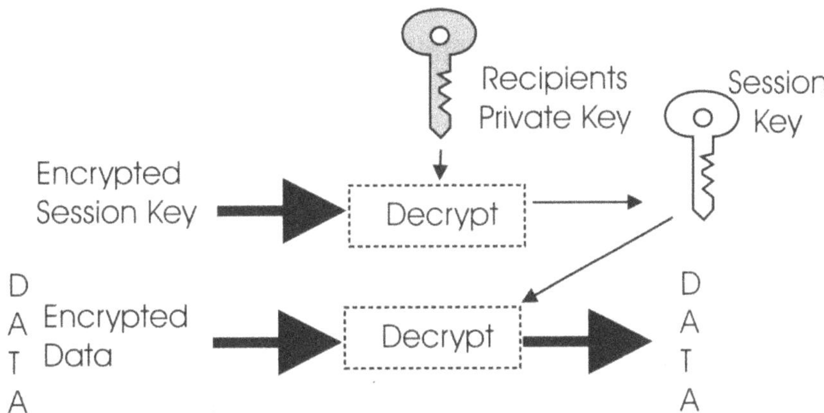

Figure 12.6. Decryption phase of the Data/Key encryption

Public-key systems, such as Pretty Good Privacy (PGP), are becoming popular for transmitting information over the Internet. They are secure and relatively simple to use. The only problem with public-key systems is that the sender must know the recipient's public key to encrypt a message for them.

In a broader sense, public key infrastructure (PKI) is an arrangement that binds public keys with respective user identities by means of a certificate authority (CA). For each user, the user identity, the public key, their binding, validity conditions and other attributes are made unique in PKI certificates issued by the CA.

12.5. Security Protocol Layers

Security protocols protect network communications against attacks by adversaries. Figure 12.7 shows the various security related protocols and the layers at which they work. The layers are loosely mapped onto the 7-layer OSI model. These protocols are briefly discussed next.

e-commerce Protocols: Protocols designed for electronic commerce are at the application layer. These differ from traditional security protocols because they need to establish if other parties to the transaction can be trusted. These protocols further ensure that the information exchanged is secure. It is essential that these desirable properties be satisfied even in the presence of site or communication failures. [103]

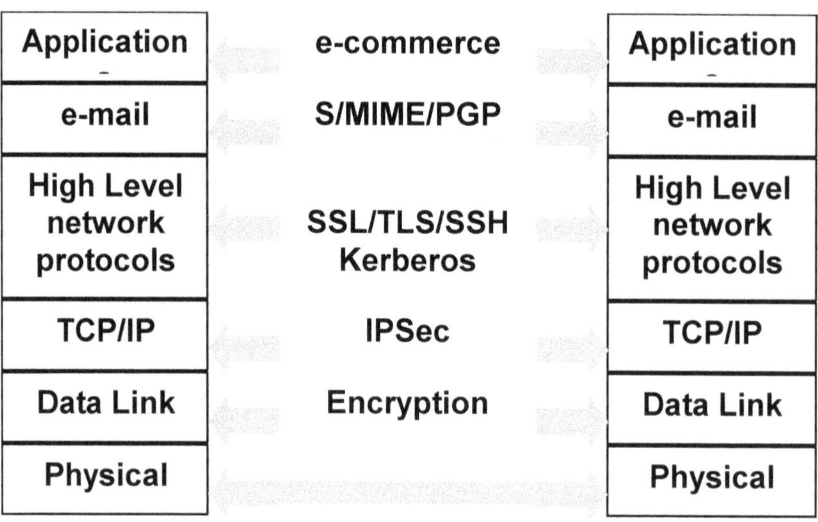

Figure 12.7. Security protocols and layers at which they operate

e-mail protocols: These include MIME and PGP [104]. MIME is short for Multi-purpose Internet Mail Extensions, a specification for formatting non-ASCII messages so that they can be sent over the Internet. Many e-mail clients now support MIME, which enables them to send and receive graphics, audio, and video files via the Internet mail system. In addition, MIME supports messages in character sets other than ASCII. PGP is one of the most common ways to protect messages on the Internet because it is effective, easy to use, and free. PGP is based on the public-key/private-key method discussed earlier. A PGP encryption package is needed in order to encrypt a message using PGP. The official repository for this package is at the Massachusetts Institute of Technology, but it available for free from a number of sources.

12.6. Security protocols (SSL, SSH, TSL and Kerberos)

These protocols operate at the higher-level network layer. SSL is short for Secure Sockets Layer, a protocol developed by Netscape for transmitting private documents via the Internet. SSL uses the public-key/private-key, cryptographic system for transmitting data securely over S-HTTP. At the same SSL creates a secure connection between a client and a server, over which any amount of data can be sent securely. SSL and S-HTTP, therefore, can be seen as complementary rather than competing technologies. The Internet Engineering Task Force (IETF) as a standard has approved both protocols.

Secure Shell (SSH)

This is a program used to remotely log into another computer over a network. It is a replacement for rlogin, rsh, rcp, and rdist and it provides strong authentication and secure communications over insecure channels. SSH protects a network from attacks such as IP spoofing, IP source routing, and DNS spoofing. An attacker who has managed to take over a network can only force ssh to disconnect. When encryption is enabled the attacker cannot play back the traffic or hijack the connection. When using ssh the entire login session, including transmission of password, is encrypted; therefore it is almost impossible for an outsider to collect passwords.

Transport Layer Security (TLS)

This protocol guarantees privacy and data integrity between client/server applications communicating over the Internet. It is made up of two layers namely,

- **The TLS Record Protocol:** This resides on top of a reliable transport protocol, such as TCP. It ensures that the connection is private by using symmetric data encryption and it ensures that the connection is reliable. The TLS Record Protocol is also used for encapsulation of higher-level protocols, such as the TLS Handshake Protocol.
- **The TLS Handshake Protocol:** This protocol provides authentication between the server and client and the negotiation of an encryption algorithm and cryptographic keys before the application protocol transmits or receives any data.

Kerberos

Kerberos is a network authentication protocol that enables two parties to exchange private information across a public network. It works by assigning a unique key, called a ticket, to each user that logs on to the network. The ticket is then embedded in messages to identify the sender of the message. [105] Kerberos, as defined in RFC 4120, uses symmetric cryptography. In this kind of cryptography, there is only one key, which is shared by the two endpoints. The key is used to encrypt a message, and on the other end, the same key is used to decrypt that message (hence the name, symmetric cryptography). This is in contrast to public-key cryptography, which uses two keys (i.e. private and public). Because of the two different keys, public-key cryptography is sometimes known as asymmetric cryptography.

Internet protocol security (IPsec)

This is a suite of protocols developed by the IETF to support secure exchange of packets at the IP layer. IPsec has been deployed widely to implement Virtual Private Networks (VPNs). It supports two encryption modes namely, transport and tunnel. Transport mode encrypts only the data portion (payload) of each packet, but leaves the header untouched. The more secure of the two is the tunnel mode, which encrypts both the header and the payload. On the receiving side, an IPSec-compliant device decrypts each packet.

For IPsec to work, the sending and receiving devices must share a public key. This is accomplished through a protocol known as Internet Security Association and Key Management Protocol/Oakley (ISAKMP/Oakley), which allows the receiver to obtain a public key and authenticate the sender using digital certificates. [106]

12.7. Encryption algorithms

An encryption algorithm defines a process by which data is modified so that it can be made secure. In order for someone to access the encrypted data they need to know the encryption algorithm so that they can decrypt it. A useful website for background reading on this topic is given at The International Cryptographic Software Pages. [107] However, a brief description is given here simply to illustrate the principles.

Encryption dates back to Roman times where Caesar cipher was used to hide the contents of a written message. An example is given below, where for example a letter in the alphabet is replaced by one that is three places after it in the alphabetical order. The principle folds back so that the letter ***z*** will be represented by the letter ***c***.

Caesar cipher

For example, letter = letter + 3, which maps 'meat' to 'phdw'. An example of Caeser's cipher is rot13 [108], which is used in Usenet news reading and posting programs. It replaces each letter in the English alphabet with the one 13 places forward or back along the alphabet. The process of 'Add 13/swap alphabet halves' means that applying it twice restores the original text.

One-time Pad

One-time pad (OTP) is an encryption algorithm where plaintext is combined with a random key or 'pad' which is the same length as the plaintext and used only once. For binary data, the exclusive OR operation (XOR) is used to encrypt the plaintext. This is shown in table 12.1, where it is seen that applying the XOR twice returns the original data.

If the key is truly random, never reused, and kept secret, the one-time pad provides perfect secrecy. It has also been proven that any cipher with perfect secrecy must use keys with the same requirements as OTP keys. OTP is considered to be unbreakable provided that,

- Pad is never reused.
- Unpredictable random numbers are used (physical sources, e.g. radioactive decay).

Stream Ciphers

Stream ciphers are based on OTP but the key used to encrypt is smaller. Thus, a stream cipher could use a much smaller key comprising for example of 128 bits. Based on this key, it generates a pseudorandom keystream, which can be combined with the plaintext digits in a similar fashion to the one-time pad. However, this comes at a cost, because the keystream is now pseudorandom and not truly random the proof of security associated with the one-time pad no longer holds. Consequently, it is quite possible for a stream cipher to be completely insecure. However variations on the basic principle can render data secure to different levels depending on complexity. [109]

Table 12.1

Binary pad (keystream), use XOR instead of addition	PAD	1010 1100 0110
Plaintext = original, unencrypted data	DATA	0101 0100 1000
Ciphertext = encrypted data	PAD XOR DATA	1111 1000 1110
Two XORs with the same data always cancel out	RESULT XOR PAD	0101 0100 1000

RC4

This is a relatively fast and strong cipher with a key size of up to 2048 bits (256 bytes). It is a 'stream'cipher, creating a stream of random bytes and XORing those bytes with the text. Using it with the same key on two different messages makes it very weak. It is thus useful in situations in which a new key can be chosen for each message. It was reverse-engineered and posted to the net in 1994. [110]

Block Ciphers

Block cipher is a symmetric key cipher, which operates on fixed-length groups of bits, termed blocks, with an unvarying transformation. An early and highly influential block cipher design was the Data Encryption Standard (DES), developed at IBM and published as a standard in 1977. A successor to DES, the Advanced Encryption Standard (AES), was adopted in 2001. When encrypting, a block cipher might take (for example) a 128-bit block of plaintext as input, and output a corresponding 128-bit block of ciphertext. The exact transformation is controlled using a second input, which is the secret key. Decryption is similar; the decryption algorithm takes, in this example, a 128-bit block of ciphertext together with the secret key, and yields the original 128-bit block of plaintext.

Block ciphers can be contrasted with stream ciphers; a stream cipher operates on individual digits one at a time and the transformation varies during the encryption. The distinction between the two types is not always clear-cut; a block cipher, when used in certain modes of operation, acts effectively as a stream cipher. [111]

12.8. Network Security Components

Network security begins with authenticating users. Once authenticated, a firewall enforces access policies to deny or permit user access to network resources. After a user has been authenticates an intrusion prevention system (IPS) helps detect and prevent any potentially harmful contents such as computer worms being transmitted over the network.

As mentioned earlier, messages travel along the Internet as standard size packets. Once the message is broken down into packets, each one is transmitted to the destination computer individually. Packets that make up the same message are often sent along different routes to the destination by the router depending on the amount of traffic on any given channel at the time of transmission. Upon arrival at the destination computer, packets are recombined into the original message. A large number of tools are available that can examine these packets and decide if any of them pose a security threat. Each packet has a header that contains important information to guide the packet over the network, and packet filters are used to read the headers in order to determine security issues.

First generation packet filters. Packet filters act by inspecting the 'packets', which represent the basic unit of data transfer between computers on the Internet. If a packet matches the set of rules of the packet filter, the packet filter will accept the packet, or reject it (discard it, and send 'error responses' to the source).

Second generation. 'Stateful' filters or 'stateful firewall' maintains records of all connections passing through the firewall, and is able to determine whether a packet is the start of a new connection, or part of an existing connection. Though there is still a set of static rules in such a firewall, the state of a connection can in itself be one of the criteria, which trigger specific rules.

Third generation (application layer). These are also known as proxy based firewalls. The key benefit is that they can 'understand' certain applications and protocols (such as File Transfer Protocol, DNS or web browsing), and can detect whether an unwanted protocol is being sneaked through on a non-standard port, or whether a protocol is being abused in a known harmful way. Proxy servers can carry out this type of filtering, but if the filtering is done by a standalone firewall, or used in a device for traffic shaping, the technology is likely to be referred to as 'deep packet inspection'.

Network address translation. Firewalls often have network address translation (NAT) functionality, and in this case the hosts protected behind a firewall commonly have addresses in the 'private address range'. The function of the NAT is to re-write the source and/or destination addresses of IP packets as they pass through a router or firewall. As mentioned in earlier chapters, most systems using NAT do so in order to enable multiple hosts on a private network to access the Internet using a single public IP address.

Access Control Lists (ACL). These were described earlier but as a brief reminder an ACL is a list of permissions attached to an object. The list specifies who is allowed to access the object and what operations are supported. In an ACL-based security model, when a subject requests to perform an operation on an object, the system first checks the list for an authentic entry in order to decide whether or not to proceed with the operation.

Spyware

When any software is downloaded for free from the Internet, it is possible that it may be spyware. This means that the software can gather information about your computer and how you use it and send that information to marketing companies. Those companies can gather information such as your email address, calendar data, web sites you have visited, or what music you listen to. [112] Although it will not harm the data, Spyware will cause the machine to run slower. Anti-spyware software can be installed to deactivate the spyware. For example, Windows Defender is software that helps protect your computer against pop-ups, slow performance, and security threats caused by spyware and other unwanted software by detecting and removing known spyware from your computer.

Viruses

A computer virus is a computer program that can copy itself and infect a computer without permission or knowledge of the user. Many personal computers are now connected to the Internet and to local area networks, facilitating the spread of malicious code. Today's viruses may also take advantage of network services such as the World Wide Web, e-mail, and file sharing systems to spread, blurring the line between viruses and worms. A computer worm is a self-replicating computer program. It uses a network to send copies of itself to other. Unlike a virus, it does not need to attach itself to an existing program. Worms almost always cause at least some harm to the network, if only by consuming bandwidth, whereas viruses almost always corrupt or devour files on a targeted computer. Furthermore, some sources use an alternative terminology in which a virus is any form of self-replicating malware. [113]

In a computer network, dealing with computer viruses requires an approach that includes policy, delegation of responsibility as well as configuring and upgrading anti-virus software. Some general points to consider are as follows,

- Install anti-virus software.
- Avoid using floppy disks to transfer files from one computer to another.
- Do not open files from any email before checking the file with an anti-virus program. If a file is received via email, be careful to check the file extensions. Avoid opening any file that has the .exe extension. These are usually programs that can either be spyware, viruses, or trojans. Trojans are malicious software programs (also called 'malware') that can erase files from your hard drive.
- Install only the software that is authentic. Pirated versions of programs can have viruses and when the application is installed, so is the virus software.
- Do not download free music, movies, or media files. These types of files (along with other types of free images, media files or movies) often have viruses embedded within.

12.9. Managing Network Security

A very important aspect of security is the planning of the manner in which it is deployed. Network operating systems such as Microsoft 2003 Server offer built in tools to manage the network. [114] Security is managed through features embedded in the Group Policy objects that are used to secure the User Environment. This shown in figure 12.8, where a group policy that is defined at domain level is used to configure account policies.

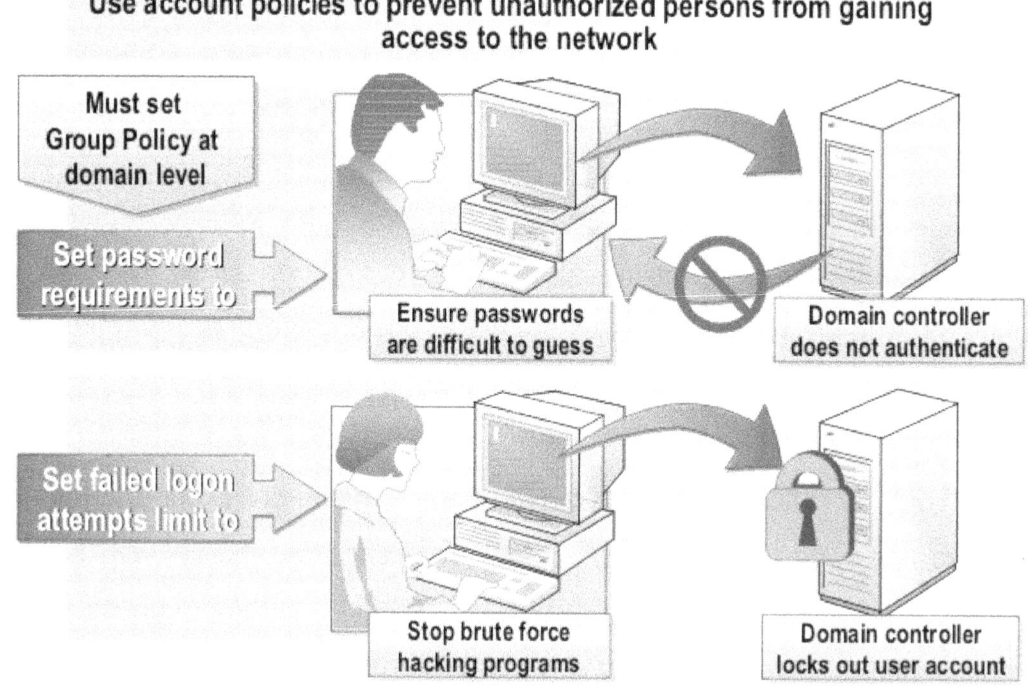

Figure 12.8. Account policies provide for access control to resources

Any security issues can be analysed using Security Log Files to Detect Security Breaches. Components of the security management include the following,

- Securing the Logon Process.
- Examining Service Packs.
- Hotfixes and antivirus software.

- Monitoring events such as Change of File Ownership, Clearing of the Security Log, System Shutdown.

As with any major project, planning for security requires an appropriate level of documentation. For any security system it is necessary to have the documentation to cover the following aspects, [115]

Day-to-day documentation: These are project structure documents that are revised throughout the remaining project phases.

Capacity Plan: Planning for capacity is fundamental in providing the required services at an affordable price. Detailed analysis of every user and their bandwidth requirements needs to be performed in order to arrive at a figure for combined bandwidth. Capacity management is the process of planning, analysing, sizing, and optimising capacity to satisfy demand in a timely manner and at a reasonable cost. An example analysis provided by Microsoft is given in table 12.2. [115] Here the various roles such as sales assistants and human resources etc. are analysed for their average network traffic usage per hour. This is multiplied by the actual value for each user in this role to arrive at the average network usage per hour for that role of user. A sum total for all the roles gives the capacity that the network is required to support.

Table 12.2 Example loads for capacity planning

Role	Average Net Traffic p/hour	Total No: of Users	Average Net. Traffic per Hour
Sales Assistants	700 K	420	294 Mb
Managers	60 K	40	2.4 Mb
Stock Clerks	6 Mb	26	156 Mb
Secretarial	2 Mb	8	16 Mb
Human Resources	4 Mb	6	24 Mb
Warehouse staff	400 K	30	12 Mb
Maintenance	20 K	20	400 K
TOTAL			**504.8Mb/hour 140kbps**

Deployment Plan: This will need input from the senior management because there will be an impact on performance during the various stages of deployment. Clearly any specific issues have to be addressed and this will necessarily mean that each plan is effectively a bespoke solution. Nevertheless some general guidelines on key deployment areas and techniques provided by Microsoft are given in table 12.3. These can be used as a starting-point template and revised to suit a particular deployment.

Table 12.3 Deployment plan considerations

Key areas	**Techniques**
Installation strategy	Phased or all at once, site by site or department by department. Contingency planning:
Site/line-of-business	All at once during planning phase, or site by site during deployment phase
Mechanisms	Fully automated network installation, partially scripted installation, or manual
Resources	Internal IT staff, or contractors
Support	Tiered support, or pilot and roll out support

Security Plan: The actual security plan needs to be documented. This plan should consider all the security needs and should de designed to maintain the integrity of the solution, prevent data loss and any compromise of data, resources or services. It would be unwise to implement any security on the whole system without testing it on a pilot-system. The basic features that a pilot plan should cover are given in table 12.4. The corresponding test plan is described in table 12.5.

Table 12.4 Pilot plan features and techniques

Key areas (pilot)	**Techniques**
Participant selection	Focus on urgent business needs, the visibility or influence of user group, or the risk of failure
Scope	Test of solution functionality and deployment processes, or full test of solution and deployment processes
Number of participants	Small number of participants, or an entire department or entire site
Number of projects	Complete network installation, partially scripted installation, or manual
Resources	Single or multiple allocation of resources
Feedback mechanisms	One time only planning phase, or site by site during deployment phase

Table 12.5 Test plan features and techniques

Key areas (Test plan)	Techniques
Types of testing	Unit test, integrated system test, performance test, stress test, usability test, and regression test
Test format and criteria	Fully documented test scenarios and test results, and informal testing with verbal agreement from key stakeholders
Change control	Programmatic check-in of a change management process
Configuration management	Centralised management of hardware, software, and documentation standards, and local management of configurations
Issue and bug tracking	Prioritisation of issues, and tracked in bug-tracking database, or issues tracked through e-mail

Development and Test Environment Process: Having identified the components to include in the pilot test, and specifying how these will be tested the system is ready for full deployment. Clearly, if any issues are identified that need attention during the pilot testing stage, they need to be resolved before final deployment. During the testing phase it is further necessary to establish a baseline for performance. This can be used for comparison so that any changes made to the system can be evaluated in comparison with the baseline performance. The basic flow for pilot testing and development is illustrated in figure 12.9

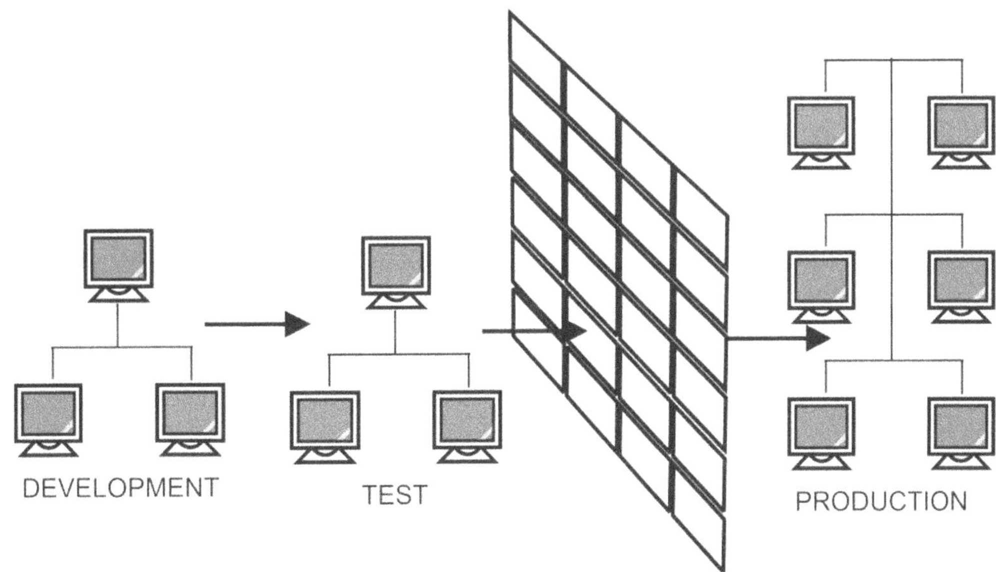

Figure 12.9. Development, testing and production

Exercises

12.1. Discuss how usability of the system is affected by security measures.

12.2. What are the essential elements of a security system?

12.3. It is said that, confidentiality, access control, authentication, non-repudiation, availability and integrity are the essential elements of a security system. Explain how you would implement each of these in a typical network.

12.4. Describe the security protocols (SSL, SSH, TSL and Kerberos) and their applications.

12.5. Discuss the basic characteristics of encryption, as a means of protection in computer networks.

12.6. What are hash functions, and how are they used?

12.7. What considerations should be taken into account when deciding to encrypt data?

12.8. Discuss the PKI system and algorithms that are commonly applied?

12.9. Explain the security protocols and the layers at which they operate.

12.10. How are ciphers applied to encryption?

12.11. Discuss packet filters as security measures.

12.12. What is deep-packet inspection?

12.13. What is spyware and how can it be countered?

12.14. List the essential steps to protect your network against viruses.

12.15. You are the administrator of a corporate network with 2000 users in a single building. The network is arranged as single domain and all Internet traffic is through a single Firewall installed as a proxy server. Discuss the elements of a security plan that you would recommend for this network. Include details of the documentation that you would provide.

References

Please note: All web pages accessed between June 2007 and November 2007.

[1] Linux wireless networking: A look at WLAN, Bluetooth, GPRS, GSM, and Infrared Data on Linux.
http://compnetworking.about.com/gi/dynamic/offsite.htm?zi=1/XJ/Ya&sdn=compnetworking&cdn=compute&tm=22&f=00&su=p284.8.150.ip_&tt=14&bt=1&bts=0&zu=http%3A//www-128.ibm.com/developerworks/library/wi-enable.html%3Fca%3Ddgr-lnxw09Linux4Wireless].
Accessed [11/07].
[2] A History of Apple's Operating Systems © Amit Singh. All Rights Reserved.
http://www.kernelthread.com/mac/oshistory/
[3] NetWare® The future of NetWare - Open Enterprise Server. Open Enterprise Server combines the best of NetWare and Linux.
http://www.novell.com/products/netware/
[4] OS/2 Warp.
http://www-306.ibm.com/software/os/warp/
[5] Operating systems for IBM mainframes z/OS.
http://www-03.ibm.com/systems/z/os/
[6] Cisco IOS Software Release 12.4(15)T.
http://www.cisco.com/en/US/products/ps8258/index.html
[7] IBM X-Architecture technology.
[http://www-03.ibm.com/systems/x/about/]
[8] SAP enterprise software.
http://www.sap.com
[9] Application programming definition.
http://en.wikipedia.org/wiki/Application_programming
[10] David Solomon, Mark Russinovich, Windows Internals and Advanced Troubleshooting Tutorial.
[11] What Is the Definition of a TTL (Transistor-Transistor Logic) Compatible Signal?
http://digital.ni.com/public.nsf/3efedde4322fef19862567740067f3cc/acb4bd7550c4374c86256bfb0067a4bd
[12] Power Macintosh: L1 and L2 Cache Explained.
http://docs.info.apple.com/article.html?artnum=14750
[13] XDR™ Memory Architecture.
http://www.rambus.com/us/products/xdr_xdr2/index.html
[14] Intel® Pentium® 4 Processor Family.
http://www.intel.com/design/Pentium4/documentation.htm
[15] eMIPS, A Dynamically Extensible Processor, Richard Neil Pittman, Nathaniel Lee Lynch, Alessandro Forin, Microsoft Research, October 2006
Technical Report, MSR-TR-2006-143.
http://research.microsoft.com/research/EmbeddedSystems/eMIPS/eMIPSreport1.pdf
[16] Compute Cluster Network Requirements, Microsoft TechNet.
http://technet2.microsoft.com/windowsserver/en/library/f49b19ee-aa05-4f16-8132-36ee09f631c11033.mspx?mfr=true
[17] Overview, Stars cluster beautifully. So do computers.
http://www.myri.com/myrinet/overview/
[18] Technological impact of magnetic hard disk drives on storage systems by E. Grochowski and R. D. Halem.
http://www.research.ibm.com/journal/sj/422/grochowski.html
[19] The Memory Management Glossary.
http://www.memorymanagement.org/glossary/m.html
[20] baseband definition.
http://wi-fiplanet.webopedia.com/TERM/b/baseband.html
[21] baseband definition 2.
http://www.techweb.com/encyclopedia/defineterm.jhtml?term=Baseband
[22] X.25 Description by Cisco Systems.

http://www.cisco.com/univercd/cc/td/doc/cisintwk/ito_doc/x25.htm
[23] Time-Based ISDN/Async (Legacy) DDR.
http://www.cisco.com/en/US/tech/tk801/tk133/technologies_configuration_example09186a0080094089.shtml
[24] Cisco 700 Series ISDN Access Routers.
http://www.cisco.com/en/US/products/hw/routers/ps331/tsd_products_support_eol_series_home.html
[25] B-ISDN and ATM.
http://www.doc.ic.ac.uk/~nd/surprise_95/journal/vol2/vm4/article2.html
[26] What is ATM by Cisco Systems.
http://www.cisco.com/univercd/cc/td/doc/product/atm/c8540/12_0/13_19/atg/basics.htm#wp1019851
[27] SONET Telecommunications Standard Primer.
http://www.tek.com/Measurement/App_Notes/SONET/
[28] The Get IEEE 802® program makes IEEE 802® standards available at no charge in PDF format
http://standards.ieee.org/getieee802/
[29] Search Networking Ethernet definition.
http://searchnetworking.techtarget.com/sDefinition/0,,sid7_gci212080,00.html
[30] Copper Distributed Data Interface by Cisco Systems.
http://www.cisco.com/univercd/cc/td/doc/cisintwk/ito_doc/fddi.htm#wp1020678
[31] ATM definition.
http://en.wikipedia.org/wiki/Asynchronous_Transfer_Mode
[32] Frame Relay.
http://www.cisco.com/univercd/cc/td/doc/cisintwk/ito_doc/frame.htm
[33] The Internet Engineering Task Force.
http://www.ietf.org/]
[34] RFC Title Index 2601 - 2700.
http://www.faqs.org/rfcs/rfc-sidx27.html
[35] RFC 1180 (A TCP/IP Tutorial, January 1991).
http://tools.ietf.org/html/rfc1180, RFC 1580 (Guide to Network Resource Tools, March 1994)
http://www.faqs.org/rfcs/rfc1580.html
[36] networking glossary of terms: http://www.javvin.com/protocol/index.html
[37] RFC 2151 (A Primer on Internet and TCP/IP Tools and Utilities, June 1997)
http://www.ietf.org/rfc/rfc2151.txt
[38] RFC 2700 (Internet Official Protocol Standards, August 2000)
http://www.faqs.org/rfcs/rfc2700.html
[39] Hubert Zimmermann. OSI Reference Model - The ISO Model of Architecture for Open Systems Interconnection. IEEE Transactions on Communication, 28(4):425-432, April, 1980.
http://www.comsoc.org/livepubs/50_journals/pdf/RightsManagement_eid=136833.pdf
[40] Cisco Systems Home.
www.cisco.com
[41] OSI Model and Communication Between Systems by Cisco Systems.
http://cisco.com/univercd/cc/td/doc/cisintwk/ito_doc/introint.htm#wp1020618
[42] Microsoft Developer Network, ICMP Router Discovery Messages
http://msdn2.microsoft.com/en-us/library/ms817885.aspx
[43] Bluetooth Home.
http://www.bluetooth.com/.
[44] Microsoft Windows 2003 Server R2, Server Role Configuration Options.
http://www.microsoft.com/windowsserver2003/evaluation/serverroles/options.mspx Published: March 25, 2003
[45] Blade server Definition.
http://searchdatacenter.techtarget.com/sDefinition/0,,sid80_gci770169,00.html
[46] HP Blade System p-Class System Overview and Planning
http://h20000.www2.hp.com/bc/docs/support/SupportManual/c00263417/c00263417.pdf
[47] Atlantech Software Development.
http://www.atlantech.co.nz/SoftwareDevelopment___479d87d388d0.html

[48] Mountainous Investment Transforms Enterprise Management, Software Vendor, P.J. Jakovljevic - July 11, 2006
http://www.deltek.com/pdf/news/analyst_briefings/MountainousInvestment_article_final.pdf
[49] WebSphere Application Server.
http://www-306.ibm.com/software/webservers/appserv/was/
[50] Thin Client Computing Without 'the Bill'
http://software.ivertech.com/_ivertechArticle6114_ThinClientComputingWithouttheBill.htm
[51] ASP Model issues and solving them via hybrid Client/server plus ASP approach
http://www.mycustomer.com/cgi-bin/library.cgi?action=detail&id=1327&dir_publisher_varid=10
[52] Workstation definition
http://en.wikipedia.org/wiki/Workstation
[53] RFC 2131
[54] The TCP/IP Guide is a reference
http://www.tcpipguide.com/free/t_DHCPMessageRelayingandBOOTPRelayAgents.htm
[55] Hewlett Packard Setting Up a DHCP Server
http://www.docs.hp.com/en/B2355-90153/apas04.html
[56] IBM System I, Networking, Dynamic Host Configuration Protocol, Version 5 Release 4
http://publib.boulder.ibm.com/infocenter/iseries/v5r4/topic/rzakg/rzakg.pdf
[57] CISCO DHCP OPTION 43 for Lightweight Cisco Aironet Access Points Configuration
http://www.cisco.com/en/US/tech/tk722/tk809/technologies_configuration_example09186a00808714fe.shtml
[58] RFC 1542, http://www.ietf.org/rfc/rfc1542.txt
[59] RFC 1035
[60] DNS Resource Record (RR) Types & DNS Parameters (IANA),
http://www.bind9.net/dns-parameters
[61] Oversimplified DNS, Check CNAME Record
http://rscott.org/dns/cname.html
[62] Canonical Name Record (CNAME)
http://www.zytrax.com/books/dns/ch8/cname.html
[63] Microsoft TechNet, Server planning for DNS, Updated: January 21, 2005
http://technet2.microsoft.com/windowsserver/en/library/949f3a45-84e2-487f-80d7-bce184b28a061033.mspx?mfr=true
[64] PF: Packet Filtering
http://www.openbsd.org/faq/pf/filter.html
[65] Firewalls and how they work
http://computer.howstuffworks.com/firewall4.htm
[66] Microsoft, Description of a Personal Firewall
http://support.microsoft.com/kb/321050
[67] How Virtual Private Networks Work, by Jeff Tyson
http://computer.howstuffworks.com/vpn.htm
[68] Virtual Private Networking: An Overview, White Paper,
http://www.microsoft.com/technet/network/vpn/vpnfaq.mspx]
[69] Resolve IP Fragmentation, MTU, MSS, and PMTUD Issues with GRE and IPSEC
Document ID: 25885
http://www.cisco.com/en/US/tech/tk827/tk369/technologies_white_paper09186a00800d6979.shtml#t16
[70] RFC792
[71] RFC 3222
[72] Microsoft technet library RIP protocol
http://technet2.microsoft.com/windowsserver/en/library/5e40738f-7c26-4b25-aa4b-35f9605c44ea1033.mspx?mfr=true
[73] Microsoft TechNet library OSPF protocol
http://technet2.microsoft.com/windowsserver/en/library/5e40738f-7c26-4b25-aa4b-35f9605c44ea1033.mspx?mfr=true
[74] RFC 1058, 'Routing Information Protocol,' RFC 2328, 'OSPF Version 2,' and RFC 2453, 'RIP Version 2,'
[75] Protecting Your Core: Infrastructure Protection Access Control Lists
Document ID: 43920

http://www.cisco.com/warp/public/707/iacl.html
[76] GSR: Receive Access Control Lists, Document ID: 43861
http://www.cisco.com/en/US/tech/tk648/tk361/technologies_white_paper09186a00801a0a5e.shtml
[77] Configuring Commonly Used IP ACLs, Document ID: 26448
http://www.cisco.com/en/US/tech/tk648/tk361/technologies_configuration_example09186a0080100548.shtml
[78] Access control lists (ACLs) and ACL profiles
http://publib.boulder.ibm.com/infocenter/lmc/v6r1/index.jsp?topic=/com.ibm.lmc.doc/HowTo/acl.htm
[79] Cisco - Access Control Lists and IP Fragments White paper
http://whitepapers.zdnet.co.uk/0,1000000651,260104249p,00.htm
[80] Access Control Lists, www.bitpipr.com
[81 RFC 2544, http://www.faqs.org/rfcs/rfc2544.html
[82] RFC 1242
[83] Course map and OSI model
http://www.erg.abdn.ac.uk/users/gorry/eg3561/road-map.html
[84] RFC 2544 Benchmarking Methodology for Network Interconnect Devices,
http://www.ietf.org/rfc/rfc2544.txt, [85] RFC 2544 Testing of Ethernet Services in Telecom Networks, White Paper
http://cp.literature.agilent.com/litweb/pdf/5989-1927EN.pdf
[86] Planning and Maintaining a Microsoft Windows Server 2003 Network Infrastructure Course 2278
http://www.microsoft.com/learning/syllabi/en-us/2278Bfinal.mspx
[87] RFC 2544 Testing with Aurora Tango, Application Note describing Aurora Tango used to perform the RFC 2544 tests to measure network performance.
http://www.trendcomms.com/trendweb/resource.nsf/vlFileURLLookup/en%5E%5ERFC+2544+testing/$FILE/GbEnet.2544.test.pdf
[88] Network performance measurement
http://www.intellipool.se/
[89] WinDump: tcpdump for Windows
http://www.winpcap.org/windump/]
[90] Sniffers: What They Are and How to Protect Yourself, by Matthew Tanase, last updated February 26, 2002 http://www.securityfocus.com/infocus/1549
[91] Internet Assigned Number Authority
http://www.iana.org/
[92] Toward an Internet Standard Scheme for Subnetting
http://www.faqs.org/rfcs/rfc940.html
[93] RFC 1519 - Classless Inter-Domain Routing (CIDR): an Address Assignment and Aggregation Strategy
http://www.faqs.org/rfcs/rfc1519.html
[94] FRTR: A Scalable Mechanism to Restore Routing Table Consistency, Lan Wang, Daniel Massey, Keyur Patel, and Lixia Zhang
http://wiki.netsec.colostate.edu/images/8/8a/Netsec_uclatr030054.pdf
[95] IP Addressing and Subnetting for New Users, Document ID: 13788
http://www.cisco.com/warp/public/701/3.html
[96] CMMI for Systems Engineering/Software Engineering/Integrated Product and Process Development, V1.1, Tech. Rep. CMU/SEI-2002-TR-004, Carnegie Mellon University, Software Engineering Institute, Pittsburgh, PA, 2002
[97] Copper Cabling Standards and Technical Aspects, The Evolution of Copper Cabling Systems from Cat5 to Cat5e to Cat6, White Paper – 2/27/04
http://www.panduit.com/products/WhitePapers/098765.pdf
[98] Fibre Distributed Data Interface
http://www.cisco.com/univercd/cc/td/doc/cisintwk/ito_doc/fddi.htm
[99] FDDI-II capacity analysis, Krishnamurthy, B., TENCON 90. 1990 IEEE Region 10 Conference on Computer and Communication Systems, Volume, Issue, 24-27 Sep 1990 Page(s): 546 - 550 vol.2, Digital Object Identifier 10.1109/TENCON.1990.152669
http://ieeexplore.ieee.org/Xplore/login.jsp?url=/iel5/498/3989/00152669.pdf

[100] http://www.pcmag.com/encyclopedia_term/0,2542,t=FDDI&i=43061,00.asp
[101] Definition of: FDDI, http://www.rhyshaden.com/fddi.htm
[102] Public Key Encryption and Digital Signature: How do they work? White Paper http://www.cgi.com/cgi/pdf/cgi_whpr_35_pki_e.pdf
[103] Failure analysis of an e-commerce protocol using model checking
Ray, I., Advanced Issues of E-Commerce and Web-Based Information Systems, 2000. WECWIS 2000. Second International Workshop on Volume, Issue, 2000 Page(s): 176 – 183, Digital Object Identifier 10.1109/WECWIS.2000.853873
http://ieeexplore.ieee.org/Xplore/login.jsp?url=/iel5/6886/18539/00853873.pdf
[104] Encryption for enterprise data solutions, http://www.pgp.com/
[105] Kerberos: The Network Authentication Protocol, http://web.mit.edu/Kerberos/
[106] ISAKMP/Oakley White Paper, Industrial strength key exchange http://www.ipadventures.com/docs/IKE.pdf
[107] Cryptography, http://axion.physics.ubc.ca/crypt.html
[108] The purpose of this page is to collect and display various ROT13, http://www.miranda.org/~jkominek/rot13/
[109] Stream Cipher definition, http://en.wikipedia.org/wiki/Stream_cipher
[110] CR4 code in the C programming language http://www.cypherspace.org/adam/rsa/rc4.c
[111] Block Cipher definition
http://en.wikipedia.org/wiki/Block_cipher
[112] Antispyware download centre, http://www.spyware.co.uk/
[113] Computer Virus definition http://en.wikipedia.org/wiki/Computer_virus
[114] Microsoft Home. www.microsoft.com
[115] Service Management Functions, Capacity Management
http://www.microsoft.com/technet/solutionaccelerators/cits/mo/smf/smfcapmg.mspx
[116] The traditional approach to terminating DDS, T1/FT1 and T3 circuits at each location is to use a standalone or high density rack mounted Channel Service Unit/Data Service Unit (CSU/DSU)
http://www.gdc.com/inotes/pdf/sc5000wp.pdf
[117] Network operating systems http://www.redbooks.ibm.com/redbooks/pdfs/sg244786.pdf Hubert Zimmermann. OSI Reference Model - The ISO Model of Architecture for SG24-4786-00, OS/2 Warp Server, Windows NT, and NetWare: A Network Operating System Study December 1996, First Edition (December 1996). Comments may be addressed to: IBM Corporation, International Technical Support Organization, Dept. JN9B Building 045 Internal Zip 2834 11400 Burnet Road, Austin, Texas 78758-3493
[118] Matthias Jung and Ernst W. Biersack. How Layering Protocol Software Violates Separation of Concerns. In ECOOP 2000 Workshop on Aspects and Dimensions of Concerns, Cannes, France, June 2000. http://trese.cs.utwente.nl/Workshops/adc2000/papers/Jung.pdf
[119] RFC2396, Tim Berners-Lee, Roy T. Fielding, and Larry Masinter. Uniform Resource Identifiers (URI): Generic Syntax. Internet draft standard RFC 2396, August 1998. http://www.ietf.org/rfc/rfc2396.txt
[120] TCP, Transmission Control Protocol. DARPA Internet Program Protocol Specification, September 1981. http://www.ietf.org/rfc/rfc793.txt
[121] T. Dierks, C. Allen. The TLS Protocol Version 1.0. Internet Engineering Task Force RFC 2246, January 1999. http://www.ietf.org/rfc/rfc2246.txt
[122] John Postel. User Datagram Protocol. Internet Draft Standard RFC 768, August 1980. http://www.ietf.org/rfc/rfc768.txt
[123] Tim Bray, Jean Paoli, C. M. Sperberg-McQueen, Eve Maler, and François Yergeau. Extensible Markup Language (XML) 1.0 (Third Edition). World Wide Web Consortium, Recommendation REC-xml-20040204, February 2004. http://www.w3.org/TR/2004/REC-xml11-20040204/
[124] VPN Resources, Microsoft VPN Position White Paper:
http://www.microsoft.com/windows2000/library/howitworks/communications/remoteaccess/nwpriv.asp
[125] Windows Communications: http://www.microsoft.com/communications
[126] Compaq/Microsoft Network Security Briefings:
http://www.securitybriefing.com/

[127] Windows 2000 Server: http://www.microsoft.com/windows/server/
[128] 3DES support in IPSec is obtained by installing the High Encryption Pack at: http://www.microsoft.com/windows/server/beta/downloads/128bit/default.asp
[129] Windows 2000 IPSec Interop external Web site: http://w2kipsec-pub.rte.microsoft.com
[130] IETF specifications: RFC 2637 (PPTP), RFC 2661 (L2TP)
http://www.ietf.org/internet-drafts/draft-aboba-ipsra-req-00.txt
http://www.ietf.org/internet-drafts/draft-ietf-pppext-l2tp-security-05.txt
http://www.ietf.org/internet-drafts/draft-ietf-ipsec-dhcp-04.txt

INDEX

G

H

I

J

K

L

M

N

O

www.ingramcontent.com/pod-product-compliance
Ingram Content Group UK Ltd.
Pitfield, Milton Keynes, MK11 3LW, UK
UKHW050615260726
13967UKWH00008B/2878

9 780955 815300